Exchange Traded Funds

Structure, Regulation and Application of a New Fund Class

Elisabeth Hehn
Editor

Exchange Traded Funds

Structure, Regulation and Application of a New Fund Class

With 44 Figures and 70 Tables

Springer

Dr. Elisabeth Hehn
Eichhofweg 1
6318 Walchwil
Switzerland
info@vipag.com

Cataloging-in-Publication Data
Library of Congress Control Number: 2005924632

ISBN 3-540-24124-8 Springer Berlin Heidelberg New York

Springer is a part of Springer Science+Business Media

springeronline.com

Printed in Germany

Hardcover-Design: design & production, Heidelberg

SPIN 11369097 43/3153-5 4 3 2 1 0 – Printed on acid-free paper

Preface

The organization of traditional mutual funds as Exchange Traded Funds (ETFs) produced revolutionary changes in the fund industry. These changes, and the subsequent events to which they led, have greatly increased the practical way of trading funds. Traditional mutual fund markets were fragmented, and transactions were both costly and from time to time difficult to arrange. Investments in emerging markets for example were anything but efficient. As a consequence of establishing ETF funds market segments, the efficiency of transactions has been broadly increased as well as transaction costs dramatically reduced. All this changed in the early Nineties with the introduction of the first ETF for the purpose of trading funds.

Exchange Traded Funds – Structure, Regulation and Application of a New Fund Class is a comprehensive summary of articles covering all aspects of the Exchange Traded Fund industry. Similar to several publications of the last few years this book includes articles form academia as well as the banking, investment, and insurance industry, this combining theoretical evolution and practical implementation of Exchange Trades Funds.

The present book is divided into four parts:

The opening part, containing *ETFs – A Leading Financial Innovation* and *From Continent to Sectors: Challenges and Uses of ETFs in Europe,* is designed to give the reader broad insight into the industry, developments and trends. Further, the article *Spiders: Where Are the Bugs?* examine the characteristics and performance of these instruments from an academic point of view.

The second part gives the reader a full guide to the different asset management concepts with ETFs. It also addresses the controversial problem involved with asset allocation techniques. *Xetra Active Funds (XAF) – More Than "Just" Index Tracking, The Role of Exchange Traded Funds in the Active vs. Passive Debate* and *ETFs – Tactical Asset Allocation Tools.*

Part three, Jurisdiction, Regulation and Trading of ETFs, with the two contributions, *Exchange Traded Funds from a Lawyer's Perspective – The Case of Germany* and *Liquidity and Innovation – Nothing Else Matters*, introduces the jurisdiction of ETFs and the XTF platform, a fully electronic Xetra trading system.

Finally the last two articles in this book, *The Gateway to International Islamic Investing* and *Review: Facts & Figures on ETFs* provide an innovative product example as well as statistical analysis.

In the attached appendices the interested reader can find a detailed glossary, further statistics on ETFs and a prospectus.

I would like to thank all contributors to realize the book. Especially I like to thank debating ideas as well as providing the data used for the statistics. Further thanks go to Dr. Martina Bihn for her ongoing support during the whole project.

Walchwil, March 2005 Elisabeth Hehn

Table of Contents

Introduction

Elisabeth Hehn

ETFs are known by a variety of sometimes quirky names — Spiders, Diamonds, OPALs, WEBS (now iShares), Qubes, VIPERs, HOLDRs and streetTracks are just a few. ETFs are a simple, low cost and flexible way to access the potential rewards of market segments. In essence, it brings important advantage in combining index diversification with the flexibility of trading shares. The market growth continued rapidly despite the disappointing investment climate between 2000 and 2003. Therefore ETFs are regarded as the hottest investment product of the new century.

Performance and fees have been the rationale behind index investing for years. In accordance to many investigations only a few actively managed portfolios outperform the broad market over the long run. That's enough to make investors think twice about paying high fees or pricey sales loads for a fund manager's supposed expertise.

Like conventional index investments, ETFs allow investors to be as active or passive as they wish. Entire portfolios can be built using plain-vanilla index ETFs that offer broad exposure to stocks and bonds. Further, investors might instead choose to cobble together portfolios based on a dozen or more sector ETFs. Unlike traditional index funds, ETFs can be bought and sold throughout the trading day at intraday prices, rather than based on a fund's net asset value at a given day and time. ETFs are an evolutionary advance, bringing institutional-quality products to all investors.

In recent years, these unique features and benefits have helped exchange traded funds explode in popularity and emerge as one of the most flexible, multi-purpose investment vehicles available. Ever since the American Stock Exchange pioneered the concept of a tradable basket of stocks with the creation of the Standard & Poor's Depositary Receipt (SPDR) in 1993, exchange traded funds have evolved into an entirely new investment category. Today, the number of ETFs listed and traded in the US has grown to more than 150 and continues to grow — not only in the number of products and their variety — but also in terms of assets and market value. Currently, there are about 30 ETF managers in more than 25 countries with listings on almost 30 exchanges.

The U.S. Securities and Exchange Commission defines ETFs as "a type of investment company, whose investment objective is to achieve the same return as a particular market index". An ETF is similar to an index fund in that it will primarily invest in the securities of companies that are included in a selected market index. An ETF will invest in either all of the securities or a representative sample of the securities included in the index. For example, one type of ETF, known as Spiders or SPDRs, invests in all of the stocks contained in the S&P 500 Composite Stock Price Index.

Typically ETFs are issued for institutions in large blocks, known as "Creation Units". Payments do not use cash but baskets of securities that generally mirror the ETF portfolio. Creation Units are often split up and sold to individual investors, who are willing to buy shares on a secondary market. Further it is possible to redeem a Creation Unit back to the ETF by giving investors the securities that comprise the portfolio instead of cash. *Ref.: http://www.sec.gov/answers/etf.htm*

Each ETF is a basket of securities that is designed to generally track an index — broad stock or bond market, stock industry sector, or international stock — yet trades like a single stock. The unique combination of many of the best features of other investments presents financial opportunities for both individual and institutional investors, including:

- a wide array of investment strategies
- all day tracking and trading
- buying and selling flexibility
- cash management
- core investment
- dividend opportunities
- diversification

- hedging
- lower costs (ordinary brokerage commissions apply)
- rebalancing
- tax efficiency / tax loss strategy
- transparency

As a pioneer in the creation of ETFs, the American Stock Exchange launched a whole new class of securities that has grown to $150 billion in assets in less than a decade. Today, the Amex remains the centre of development and the global market leader, with more than 120 listed ETFs". *Ref.: http://www.amex.com*

The European ETF Industry

Because ETFs are funds, they need to be registered (listed) for marketing purposes in the various jurisdictions in Europe. As a strategic decision, issuers from all over the world are entering the European market issuing ETFs which are in line with the local regulatory requirements. Cross-listings of ETFs are implemented on multiple exchanges in pursuit of a better market penetration.

Further the majority of pan European indices are the underlying for ETFs distributed abroad.

From inception in the early 1990s, mainly as private placement, the European ETF industry did increase substantially during the last years. The ETF segment of the Deutsche Börse "XTF", Europe's first ETF Segment has been in existence since April 2000. Since then the number of funds and assets deployed as well as growth rates rose dynamically. Germany, before XTF was introduced in April 2000, foreign Funds of German origin in Luxembourg, has now become a well – established and important market segment within the European environment.

The following figure shows growth rates as well as market shares and assets under administration (circles) in 1998.

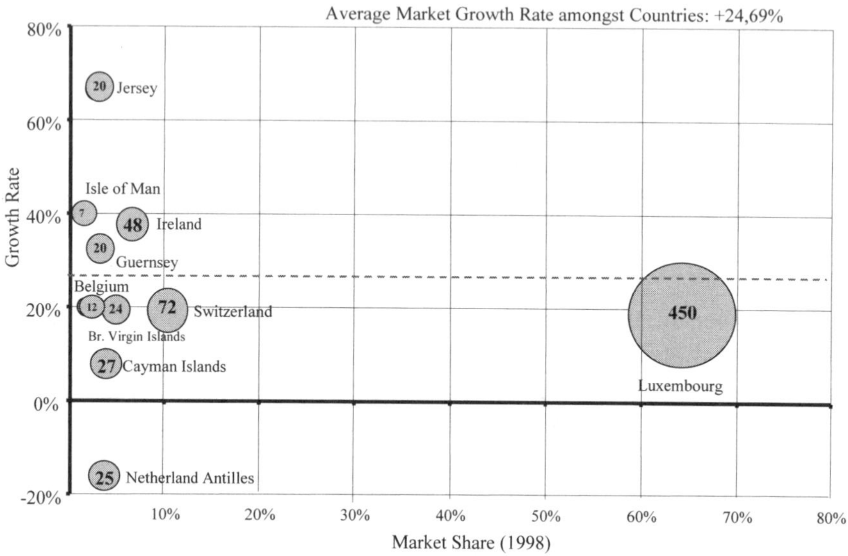

Figure 1: International market (1998, Figures in USD). Source: Clifford Chance, Deloitte Consulting

The late 1990s saw a market change with a rapid acceleration of growth in both the number of funds and assets, albeit from al low base. The European ETF industry had an increase in value terms with 60.7% (May 04, YoY) in assets under management. As at the end of June 2004 the European ETF industry was at 21.504 MEUR a phenomenal increase in assets under management of more than 80 % since 2000. *Ref.: XTF Exchange Traded Funds, Deutsche Börse AG.*

Figure 2 demonstrates how the AUM of European ETFs is shared between different providers. LDRS by Merrill Lynch are liquidated in October 2003 whilst Dexia just came into the market in June 2003. As shown in figure 2 the total AUM of European ETFs comes to 21.504 MEUR in June 2004 (20.731 in May 2004).

Due to the advantages of ETFs as well as the key trends of that industry further capital, providers, new instruments and products will be attracted during the next years to meet investor's needs.

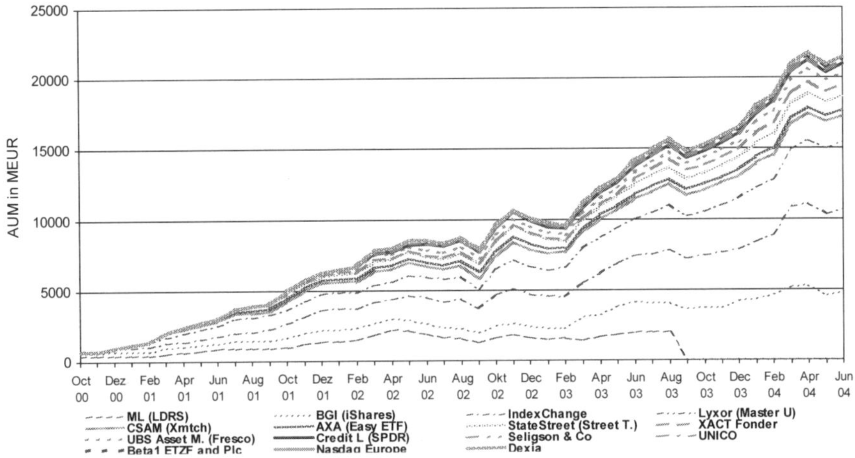

Figure 2: European ETFs – AUM by Provider (in MEUR). Source: STOXX Ltd.

ETFs – A Leading Financial Innovation

Elisabeth Hehn

1. Introduction

In a relatively short period of time, the market for Exchange Traded Funds (ETFs) has become popular, especially in Europe, and has established itself firmly in the minds of investors. ETFs have been growing faster in Europe than in the US. This is attributed to the fact that many Europcan managers were already familiar with the concept of ETFs before they were made available in Europe. ETFs are now widely used investment vehicles and considered to be an integral component of the overall asset allocation. ETFs might well be considered the leading financial innovation of the past decade.

During the last few years, ETFs have clearly conquered Europe. At the end of October 2004, there were 326 ETFs with assets of US$ 260 billion, managed by 38 managers and listed on 29 exchanges around the world. Year to date, the overall assets under management of ETFs increased by 5% – the US increased by 4.6%, Europe by 15.7%, while Japan declined by 3.9%. During 2004, 45 new ETFs were launched, a further 66 are planned and six ETFs were delisted. The average daily trading volume in US dollars has increased 50.6% to US$ 13.4 billion. This represents a dramatic increase from 1993, when there were just three ETFs with US$ 811 million in assets. January 29, 2003 marked the 10th anniversary of the first ETF listing in the US.[1]

The attraction of an ETF is that it provides access to a whole index, market or predefined portfolio strategy, but is much less complicated. An ETF behaves like an ordinary share that can be traded on a daily basis, but its un-

---

[1] Source: Morgan Stanley ETF Worldwide Guidebook, Global Summary as of October 29, 2004.

derlying assets are an entire index or portfolio, thereby providing diversification. Their investment objective is to replicate the price and yield performance of an independently published index. This explains why they are often described as index shares.

ETFs allow investors to gain broad exposure to specific segments of equity and fixed income markets with relative ease, on a real-time basis, and at a lower cost than many other forms of investing. Essentially, ETFs opened a new, broad range of investment opportunities in large-cap, mid-cap, small-cap, value, growth, domestic, international, country and regional equity indices as well as in corporate and government fixed income indices. Additionally, a trend towards setting up sector ETFs could eventually include style-based offerings and actively managed funds.

Key benefits of return enhancement and the ability to offset custodial and administrative fees help funds squeeze a few extra basis points out of their performance. This can be anywhere between five and thirty basis points on a portfolio, and can often mean the difference between first and second quartile performance.

2. Characteristics

It is believed that growth in the use of ETFs reflects their superior characteristics. The characteristics of ETFs essentially are comparable to index tracker funds that are listed and trade on-exchange like stocks. Most ETFs are structured as open-ended mutual funds, registered under the local jurisdiction. The open-ended mutual fund structure allows ETFs to lend stock, which may generate extra income. In addition, these funds can hold other securities and financial instruments, including cash, fund equivalents, and futures. Dividends are reinvested in the fund on the day of receipt and are paid to ETF investors quarterly, semi-annually or annually.

Since the objective of exchange-traded funds is to give exposure to indices, ETFs may be useful to investors who want to passively track an index. Factors such as fees and expenses, taxes, corporate actions, differences in trading hours between the ETFs and the underlying stocks and adjustments to the underlying index may cause tracking error to the benchmark. ETFs can be bought and sold on margin or a commission basis like any other share – at market, limit or stop order. Further, ETFs are lendable and they are used as underlyings for derivatives. Index-linked ETFs have distinctive features. Each ETF is designed to track a specific index or basket of securities. They provide access to a wide spectrum of investment styles, asset classes, markets, and individual sectors.

Although ETFs typically replicate their underlying index exactly, they have the capacity to employ optimization and sampling techniques. ETFs utilise two types of investment strategies to track indices: replication and representative sampling.

Replication – ETFs using this strategy attempt to closely track their underlying index by holding substantially all the index constituents in the same weights as the underlying benchmarks. The streetTRACKS MSCI Europe sector ETFs for example utilise this strategy.

Representative sampling – is used when a full replication strategy is difficult to implement. For instance indices with several hundred constituents, some of which are relatively illiquid, are not easy to replicate. ETFs that apply this strategy hold a sample of stocks that have similar characteristics in terms of performance, industry weights, market capitalisation, and liquidity to the underlying index. ETFs and funds that use this strategy tend to have more tracking risk than funds using the full replication strategy. As an example, the iShares MSCI index funds utilise this strategy.

Small divergences in performance are possible between an ETF and the index it tracks. This can be due to fund fees and expenses, a slight premium or discount, a tracking error because of optimised replication of the tracked index, rebalancing due to index changes, or the dividend reinvestment policy of the fund. In addition to the index strategy, some other sources of tracking risk are portfolio rebalancing frequency, composition guidelines, dividend payout schedules and trading hours. The greater majority of ETFs listed have exhibited very low tracking risk over the past year. However, the actual tracking risk going forward may be higher, depending on the implementation of the fund manager's tracking strategy.

ETFs promote tracking efficiency through their arbitrage mechanism. ETFs tend to trade at or close to their underlying NAVs. This is because there are arbitrageurs waiting to take advantage of a significant premium or discount relative to the underlying index. An arbitrageur will buy/sell the ETF and place an offsetting buy/sell transaction in the underlying basket of component stocks or futures.

Tracking Risks – index-linked ETFs are subject to 'tracking error' risks. Factors such as transaction costs, expenses, imperfect correlation between an ETF's stocks and those in its underlying index, rounding, changes to indices, and regulatory policies may cause an ETF's performance to deviate from that of its underlying index.

Major sources of tracking error are:

- Transaction costs, fees and expenses will cause an underperformance over time. Further premiums / discounts relative to the NAV have an influence on the performance of the ETF versus its index for periods ending on that specific date.
- Optimisation and replication use several techniques to create ETF portfolios to closely track the index while minimizing transaction costs. Using representative sampling, an ETF typically has different weights to the index in some stocks or even omits certain stocks entirely. All in all Optimisation / representative sampling therefore lead to deviations, affecting relative performance.
- Rebalancings of index-linked ETFs are required due to changes in the composition of the index when stocks are added or dropped. The timing, market impact, and transaction costs of the changes can affect relative performance.
- Non-concurrent trading hours are an issue if ETFs are traded when their underlying markets are closed. For example, the Japanese market is closed while an ETF tracking the Japanese market is trading on the American Stock Exchange. Given increased correlation between markets, ETFs based on the Japanese market may appear to be at a premium prior to the start of the trading day in Japan when the US market is up in anticipation that the Japanese market will rally. Similarly, on a down day in the US, the ETF on the Japanese market may appear to be at a discount.

  Dividend reinvestments can be an issue. In accordance with the product specification, some ETFs hold dividends in cash and only pay them out to investors on a periodic basis. These ETFs accumulate the dividends paid by the shares held in the fund on an ongoing basis. The dividends become part of the NAV and add to the ETF assets, until the ETF pays out cash to its investors as dividend. At the ETF dividend ex-date, the ETF NAV only contains the value of the underlying shares, and mirrors the value of the price index more closely. The chart below displays this mechanism.

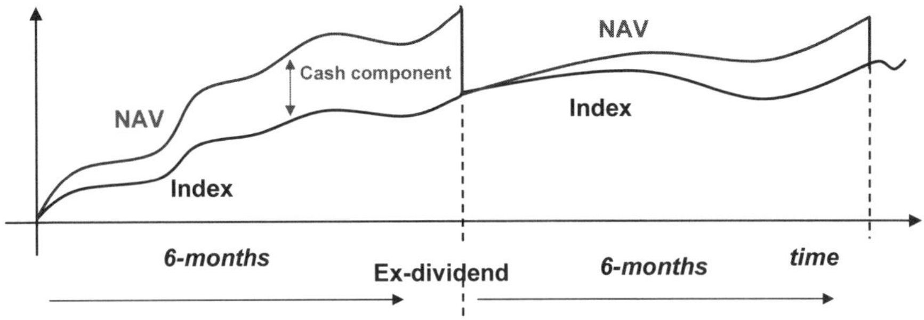

Figure 1: Dividend accumulation and pay-out of an ETF NAV. Source: Merrill Lynch ETF Research

- The dividend payments accumulated in the NAV add to the statistical tracking error between the ETF and the underlying price index (but in a positive way: the NAV outperforms). The dividend drops incurred at the ex-date further add to the statistical tracking error. Using a total return index, rather than the price index, does not solve this problem: the total return index assumes that dividends are re-invested, rather than taken along as cash. Furthermore, differences in tax assumptions between ETF and index provider, as well as in dividend adjustment (ex date) and payment dates add to discrepancies between total return index and NAV. This and the dividend drop add to statistical tracking error even between the NAV and the total return index. Management fees are deducted from the NAV on a daily basis.
- In contrast to this procedure, some ETFs reinvest dividends daily. A lag dividend reinvestment can cause small underperformance in rising markets and small outperformance in falling markets.

However, in contrast to index funds in particular, ETFs have huge advantages in terms of costs, liquidity, transparency and trading efficiency.

Why would investors care about something as basic as an index fund offered as a share? In itself, it is nothing to get especially excited about, however, looking deeper the functions of ETFs are remarkable. Unlike regular index funds, ETFs are proving to be highly flexible tools that can be used in radically different ways. The most obvious benefit for all investors is the set up of a diversified instrument – the underlying ETF – with one or several transactions. Alternatively, an investor could buy individual stocks. But in buying 100 stocks, for example, you then have to administer the dividend payments, corporate actions, stock splits and so forth for all those stocks. Therefore ETFs can be used as an alternative to programme trading. Taking a closer look at programme trading, a basket requires the ability to trade and settle numerous stocks and the consequent administration of all the holdings – although difficult to generalise, the reduction in custody costs can be significant. Stock baskets also have to manage to track the index accurately, which results in additional settlement tickets and the associated costs.

Indicative net asset values (iNAVs) are calculated on a continuous basis for ETFs, allowing investors to buy and sell them at stated market prices. This helps to reduce the uncertainty inherent in traditional open-ended funds of buying shares intraday at prices to be determined at the close. Therefore buying and selling ETFs is much more efficient and transparent than trading mutual funds.

ETFs do not have any sales loads whatsoever, although they do – like mutual funds – have management fees as well as transaction costs. In fact, ETFs have some of the lowest expense ratios among registered investment products. The annual expenses are deducted from dividend payments, which are, according to each product's individual specifications, paid once or twice a year on predefined dates.

Further important benefits of ETFs are choice and transparency. The exchange-traded fund class now covers a panorama of underlying indices, market segments and portfolio strategies – offering both broad diversification as well as a variety of imaginative ways of investing. For example, the euro made people reconsider the whole idea of how to invest and the benefits of investing on a sectoral rather than a geographical basis became more apparent.

ETFs are also transparent, in that the constituents of ETF portfolios are disclosed every trading day. Consequently, investors are provided with a continuous overview of the weighting of the individual shares in the portfolio based on the prior day's closing prices. By contrast, traditional mutual funds usually reveal their entire holdings just twice a year.

Further, liquidity plays an important role. ETFs afford investors two forms of liquidity. The first is through trading the shares on a secondary basis on the exchange. The second is via the 'creation unit' process (please refer to the next section of this article on the following pages for details), whereby an 'authorised participant' purchases the underlying basket of shares in the local market and deposits the basket 'in kind' into the ETF, creating more shares in that ETF. The unique creation / redemption process means that the liquidity in the ETF is driven by the liquidity in the underlying shares.

While small divergences in performance between an ETF and the index it tracks occur due to fund fees and expenses, optimised replication of the tracked index means that ETF performance is generally close to that of the index, regardless of the volume of trading. This is because the liquidity of ETFs is driven by the liquidity of the underlying shares rather than demand for the ETF itself.

Another aspect that leads to divergences in performance between ETF and underlying index is transaction costs. The actual performance that investors achieve is affected by both buying and selling ETF shares. Premiums / discounts and wide bid / ask spreads lead among other things to differences in market performance between an ETF's NAV and that ETF's underlying index. However, authorized participants operating as market makers reduce this impact, providing liquidity by creating or redeeming shares at or close to NAV. They quote ongoing bid and ask prices, thus guaranteeing high liquidity.

The major players in index-related markets have traditionally been large institutional investors seeking to index core holdings or pursue more aggressive market timing and sector rotation strategies. However, since smaller institutions and retail investors can trade in small lots, they can invest on essentially the same terms as larger investors. Therefore ETFs may appeal to a broad range of investors.

ETFs can be used in a similar way to futures – but with more flexibility. They are flexible non-derivative investments that allow investors to quickly react to short- and long-term needs or opportunities. Typically index futures are bought by fund managers because buying the individual components of an index would be expensive and time consuming. ETFs have several advantages over futures, and can also match the main advantage of futures, i.e. enabling investors to trade both long and short.

Futures are derivative instruments and investors are not always allowed to buy or sell them. Further practical issues are to be considered in the implementation of derivatives. There are operational complexities with account set-up, including detailed legal documentation. Ongoing position management necessitates the capacity to manage both the future position and the cash held against them as collateral, as well as the daily margin requirement. Purchasing and holding an ETF only involves one trade and the custody of a single asset. Day to day attention to such matter as maintaining the index shape or dealing with administration related to tax reclaims on dividends is minimised – in short, the cost of the investment process of tracking the index is externalised. As such, they may serve as an alternative to futures, trading baskets of stocks, and traditional mutual funds.

Futures and Options contracts on ETFs complete the product range. They are no substitute for such products; instead they form an ideal complement to the existing index derivatives segment. Futures and Options on ETFs deliver potential for arbitrage by trading on the difference between the derivatives and spot markets (ETFs and the index's underlying).

The following chart displays all components out of one hand.

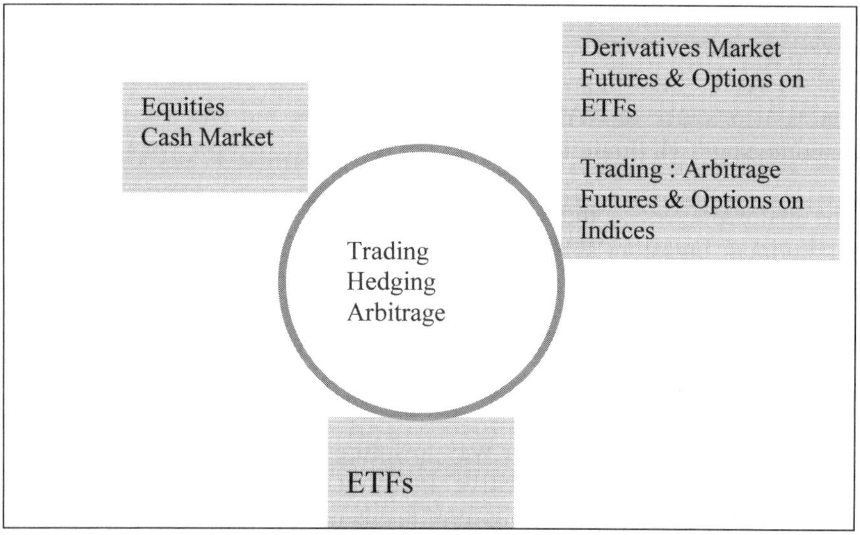

Figure 2: A complete product range out of one hand; Source: Deutsche Börse AG

3. Creation and Redemption Process

ETFs have a unique so-called creation / redemption mechanism which allows professional market participants to exchange baskets of shares with the same composition at any time for ETFs (and vice versa) with the fund. This ability to continually create or redeem shares helps keep an ETF's market price in line with its underlying net asset value. A key feature that distinguishes ETFs is that the shares are created by 'authorised participants' or creation/redemption brokers in block-size 'creation units'. The creator deposits into the applicable fund a portfolio of stocks closely approximating the holdings of the index in exchange for an institutional block of ETF shares (usually 50,000). Similarly, they can only be redeemed in redemption units, mainly 'in-kind' for a portfolio of stocks held by the fund. The redemption and creation processes are very similar. However, a key benefit is that the in-kind distribution of securities does not create a tax-event, which could occur if the fund sold securities and delivered cash. This is a special advantage of an index-linked ETF versus an open-ended indexed mutual fund, which would have to sell securities to meet cash redemptions.[2]

Creation Process at the Authorized Participation Level	Redemption process at the Authorized Participation Level
An Authorized Participant (AP) initiates the creation of ETF shares. The broker/dealer may purchase ETF shares to fulfil customer orders or for their own inventory.	The ETF portfolio value (NAV) is calculated at the close of each trading day.
The AP may purchase individual stocks contained in the ETF basket of stocks in the relevant market. I.e., unless the AP has a stock position in the S&P 500, the entire S&P 500 portfolio is purchased. The value of the portfolio is calculated at the close of each trading day.	The ETF shares are delivered to the custodian in creation unit size. At settlement, securities comprising the index plus a cost component are delivered to the AP.
The stock basket is delivered to custodian bank.	A nominal fee is charged for this transaction.
In addition, a cash component is delivered to the custodian to cover the fees for creation and	The AP will receive the basket of stocks underlying the ETF plus a cash component and
– accrued dividends, – interest on dividends, – accrued revenues from stock lending as well as – any capital gains less losses on the ETF that have not been reinvested since the last distribution less any custody and transfer charges.	– accrued dividends, – interest on dividends, – accrued revenues from stock lending as well as – any capital gains less losses on the ETF that have not been reinvested since the last distribution less any custody and transfer charges.
At settlement, the custodian delivers the ETF shares to the AP, usually an institutional block of 50,000 shares.	The fund can reduce cash by the amount equal to the dividends on any deposit security that should be paid to the fund.

Figure 3: Creation / Redemption Process; Source: Morgan Stanley ETF Strategies

2 Source: Morgan Stanley ETF Strategies.

The issuers and primary traders of index funds operate following the creation – redemption model. In order to track the underlying index, the Designated Sponsors set up a basket of stocks with a composition that mirrors the fund portfolio 1:1. They receive unit shares from the issuers, to the value of the basket, which can subsequently be sold on the market (creation of fund shares). They can also redeem unit shares in the fund, receiving stocks from the issuer in exchange (redemption)[3].

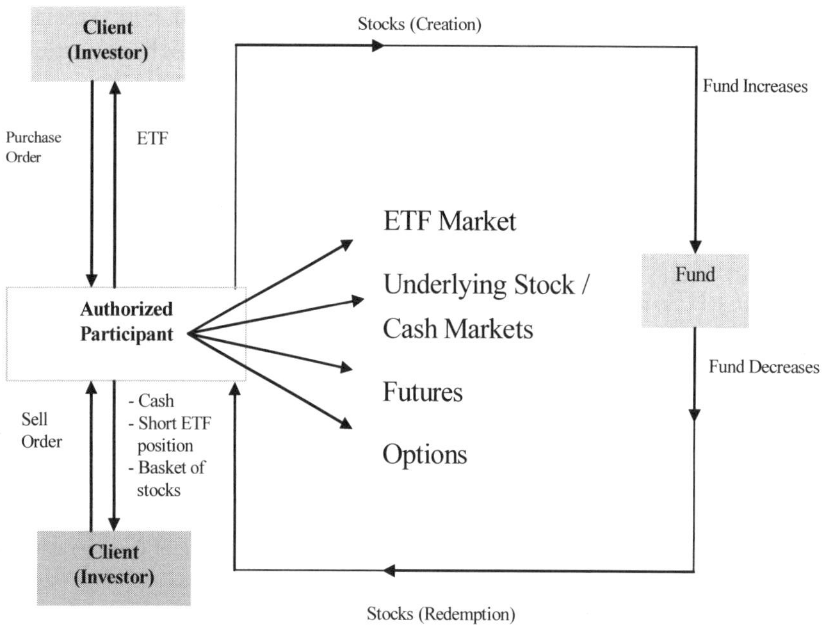

Figure 4: ETF Trading Process; Source: Morgan Stanley ETF Strategies

4. Investment Applications

ETFs offer a broad range of investment applications.

- **Asset Allocation.** As most investors will know, the key driver of investment performance is the asset allocation strategy. A study by Brinson, Hood and Beebower in 1986 showed that asset allocation is responsible for about 94% of the total return in a typical, well diversified

---

[3] Source: Morgan Stanley ETF Strategies.

portfolio. This recognition has led to the increased use of core / satellite approaches to investment structures, where the core holding of the portfolio is invested in low cost index tracking vehicles and additional returns are sought form specialist investment managers. The general suitability of these vehicles for asset allocation can be looked at in terms of long-term strategic asset allocation, short-term tactical asset allocation and very short-term speculation and other trading activities like sector rotation or more aggressive market timing strategies.

ETFs can form the core holding in a portfolio with the aim of providing global diversification as well as reducing portfolio risk. Further, ETFs can be used to target sectors where there are no futures contracts. Investors may find this appealing, as they merely have to purchase appropriate investments for each market segment in their proper weightings and occasionally rebalance their portfolios. Further, they also provide convenient investments in markets and securities that otherwise might be inaccessible. ETFs can also be used to adjust sector or country exposure and to avoid style drifts.

- **Hedge a portfolio, an index, a sector or a country**. ETFs can be used for hedging purposes. They can be sold short like individual stocks to hedge a portfolio of stocks, allowing an investor to preserve a portfolio while protecting it from overall market losses.

- **Cash management or Equitization.** Investors can use ETFs as a cash management tool. Index linked ETFs can be traded to 'equitise' cash inflows that could eventually be invested in stocks. Further they can be traded to liquidate from an investment. Transactions can be done in relatively small increments — ETFs typically trade in round lots of 1,000 shares. ETFs can be a good alternative to using futures to manage cash flow; they can be bought in smaller sizes than futures, they do not require any special documentation or accounts, and investors do not have to worry about roll costs and margin requirements. In addition, the current array of ETFs covers many benchmarks for which there is no futures contract.

- **Arbitrage.** There is a close relationship between the cash market index level and the corresponding futures price. During the lifetime of a futures contract, however, there will be fluctuations in both the cash and futures markets leading to arbitrage opportunities.

- **Lending.** The global equity finance or stock borrowing market has rapidly evolved over the past year, facilitating ETF lending and borrowing.

Limited availability and fragmented ETF holdings across European investors, mean market lending fees for ETFs often reach multiples of the TER, making ETF lending very lucrative. Lending ETFs generates welcome fee revenue while enhancing market liquidity. Particularly stable index tracking or core portfolios as well as long-term investments are ideally suited to securities lending.

5. Conclusions

ETF advantages attract both investors and traders. They have some of the lowest associated costs of any registered investment product. Their expense ratios are significantly lower than those of traditional mutual funds.

ETFs tend to be lower-risk investments than individual stocks because of their diversification. In addition, they are transparent, since the fund manager discloses the underlying basket of shares to the market every day and, unlike traditional funds, are not subject to style drift. Index-linked ETFs can also be shorted, providing extra flexibility for hedging or market-timing strategies.

ETFs typically offer strong liquidity. They also settle just like any other share traded on the exchange. Many ETFs have listed futures and options. Derivatives linked to ETFs offer strategies for managing risk or expanding opportunities for profit.

Consequently, investors increasingly appreciate the features that ETFs offer: reliable index performance, a wide array of investment strategies and strong liquidity coupled with quick buy and sell opportunities in asset management.

References

ETF Newsletter No. 4 I 2 Quarter 04, Swiss Exchange virti-x, Zürich 2004. www.swx.Com/www.virt-x.com

Pan-European Tracking – Stocks vs. Futures vs. ETFs; Barclays Global Investors 11.03 November 2003

Vision + moneyspecials; The Financial Markets Magazine of Deutsche Börse AG; October 2002. www.deutsche-boerse.com

The Euro ETF Report. An International Fund Investment Supplement. November – December 2002. www.ifiglobalonline.com

Pi Portfolio International. An Investment Guide for European Institutionals and their Advisors October 2002. www.portfolio-international.com

XTF Exchange Traded Funds – A Guide for Traders. Deutsche Börse. www.deutsche-boerse.com

Deutsche Bank – Trading & Index Strategy – Exchange Traded Funds -Weekly Analysis. www.db.com

Morgan Stanley – Exchange Traded Funds Strategies – ETF Worldwide Guidebook and new ETF Strategy reports. www.morganstanley.com

Merrill Lynch European Equity Derivatives Weekly – Merrill Lynch Global Securities Research & Economics Group – Equity Derivatives Strategy Department. www.ml.com

STOXX Limited The ETF Market STOXX LIMITED Selnaustrasse 30 CH 8021 Zurich Switzerland. A Joint Venture between Deutsche Börse AG Dow Jones & Company SWX Group. www.stoxx.com

From Continent to Sectors: Challenges and Uses of ETFs in Europe

Alain Dubois and Stephane Barthelemy

Throughout 2002, Exchange Traded Funds (ETFs), known in Europe as "Trackers" enjoyed an extensive media coverage. Fact is that the growth, both in terms of product offering and assets under management has been impressive.

In Europe, the ETFs are mainly used by institutional investors with few retail interests. Despite the rapid growth of the ETF market, an enormous educational task remains to be done. The concept, cost structure, distribution mechanism and uses are not always fully understood. It is the responsibility of the issuers and their partners to explain all the aspects of the product in the hope of ensuring steady growth in all market segments. In this article, we will highlight a few of these challenges, mainly from the issuers standpoint, attempt to provide a fair picture of the market and discuss our view on future development particularly with regards to sector funds.

1. ETFs in Europe and in US – Same Product, Different Market

ETFs are relatively new. They first one emerged in 1993 in the U.S with the S&P 500 SPDRs. The US market took time to develop, but is now well established through recognized "brands" likes the QQQ's and the SPDRs which make up 55% of the total US ETF market.

After ten years, a handful of asset management firms dominate the US market. This is not the case in Europe.

In the US, three issuers (BGI, SSGA, BONY) share 90% of the market, whereas, in Europe, the overall market is much more fragmented, with the

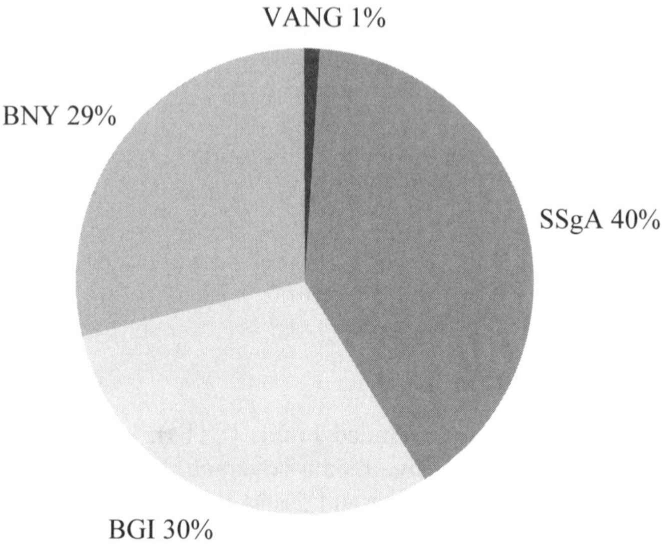

Figure 1: Issuers in the US

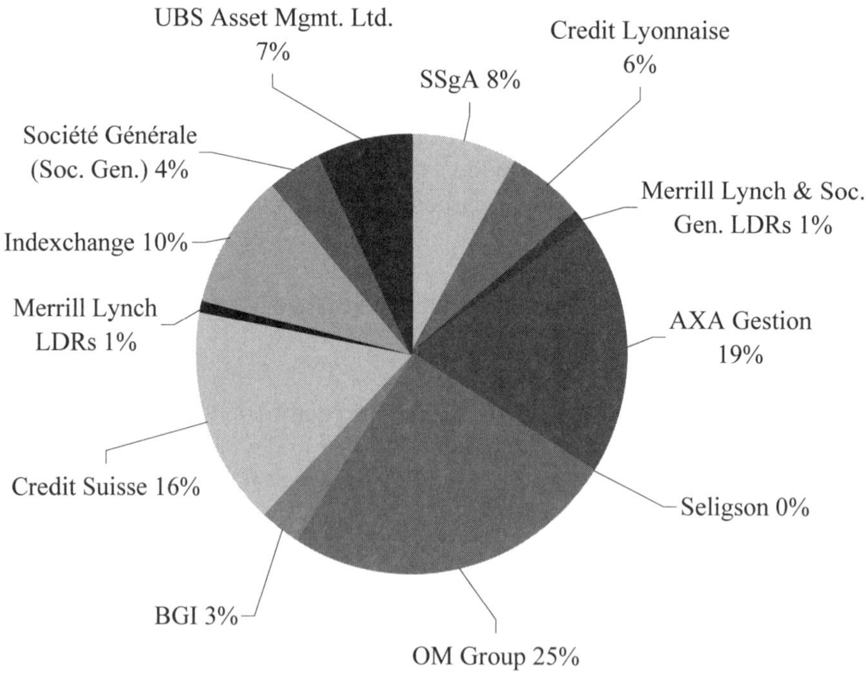

Figure 2: Issuers in Europe

three main issuers sharing 53% of the market. In addition, in terms of the pure number of sponsors, the US counts 4 firms and 113 funds present on the ETF market, compared to 14 players and 117 funds in Europe[1].

The type of firms involved in the US and in Europe also differs. In America, the main players are best known for their institutional business and have little retail presence. Their products, on the other hand, have gained recognition. Whereas most retail individuals know "the QQQs" and the SPDRs," few are aware of the actors behind the fund. In Europe, some of the largest firms involved in the ETF business have both a recognized brand name within the retail market in the institutional arena. This has a direct impact on the distribution of the ETFs and their progressive acceptance and understanding by the public.

This leads us to one of the challenges faced by the issuers of ETFs: sales and marketing. ETFs are listed real time priced index funds. As such, they are convenient and available for institutional and retail investors and are used in the implementation of passive and active strategies, e.g.: core satellite asset allocation, transition management, cash equitisation and other multiple applications.

2. Marketing of ETFs in Europe, the Who's and Why's

Because they are funds, ETFs, need to be registered for marketing in the various jurisdictions in Europe. The registration process varies depending on the markets, as does the freedom to present and discuss the products. This implies that the issuers have to make strategic choices as to where they will apply their resources and decide on the countries in which their funds will need to be registered. The majority of trackers in Europe have been registered in multiple jurisdictions to allow the sales process to be in line with local regulatory requirements. In several cases, ETFs have been cross-listed on multiple exchanges in pursuit of a better market penetration.

Since they are not only funds, but also listed securities, the ETFs can be bought on an exchange. As listed securities, market makers need to be present and to provide a spread, which varies depending on local rules and practices. The existence of primary and secondary market has a direct im-

[1] Source: SSGA 2003

pact on distribution and on asset growth. In effect, unlike classic mutual funds, large portions of the issuers do not have direct contractual relationships with the users of the fund. As a result of this, the role of the broker dealer is extremely important because he plays a key function in the sales process. Another player is the exchange, which has an important role in the education of both the public and the professional intermediaries. In effect, because of the potential importance of retail as a market for ETFs, the message needs to be effectively communicated. In several European countries, the education has been mainly handled by the exchanges which are recognized as neutral and can then focus on the concept of trackers rather than on a specific brand or index.

So far education effort has been conducted via road shows, articles and training sessions and should be continuing in the following months, if not years.

The specifics of the ETFs are such that the classic retail distribution channels are challenged. The European landscape is characterized by a large number of sponsors, some of which have their established distribution networks which can be leveraged to provide ETFs to their clients. In other cases, the fund management company does not have direct access to retail investors. The logical approach in this case would be to use third party distributors to reach the public. In the case of ETFs, this is more difficult to implement for the following reasons: firstly, low expense ratios do not provide for fee sharing of a sufficient level for a distributor to allocate time and resources. Secondly, the fact that an ETF can be traded on an exchange makes the monitoring of the outstanding shares balance more challenging, hence the calculation of rebates and distribution fees difficult to track and implement. Consequently, the lack of understanding of the product and relatively low motivation for the distributor implies that institutional investors make up the main users of the European ETFs. This affects the marketing, product design and sales process of ETFs.

One of the key drivers for an appropriate marketing strategy is to understand the market and how the funds are used by the final investors. In the case of ETFs, the lack of contractual relationships between the fund provider and the users makes this intelligence gathering more difficult than for other commingled products. Based on market research and numerous client meetings, it is possible to draft a high level profile of ETF users. The product offering can be divided into 3 main segments, each of which has its own user base and dynamics.

These categories are:

- ETFs based on domestic Indices (CAC, AEX, DAX, etc.)
- ETFs based on large indices (MSCI pan euro, STOXX, Euro STOXX, SPDR Europe 350)
- Sector ETFs (MSCI Sectors; Stoxx etc.)

During the last year, each category experienced different growth rates and degrees of acceptance. As an example, the following table compares the growth in term of assets and in number of funds belonging to each of the 3 categories:

Table 1: Growth in AUM – 3 categories

2001

Index type	Number of Funds	AUM (USD)	Percent total (AUM)	Percent Total (No of funds)
Domestic	10	1,940	35.95 %	14 %
Large	18	2,820	52.26 %	26 %
Sectors	42	636	11.79 %	60 %
Total	70	5,396	100 %	100 %

2002

Index type	Number of Funds	AUM (USD)	Percent total (AUM)	Percent Total (No of funds)
Domestic	15	3,489	33.36 %	13 %
Large	24	5,800	55.45 %	21 %
Sectors	78	1,170	11.19 %	67 %
Total	117	10,459	100 %	100 %

Overall ETFs offering and Assets under Management (AUM) have shown an impressive growth between 2001 and 2002, with the large indices keeping the leadership in term of assets.

3. Who Buys ETFs and Why

The first category – domestic index based ETFs – is used both by institutional and retail investors. The StreetTRACKS AEX index, for example, is used mainly by Dutch retail investors for long-term exposure. In effect, the index is known and recognized by the local investor community and the fees are competitive, compared to similar funds offered in the market.

The second and third category (large and sector ETFs), are used mainly by institutional investors for risk management purposes, either to equitize cash inflows or as flexible and anonymous asset allocation tools (large ETFs) or to implement a more active asset allocation (sectors).

Sector ETFs make an interesting case. The growth in fund offer has been staggering with the number of sector based ETFs rose in 2002 by 85 %, representing 67 % of the number of funds offered. From the asset size standpoint, the sector products remained at 11 % market share, far behind the other segments.

Based on the hypothesis that the sector funds are mainly used by institutionals, one should ask the following question: does sector investing add value or is it just marketing hype?

It is not the purpose of this article to discuss the advantages of sector investing versus other types of asset allocation. Nevertheless, based on available data, "sector" investing in Europe does contribute to a higher level of diversification than "country" investing. The following graph shows that since 1999, the correlation across countries in Europe increases while the correlation across sectors follows a reverse trend:

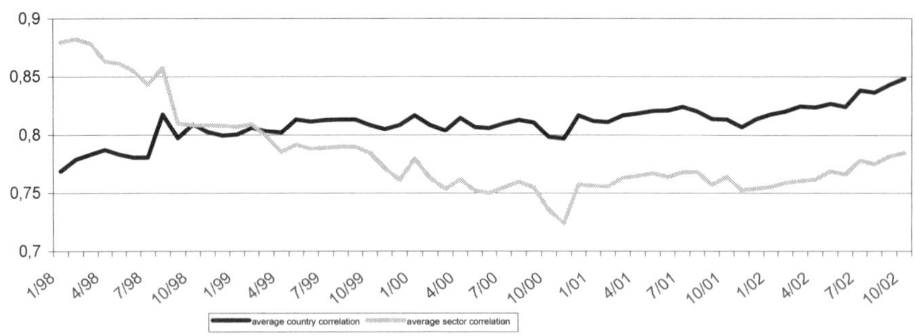

Figure 3: Correlation across countries in Europe. Source: SSGA, 2003

From the point of view of risk return, the sectors have very different behaviour as shown in the following graph:

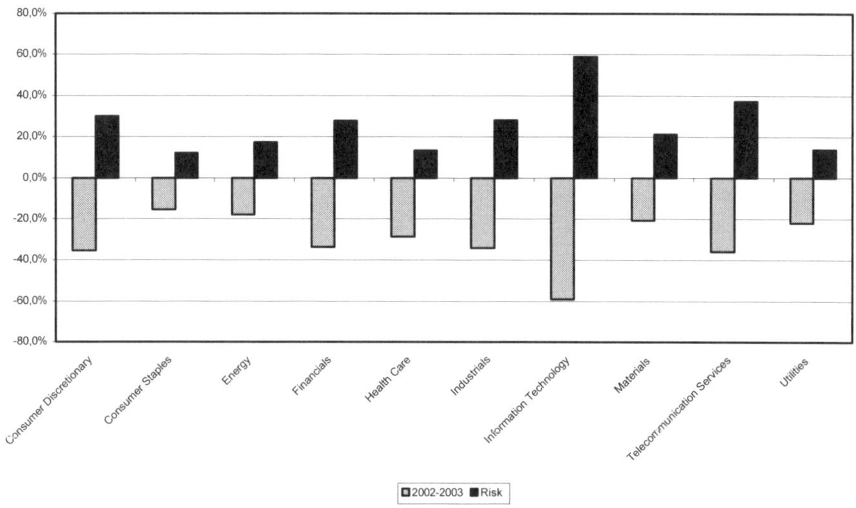

Figure 4: Risk and Returns MSCI European Sectors 2002-2003. Source: SSGA/ Barra

Based on the data above and taking the position that sector indexing does make sense, what is the role that sector ETFs can play in such a strategy? To implement a sector-based strategy several approaches are available, mainly depending on the level of risk that an investor is willing to take. Basic portfolio theory accords an important role to diversification with regard to risk control. Indeed, in the case of a sector-based strategy, the universe of stocks in a single sector is less than the available exposure in a regional index like the MSCI Europe. By taking individual sector bets, the investor is aiming at outperforming the overall benchmark of choice. More and more strategists will decide to use ETFs as a tool to implement a sector strategy by over-weighting some sectors against their weight in the index. In addition, because ETFs can be sold short, investors can take a short sell position on a less favoured sector, hoping to produce "alphas" in both long and short positions.

Nevertheless, the most active strategists believe that sector ETFs do not provide a good enough level of detail as they encompass several industries which can have different behaviours. This may be the case, for example, for "MSCI Europe Consumer Discretionary" with 12 sub industries or for the finance sector as evidenced by the "MSCI Europe Finance" with 4 sub industries. The breakdown of some sectors into industries is shown hereafter:

Table 2: Sector Breakdown: Consumers Discretionary

Consumers Discretionary	
Automobile	16 %
Automobiles Components	3 %
Distributors	0 %
Hotels, Restaurants & Leisure	13 %
Household Durables & Apparel	11 %
Internet and catalogue retail	3 %
Leisure equipment and product	1 %
Media	31 %
Multi line retail	7 %
Retailing	1 %
Specialty retail	9 %
Textile apparel and luxury goods	8 %

Table 3: Sector Breakdown: Finance

Finance	
Banks	70 %
Diversified Financials	8 %
Insurance	19 %
Real Estate	2 %

But not the case for MSCI Europe Energy witch is more concentrated:

Table 4: Sector Breakdown: Energy

Energy	
Equipment and services	1 %
Oil and Gas	99 %

For these managers, the correct approach is to invest at industry level. So, the question arises: would industry ETFs make sense to meet these needs? As often in our world, the answer is "it depends on the index of reference". If the index is broad enough, the diversification at the industry level can be implemented through ETFs. If this not the case, the number of stocks and the weights of the individual securities within the industry will not warrant the creation of a tracker. Indeed, while discussing the creation of industry based ETFs, the following should be noted:

- Some industries are too small: 46 industries out of 59 weigh less than 1 % of the MSCI Europe.
- In some industries, the number of stocks is too small to warrant the creation of an ETF: 25 Industries amongst 59 have 5 stocks or less.
- Even large industries are highly concentrated: the top 5 stocks of the second largest industry (Oils and Gas) weigh 91 % of the overall category.

The more active professional investors will prefer to implement a bottom-up approach by allocating the strategic sector weight and then making individual stock selections within the overall weight in order to "beat the sectors". In doing so in the 10 sectors, they would aim to out perform the overall index. This method carries more risk, in terms of stock specific risk and may or may not prove successful when balancing risk and reward.

It is not the goal of this paper to open the passive versus active debate. But, based on existing techniques, we would suggest that balanced approach could be implemented making the "best of both worlds". In effect, by combining ETFs at the sector level with a more active strategy, managers will be able to maintain a "risk cushion" based on their strategic asset allocation, and then, implement a fully active stock picking strategy as described above. The weight of the ETFs versus the individual stocks will be driven by both the risk budget and the sentiment present within each sector. Another advantage of using ETFs is that the manager will be able to adjust sector allocation(s) without having to cut the mid to long-term bets taken on single stocks by the active managers. We believe that this approach is widely used for sector allocation in Europe.

Further, this is an approach of choice for institutions aiming at decreasing administration costs, where a rebalancing in multiple portfolios implies numerous movements and where the administration of random stocks specific events (merger, corporate actions, tax reclaims etc.) can be an organizational and a financial burden. For these investors with multiple accounts, the costs of using ETFs –fees – is more than compensated by the indirect savings made on the overall administration.

This has several consequences: to attract such active investors, the issuers need to provide the full range of sectors, even if it implies that some ETFs will remain idle at times. But to implement an efficient sector rotation philosophy, the entire range must be available. The chart below represents the changes of weight in some sectors comparing to the larger StreetTRACKS MSCI pan euro showing that the movements within the sectors funds are much more frequent, due to their use in sector rotation techniques.

Nevertheless, despite a rapid outstanding growth, the ETFs are still surrounded by several misconceptions, mainly with regards to fees and to

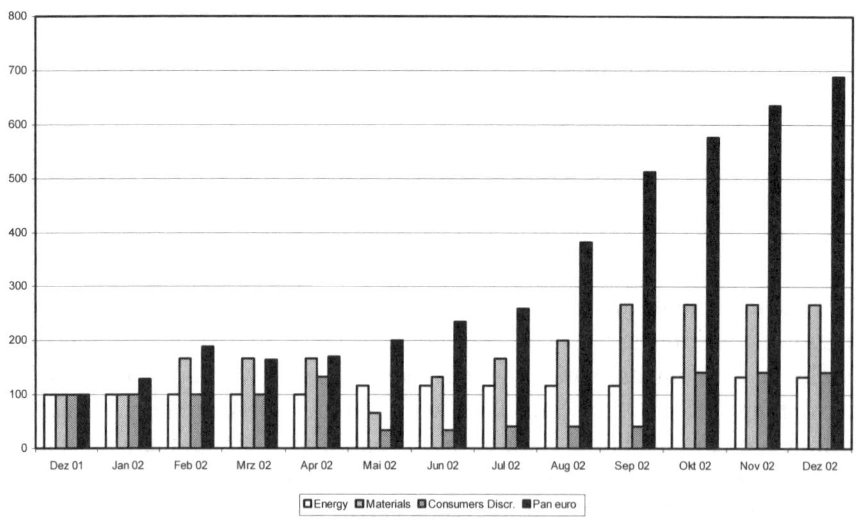

Figure 5: Sector rotation. Source: SSGA, 2003

liquidity. When comparing the ETF market in the US and in Europe, one usually focuses incorrectly on the fee differences. But the comparison does not stop there. I would advocate that lower costs in the US are far from being the rule. In effect, the arithmetic average total expense ratio in American ETFs is 45bp (versus 45.7bp in Europe). The distribution of ETFs fees in the US market is wide, ranging from a low 9bp to 84bp for some single country products. The references for ETFs are often the "Big Three", the Spider, the QQQs and the Diamonds, which together make up 52% of the US ETF market capitalization. Their size and low fees are like a beacon in the forest of ETFs; forest because the US offering is a lot more vast and mature. In fact, more than fees, it is the choice that differentiates both markets. In effect, in Europe, the ETF equity landscape is characterized by three market segments: sector indices, large or regional indices (MSCI, STOXX, S&P etc.) and domestic benchmarks (DAX, CAC 40, AEX etc.). The perception of illiquidity is a little bit more complex since it relies to the very definition of an ETF.

4. Liquidity in the StreetTRACKS MSCI Europe Sectors ETFs

ETFs are commingled investment products containing a pool of securities representing a specific index. They exhibit two form of liquidity:

- Trading of ETF units on the secondary market: ETFs are built like mutual funds but trade like stocks. They are priced continuously and can be bought or sold throughout the trading day. Their pricing for a minimum size is permanently ensured by at least two market makers who are officially committed to the quotation.

- Creation and Redemption of ETF units: contributions and redemptions of ETFs are limited to in-species baskets. Following the creation process, market makers – acting as authorized participants – purchase the underlying basket of shares in the local market and deliver the basket in kind to the ETF manager in exchange for units in the corresponding ETF. Market makers can deliver ETF units to the ETF manager and take delivery of the underlying basket of shares through the redemption process. These baskets of shares are determined and published for each ETF by the ETF manager on a daily basis.

The liquidity can be defined as the ability to sell quickly at a fair and certain price, and can be basically measured in three ways:

- Market depth and breadth: the breadth is determined by the number of participants and the depth by the size of orders in the order book. They both assert the ability to trade quickly at a certain price. However, the liquidity of ETFs is theoretically guaranteed for an unlimited amount of units through the creation and redemption process. ETFs can always be created or redeemed upon request on the primary market, in exchange for the underlying basket of stocks to meet supply and demand on the secondary market.
- Traded volume: that evaluation may only be appropriate for mature ETF markets where past volumes reflect the current conditions of trading such investment products. Moreover, a large number of ETF units can be traded over the counter and are not reported to the market place.

The following table shows some examples of both reported and unreported volumes of StreetTRACKS ETFs.

Table 5: Reported and unreported volumes

ETFs		TradedVol(units)	Turnover(mio)	Date	MarketStatus
	Pan Euro	425,600	30.2	09/25/04	reported
		900,000	81.1	10/7/2004	OTC unreported
	HealthCare	120,000	5.54	23/06/2004	reported
	Financials	70,000	2.71	16/06/2003	reported
	Info Technology	127,710	3.52	24/06/2004	reported
	Energy	100,000	6.70	22/04/2004	OTC unreported

- Bid/Ask spread: the market spread is the difference between the bid and the offer prices and provides a measure of the investors' ability to trade at a fair and efficient price. As described below, the spread of a given ETF is directly linked to the spread of the stocks constituting the index.

Market makers typically sell ETF units on the market, and simultaneously buy the shares of the underlying basket to be delivered against new ETF units. Inversely, they buy ETF units on the market, and sell the shares of the corresponding basket at the same time. Those sales are then covered by the delivery of shares in exchange for the ETF units redeemed.

To be arbitrage free, the bid price of a given ETF will then be equal to the sum of the products of the underlying shares and their bid price (converted in the currency of the ETF), divided by the fund divisor. In a similar way, the ask price of a given ETF will be equal to the sum of the product of the underlying shares and their ask price (converted in the currency of the ETF), divided by the number of ETF unit for one basket. Those prices must be adjusted for local taxes. In addition, the basket value must be adjusted for dividends through the cash component.

$$Bid\ price_{etf} = \frac{\sum_{i=1}^{n} \left(n_i * bid\ price_i * \left(1 - sell\ side\ tax_i\%\right) * bid\ spot_{etfi/i}\right) + cash\ component_{etf}}{n_{etf}}$$

$$Ask\ price_{etf} = \frac{\sum_{i=1}^{n} \left(n_i * ask\ price_i * \left(1 + buy\ side\ tax_i\%\right) * ask\ spot_{etfi/i}\right) + cash\ component_{etf}}{n_{etf}}$$

i : underlying stock i included in the basket of n stocks

n_i : number of shares i included in the basket

n_{etf} : number of ETF units per basket or fund divisor

$spot_{i/etf}$: price of 1 unit of shares i currency in ETF currency term

Table 6: ETF quotes

Fund :	StreetTRACKS MSCI Europe Energy ETF
Ticker :	STN FP
Fund data for :	01/07/02
NAV per share :	73.02 EUR
Est. Cash Component :	43.50 EUR
Fund divisor :	50,000
Number of companies :	17

	Spread	Mid	Bid	Ask
Market quotes	0.67%	73.85	73.60	74.10
Calculated	0.39%	73.74	73.60	73.89
Local time	12:40			

	Bid TotalValue	Ask TotalValue
Equity	3,679,943	3,694,402
Cash	43.50	43.50

Curr	Sedol	Company	Shares	Bid	SellTax	Ask	BuyTax	Fx Bid	Fx Ask	BidValue	AskValue
EUR	4651459	OMV Ag	85	98.63	-	98.99	-	1.00	1.00	8,384	8,414
EUR	5669354	Repsol SA	5,765	12.08	-	12.10	-	1.00	1.00	69,641	69,757
EUR	5579550	Fortum OYJ	2,130	5.83	-	5.85	-	1.00	1.00	12,418	12,461
EUR	4905413	TotalfinaElf SA	4,016	166.00	-	166.30	-	1.00	1.00	666,656	667,861
EUR	4874160	Technip-Coflexip SA	126	108.50	-	108.70	-	1.00	1.00	13,671	13,696
EUR	5475658	Hellenic Petroleum SA	576	6.06	0.26%	6.10	0.06%	1.00	1.00	3,481	3,516
EUR	7145056	ENI Spa	17,637	16.30	-	16.31	-	1.00	1.00	287,483	287,659
EUR	5202704	Royal Dutch Petroleum	13,390	57.00	-	57.05	-	1.00	1.00	763,230	763,900
NOK	4645805	Norsk Hydro ASA	923	364.00	-	365.00	-	0.13	0.13	45,232	45,386
NOK	4502029	Kvaerner ASA	3,096	6.63	-	6.65	-	0.13	0.13	2,763	2,774
NOK	4564665	Smedvig ASA A-Shares	225	49.50	-	49.90	-	0.13	0.13	1,499	1,513
NOK	5469372	Petroleum Geo-Services ASA	651	26.90	-	27.20	-	0.13	0.13	2,358	2,386
NOK	4587189	Smedvig ASA B-Shares	158	40.20	-	42.40	-	0.13	0.13	855	903
NOK	7133608	Statoil ASA	2,757	67.00	-	67.50	-	0.13	0.13	24,869	25,071
GBp	0803414	Shell Transprt&Tradng Plc	61,334	4.99	-	4.99	0.50%	1.55	1.55	472,598	475,745
GBp	0798059	BP Plc	141,320	5.53	-	5.54	0.50%	1.55	1.55	1,207,964	1,215,888
GBp	0876289	BG Group Plc	22,217	2.82	-	2.82	0.50%	1.55	1.55	96,841	97,475

A detailed calculation of a StreetTRACKS sector ETF illustrates the above principles.

While the quoted bid price matches the theoretical bid price (73.60 EUR), the market ask price is slightly above the calculated ask price (74.10 versus 73.89).

Buying and selling pressures may temporarily drive ETF quotes, but the continuous contribution from market makers keep these prices close to the indicative NAV. Moreover, neither the bid nor the ask prices can legally deviate of more than 1.5% from the indicative NAV for ETFs listed on Euronext Paris. The indicative NAV is defined as the official NAV of the previous day, continually adjusted up and down to reflect the intra-day performance of the underlying real-time index.

Market spreads and traded volumes of the sector ETFs listed on Euronext are exposed below. These informations have been observed on 12/07/02 at 15:30 local time. The degree of liquidity is enhanced by the following factors:

- Basket trading facilities: trading large amount of stocks and simultaneously trading the corresponding ETFs is required to keep large sizes of ETF units fairly priced and arbitrage free.
- Futures and options: ETFs covered by futures and options can have their spread substantially improved as futures contracts can be used as a substitute for the underlying stocks at a lower transaction cost. In a similar way, options can be combined to create synthetic baskets (or stocks).
- Repo market: negotiating repurchase agreements is necessary to have the ability to sell short securities.
- Foreign listings: securities listed on exchanges different from their local market can be used as a substitute when trading is halted on the local market. The resulting position may be hedged with the use of foreign exchange derivatives.

The following table shows average spreads and trade sizes as published by Euronext in September 2004.

Table 7: Spreads and traded volume

06/12/04	Ticker	Bid	Ask	NavEst	NavInd	Spread	EtfPerf	Tracking	Vol1D	Vol20D	Turnv1D million EUR	Turnv20D million EUR
StreetTRACKS ETFs												
AEX	AEXT NA	34.15	34.20	34.19	34.20	0.15%	-0.48%	-0.05%	5,283	19,876	0.18	0.68
PanEuro	ERO FP	91.25	91.50	91.24	91.24	0.27%	-0.39%	0.14%	1,764	22,337	0.16	2.04
StreetTRACKS MSCI Europe ETF												
Cons Discretionary	STV FP	38.50	38.78	38.62	38.62	0.72%	-0.72%	0.05%	-	47	-	0.00
Cons Staples	STS FP	47.00	47.28	47.19	47.19	0.59%	-0.95%	-0.11%	-	802	-	0.04
Energy	STN FP	70.38	70.50	70.71	70.71	0.17%	-0.58%	-0.38%	-	7,507	-	0.53
Financials	STZ FP	47.52	47.79	47.74	47.74	0.56%	-0.62%	-0.17%	-	845	-	0.04
HealthCare	STW FP	43.50	43.78	43.67	43.67	0.64%	-0.95%	-0.07%	149	2,278	0.01	0.10
Industrials	STQ FP	53.54	54.00	53.79	53.79	0.85%	-0.59%	-0.03%	-	3,618	-	0.19
Info Technology	STK FP	32.00	32.12	32.05	32.05	0.37%	-0.43%	0.02%	-	1,762	-	0.06
Materials	STP FP	68.36	68.90	68.69	68.69	0.78%	-0.80%	-0.09%	10	1,239	0.00	0.09
Telecom	STT FP	36.71	37.06	36.99	36.99	0.94%	-0.53%	-0.27%	336	6,175	0.01	0.23
Utilities	STU FP	49.01	49.40	49.19	49.19	0.79%	-0.21%	0.04%	10	1,292	0.00	0.06
				average		0.64%		0.12%			0.02	1.34
				min		0.17%		-0.38%				
				max		0.94%		0.05%				
AXA EasyETF EuroStoxx												
Utilities	SYU FP	310.8	312.6	-	311.25	0.56%	-0.09%	0.14%	130	95	0.04	0.03
Telecom	SYT FP	456.5	456.8	-	455.10	0.06%	0.31%	0.34%	10	80	0.00	0.04
Media	SYM FP	195.4	196.5	-	195.67	0.58%	-0.33%	0.13%	-	12	-	0.00
Technology	SYQ FP	288.7	290.0	-	290.09	0.46%	-0.73%	-0.25%	2,030	179	0.59	0.05
Bank	SYB FP	297.7	299.1	-	298.29	0.46%	-0.29%	0.04%	-	45	-	0.01
Energy	SYE FP	338.7	340.2	-	339.12	0.44%	-0.26%	0.09%	10	67	0.00	0.02
Health	SYH FP	419.5	420.8	-	420.13	0.30%	-0.24%	0.00%	10	162	0.00	0.07
Insurance	SYI FP	208.1	208.5	-	208.25	0.21%	-0.11%	0.01%	5	671	0.00	0.14
Auto	SYA FP	184.8	185.9	-	185.48	0.58%	-0.78%	-0.07%	-	13	-	0.00
Construction	SYC FP	241.0	242.5	-	241.28	0.61%	-0.41%	0.19%	-	264	-	0.06
					average	0.43%		0.10%			0.64	0.43
					min	0.06%		-0.25%				
					max	0.61%		0.34%				
IndEXchange DJ EuroSTOXX EX												
Banks	SX7EEX (	28.40	28.48	-	28.43	0.28%	-0.30%	0.04%	2,565	28,485	0.07	0.81
Healthcare	SXDEEX (	41.39	41.54	-	41.43	0.36%	-0.13%	0.07%	0	7,444	0.00	0.31
Technology	SX8EEX (	28.92	29.02	-	29.07	0.34%	-0.82%	-0.34%	10,765	63,410	0.31	1.84
Telecommunication	SXKEEX (	44.40	44.54	-	44.28	0.31%	0.41%	0.44%	10,400	14,468	0.46	0.64
					average	0.33%		0.22%			0.85	3.60
					min	0.28%		-0.49%				
					max	0.36%		0.44%				
IndEXchange DJ STOXX 600 EX												
Autos	SXAPEX (	18.78	18.85	-	18.78	0.37%	-0.52%	0.18%	100	13,846	0.00	0.26
Basic Resources	SXPPEX (	27.19	27.34	-	27.16	0.55%	-0.82%	0.38%	220,120	38,064	6.00	1.04
Banks	SX7PEX (	35.05	35.22	-	35.08	0.48%	-0.42%	0.15%	2,790	5,967	0.10	0.21
Chemicals	SX4PEX (	25.71	25.75	-	25.70	0.16%	-0.27%	0.10%	0	11,156	0.00	0.29
Construction	SXOPEX (	21.49	21.60	-	21.51	0.51%	-0.48%	0.18%	0	1,397	0.00	0.03
Cycl.Goods&Services	SXTPEX (	13.56	13.65	-	13.59	0.66%	-0.35%	0.12%	0	1,434	0.00	0.02
Energy	SXEPEX (	31.11	31.20	-	31.13	0.29%	-0.16%	0.07%	915	13,949	0.03	0.43
Financial Services	SXFPEX (	24.23	24.39	-	24.25	0.66%	-0.15%	0.25%	0	3,923	0.00	0.10
Food & Beverage	SX3PEX (	20.74	20.83	-	20.75	0.43%	-0.72%	0.15%	1,040	2,205	0.02	0.05
Healthcare	SXDPEX (	33.12	33.31	-	33.15	0.57%	-0.70%	0.20%	0	9,410	0.00	0.31
Industr.Goods&Services	SXNPEX (	18.94	19.03	-	18.95	0.47%	-0.34%	0.16%	1,080	12,523	0.02	0.24
Insurance	SXIPEX G	18.43	18.50	-	18.43	0.38%	-0.12%	0.18%	5,501	37,694	0.10	0.70
Media	SXMPEX (	19.91	20.04	-	19.95	0.65%	-0.63%	0.14%	0	10,991	0.00	0.22
Non-Cycl.Goods&Servic	SXQPEX (	24.67	24.79	-	24.69	0.48%	-0.63%	0.15%	0	3,476	0.00	0.09
Retail	SXRPEX (	24.31	24.44	-	24.33	0.53%	-0.52%	0.20%	3	291	0.00	0.01
Technology	SX8PEX (	25.62	25.68	-	25.68	0.23%	-0.62%	-0.11%	0	25,970	0.00	0.67
Telecommunication	SXKPEX (	28.39	28.71	-	28.51	1.11%	-0.02%	0.15%	1,330	35,339	0.04	1.01
Utilities	SX6PEX (	26.79	26.90	-	26.81	0.41%	-0.21%	0.13%	465	24,487	0.01	0.66
					average	0.50%		0.17%			6.32	6.31
					min	0.16%		-1.20%				
					max	1.11%		0.38%				
UNICO i-trackers												
MSCI World	UNMSWLI	8.71	8.78	-	8.67	0.80%	-0.53%	0.86%	90	7,870	0.00	0.07
Fresco DJ US Technology	FDUSTC !	53.70	54.40	-	53.95	1.29%	-0.84%	0.18%	2,010	4,828	0.11	0.26
MSCI US Tech Master Unit	UST FP	5.36	5.39	-	5.37	0.56%			12,500	17,690	0.07	0.10
IndEXchange DJ STOXX 50	SX5PEX (	27.93	27.98	-	27.96	0.18%	-0.62%	-0.02%	23,052	43,386	0.64	1.21
	SX5PEX F	27.91	27.98	-	27.96	0.25%			-	5,004	-	0.14
					average	0.21%		0.02%			0.64	1.35
					min	0.18%		-0.02%				
					max	0.25%		-0.02%				
iShares STOXX 50	EUN1 GR	27.61	27.66	-	27.61	0.18%	-0.52%	0.09%	119,550	107,861	3.30	2.98
	EUN VX	27.59	27.67	-	27.61	0.29%	-0.55%	0.09%	-	495	-	0.01
	EUN SW	27.61	27.69	-	27.61	0.29%	-0.47%	0.14%	20,105	13,558	0.56	0.37
	EUN FP	27.60	27.64	-	27.61	0.14%	-0.58%	0.04%	40,331	71,475	1.11	1.97

Table 8: Spreads and trade size

from 31/08/04 to 30/09/04	Ticker	AvSpread	ETFperf	IndexPerf	Diff	AvVol20D	AvTurnv20D (million eur)	AUM (million eur)	Var20D	NewSubsc (million eur)
StreetTRACKS ETFs										
AEX	AEXT NA	0.14%	0.15%	0.25%	-0.10%	26,581	0.87	129.3	0.2%	-
PanEuro	ERO FP	0.52%	1.68%	1.72%	-0.05%	7,006	0.61	585.4	1.7%	-
StreetTRACKS MSCI Europe ETF										
Cons Discretionary	STV FP	0.90%	0.03%	0.07%	-0.04%	922	0.03	15.0	14.3%	1.9
Cons Staples	STS FP	0.73%	-2.32%	-2.23%	-0.09%	642	0.03	22.3	-2.3%	-
Energy	STN FP	0.76%	3.41%	3.49%	-0.08%	5,130	0.36	60.1	9.9%	3.5
Financials	STZ FP	0.84%	2.06%	2.14%	-0.09%	1,427	0.06	26.8	2.1%	-
HealthCare	STW FP	0.71%	-0.13%	-0.07%	-0.06%	1,317	0.06	36.5	-0.1%	-
Industrials	STQ FP	0.76%	2.98%	3.06%	-0.08%	218	0.01	38.4	3.0%	-
Info Technology	STK FP	0.85%	7.31%	7.49%	-0.18%	1,380	0.04	7.4	7.3%	-
Materials	STP FP	0.74%	3.62%	3.67%	-0.05%	92	0.01	13.2	3.6%	-
Telecom	STT FP	0.97%	1.98%	2.08%	-0.10%	2,363	0.08	23.1	2.0%	-
Utilities	STU FP	0.82%	1.49%	1.58%	-0.08%	623	0.03	11.7	1.5%	-
		0.81%		1.77%			0.72	254.4	4.1%	5.4
European sector exposure										
IndEXchange DJ STOXX 600 E		na					3.66	562.0	-1.2%	-21.7
IndEXchange DJ EuroSTOXX E		na					1.86	99.3	14.0%	7.9
EasyETF EuroStoxx		0.64%					0.43	233.5	-14.6%	-48.7
StreetTRACKS + European sector exposure										
Cons Discretionary								96.5	-20.9%	-26.5
Cons Staples								74.1	-6.5%	-4.0
Energy								166.4	2.4%	-2.8
Financials								275.4	-2.2%	-13.6
HealthCare								118.8	-3.2%	-7.3
Industrials								77.4	4.1%	0.9
Info Technology								74.9	-7.8%	-12.9
Materials								61.6	10.8%	3.8
Telecom								145.5	6.2%	5.1
Utilities								58.5	2.1%	0.0
								1,149.1	-2.1%	-57.1
Paneuropean exposure										
IndEXchange DJ STOXX 50		0.28%					2.87	233.7	2.6%	0.0
EasyETF STOXX 50 Europe		0.69%					0.01	18.3	1.8%	0.0
iShares STOXX 50		0.26%					1.36	514.6	2.3%	0.0
iShares FTSE EuroTop 100		0.91%					0.04	54.2	4.4%	0.0
SPDR Europe 350		0.84%					0.31	414.6	5.5%	10.7
Others										
CAC 40 Master Unit		0.07%					10.92	1,900.2	-9.6%	-226.2
FTSEurofirst 80 Master Unit		0.14%					0.50	252.0	2.4%	0.0
iShares EuroSTOXX 50		0.14%					10.37	2,214.0	2.1%	-22.0
iBoxx EUR Liquid Corporates		na					0.46	343.2	6.3%	22.2

As a conclusion, the liquidity in the ETFs is driven by the liquidity in the underlying shares through the unique creation and redemption process of ETF units, and StreetTRACKS sectors ETFs exhibit one of the best market exposure.

5. Conclusion and Remarks

Looking at issuers and investors, the ETF markets in the US and Europe show different profiles. ETFs are instruments to implement the asset allocation in an efficient way. The ETF market covers world wide stocks and bond indices. Arbitrage mechanisms lead to an efficient pricing of ETFs.

Spiders: Where Are the Bugs?[1]

Edwin J. Elton, Martin J. Gruber, George Comer, and Kai Li[2]

One of the clearest trends in asset management is the rapid increase in the amount of individual and institutional money invested in indexed products. By far the most popular index which investors want to replicate is the S&P 500 index. While many academic studies have examined the characteristics of two instruments frequently used to replicate the S&P, index funds and futures, very little has been written about the newest way to replicate the S&P 500 index: Standard and Poors Depository Receipts (SDPR) commonly referred to as Spiders. The importance of Spiders can be seen by the fact that at the end of 1999 there were 19.8 billion dollars invested in Spiders and that in 1998 *daily* shares traded in Spiders exceeded any other stock except Compaq and daily dollar volume was the highest of any share traded. This is all the more surprising given the fact that Spiders have not been around very long.

There are three major reasons why this analysis is useful. First, the principal advantage of Spiders versus index funds is that they can be purchased and sold at prices which exist at any time during the trading day. As we will show, low-cost index funds produce higher returns than Spiders. Given that investors can use either vehicle, the difference in return gives a measure of the value of immediacy. The value of immediacy is an important issue in the literature on market microstructure. Second, since Spiders

---

1 This chapter was first published in The Jounal of Business 75 (2002), pp. 453-472. Reprint with the permission of The University of Chicago Press.

2 Edwin J. Elton, Martin J. Gruber, Nomura Professors of Finance, Stern School of Business, New York University; George Comer, Kai Li, Doctoral Students, Stern School of Business, New York University.

We would like to thank Michael Babel for providing some of the data used in this study and Yakov Amihud, Deepak Agrawal, David Yermack, Menachem Brenner, and Joel Hasbrouk for helpful comments on an earlier draft of this paper.

have become an important investment vehicle in terms of both trading volume and dollar value outstanding, their performance and characteristics are of interest by themselves. Third, the organizational form of Spiders is seen as the prototype for index funds of the future, and thus it is important to understand both their performance and the affect of the organizational structure on that performance.

Before analyzing Spiders, we will briefly review their history and important characteristics. Each Spider represents an ownership interest in the SPDR Trust. The Trust as stated in the prospectus holds all of the common stocks in the S&P 500 composite stock price index and is intended to provide investment results that, before expenses, generally correspond to the price and yield performance of the S&P 500 Index. Spiders are traded on the American Stock Exchange and can be bought and sold like any stock at any time during the day. One Spider has a price equal to approximately 1/10 of the price of the S&P Index. The initial deposit creating Spiders was made on January 22, 1993. The Spider was organized as an investment trust and has a mandatory termination date of January 22, 2218[3]. Any trust is governed by a trust agreement and there are certain aspects of the trust agreement governing Spiders which are important to understand. First, Spiders charge an expense ratio to holders of the Spider. This has historically been 18.45 basis points per annum. Second, a specific mechanism exists for changing the number of Spiders outstanding. Investors can create or delete Spiders in minimum units of 50,000 shares by engaging in transactions in kind plus getting or receiving certain sums of cash. For example, investors can turn in a bundle of stock matching the S&P Index plus cash equal to the accumulated dividends less management expenses and receive Spiders in return. Investors can do so for a payment of $3,000 (regardless of the size of the transaction).

There is another peculiar aspect of Spiders that arises from their organizational form. Spiders pay out the dividends the trust receives on the stocks that it holds quarterly; on the last business days of April, July, October and January (though the ex-dividend day of the trust occurs in the previous month). What is unusual is that the dividends the trust receives from the underlying stock is held in a non-earning account between the time it is received and the time it is paid out.

---

[3] There are several circumstances, none of which in our judgement is ever remotely likely, that cause the trust to dissolve earlier.

Having provided background on Spiders, we turn to the purpose of this article: to study the performance of Spiders and to compare Spiders with other methods of indexing. This paper proceeds as follows: In the first section we examine the performance of Spiders as an investment vehicle. We start by examining the return from holding Spiders compared with the return from holding the S&P Index. In this section we first examine Spider returns as if Spiders could be bought and sold at their net asset value. We then examine the magnitude and time path of the differences between Spider price and NAV. Since Spiders are not the only way of holding an index, we next compare the return on Spiders with the return on other methods of indexing, index funds and futures. One of the unique aspects of Spiders is the ability of investors to create and delete them by turning in or receiving bundles of securities. We briefly examine this phenomenon in Section 2 of this paper. The third and last section examines the determinants of volume in Spider trading. The determinants of volume provide us with insight into who is trading Spiders, and why.

1. Performance of Spiders

The purpose of this section is to examine the return on Spiders to see if they appear to be a reasonable investment instrument. Since a Spider has its basic value determined by the S&P Index, we will compare the return on Spiders to the return on the S&P Index and then try to decompose any differences in return to see what accounts for them. In what follows, we break Spider return into two components:

- the return due to changes in NAV and
- the return due to deviations of NAV from price.

This decomposition allows us to estimate return without having it depend on deviations that occurred at a particular point in time. Over long periods the difference between price and NAV is unimportant because, through the ability to create and delete Spiders, arbitrage limits deviations. For example, over our sample period the average annual return from holding Spiders was 21.91 % while the return on NAV was 21.89 %.[4]

[4] We show later that differences between price and NAV are small and extremely shortlived.

After examining overall return we will examine the reasons Spider returns differ from the S&P index. Later we will compare Spiders to other instruments whose performance is also directly related to the S&P Index.

1.1 Overall Return on Spiders

We begin our analysis by examining the overall return an investor could have earned from holding Spiders if Spiders were purchased and sold at their net asset value (NAV). It is important to note that the NAV of a Spider is equal to the market value of the securities which back the Spider plus an accumulation unit which is equal to accumulated dividends minus accumulated management fees. Later we will examine the impact on return of deviations of Spider price from NAV.

In Table 1 we report the NAV return from holding a Spider for each year from 1993-1998.[5] Since we are interested in total return, we computed return as change in NAV plus dividends *paid to the Spider holder,* all divided by NAV. The yearly return was computed by first computing daily returns and then compounding up to the yearly return. Cash payments to holders of the Spiders are assumed reinvested in the Spider on the payment date.

The first step is to compare these returns to the returns on the S&P Index with dividends reinvested *daily*. This left us with a problem: to estimate return on the S&P Index we had to estimate both the *daily* dividends and the price level of the S&P Index. Dividends were estimated by taking the *daily* dividends for the S&P Index computed by CRSP. To compute prices we considered two alternatives. One was simply to use the value (price) of the S&P Index computed by Standard & Poors. This is the official measure of the S&P Index and is the value that any investor will see reported in a public source. The second possible value is that reported by CRSP. The two values can be different because of differences in pricing or weighting of the component stocks. Prices can differ because of different treatment of the stocks where prices are not available (non-trading) or where multiple prices are available. Weighting can differ where when-issued-stocks exist, or where mergers or acquisitions are taking place, or

[5] 1993 is a partial year. Throughout, when we refer to 1993 return it is from February 1, 1993 to the end of the year.

because of different recognition of capital changes (such as new issues or stock dividends). While the Index value computed by S&P seems appropriate because this is the price most investors will look at when considering investment or arbitrage, the index value reported by CRSP might or might not be closer to the price at which investors can complete transactions in attempting to duplicate the S&P Index.

We will perform our analysis in terms of both index values for the time being. Later we will examine differences in more detail. We shall refer to returns based on the commonly reported S&P Index as standard S&P returns while those based on the CRSP data as CRSP S&P returns.

When we examine the standard definition of S&P return with dividends (Section A of Table 1), we see that on average the NAV return underperforms the S&P return by 28 basis points per year (column 6). The NAV is outperformed in every year and the yearly range of outperformance is 17 to 36 basis points. Comparison with the CRSP S&P Index (Section B) shows a larger discrepancy. The average underperformance of the NAV return is 40 basis points a year, and the range is from 5 to 71 basis points. The return earned on the assets by holders of Spiders are clearly smaller than the returns on the indexes. What can account for these differences?

Table 1 shows the annual return from investing in Spiders relative to the return of the standard S&P 500 index and the CRSP value weighted S&P 500 index. The returns are compared with and without dividends included. NAV represents the return on the net asset value of the Spiders. The standard index represents the return on the S&P Composite Price Index. The CRSP S&P index is the value weighted return on the S&P index as constructed by CRSP. The total shortfall represents the difference between the return from the S&P and the return on the NAV of the Spider with dividends taken into account. This shortfall can be separated into two factors:

1. the difference between the NAV return without dividends and the S&P return without dividends and
2. the effect of management expenses and the lack of dividend reinvestment.

Table 1: The Annual Performance of Spiders Relative to the S&P 500

Standard Index							
	With Dividends		Without Dividends and Management Fee		Shortfall in Performance		
(1)	(2)	(3)	(4)	(5)	(6)	(7)	(8)
					(2)-(3)	(4)-(5)	(6)-(7)
Year	NAV	S&P	NAV	S&P	Total	Tracking[1]	Expenses and Dividends
1993*	8.92	9.19	6.25	6.30	-0.27	-0.06	-0.21
1994	1.15	1.32	-1.46	-1.53	-0.17	0.08	-0.25
1995	37.20	37.56	34.12	34.11	-0.36	0.01	-0.37
1996	22.72	22.97	20.26	20.26	-0.25	0.00	-0.25
1997	33.06	33.40	31.03	31.01	-0.34	0.03	-0.37
1998	28.28	28.57	26.64	26.67	-0.29	-0.03	-0.26
Average	21.89	22.17	19.47	19.47	-0.28	0.00	-0.28

CRSP S&P Index							
	With Dividends		Without Dividends and Management Fee		Shortfall in Performance		
Year	NAV	S&P	NAV	S&P	Total	Tracking[1]	Expenses and Dividends
1993*	8.92	8.97	6.25	6.08	-0.05	0.16	-0.21
1994	1.15	1.37	-1.46	-1.49	-0.22	0.03	-0.25
1995	37.20	37.62	34.12	34.16	-0.42	-0.05	-0.37
1996	22.72	23.28	20.26	20.57	-0.56	-0.31	-0.25
1997	33.06	33.49	31.03	31.10	-0.43	-0.06	-0.37
1998	28.28	28.99	26.64	27.08	-0.71	-0.44	-0.27
Average	21.89	22.29	19.47	19.59	-0.40	-0.11	-0.29

* partial year

[1] doesn't equal difference in columns since calculations were carried to more decimals than reported in the table.

1.1.1 Cost Disadvantages of Spiders

It is obvious that Spiders have certain cost disadvantages relative to the indexes. First there is an amount for management expenses, including management fee which is charged every day. The expense ratio on Spiders is 18.45 basis points per year.[6] Second, the dividends received from the underlying stock are not reinvested, but rather are held in a non-interest-bearing account. Next, Spiders also have their return reduced by the trans-

[6] The expense ratio is frequently reported as 18 basis points because for many purposes it is legally acceptable to round to the nearest whole basis point. The expense ratio has recently been lowered to 12 basis points.

action costs they incur in replicating the index. While the Spiders do not have transaction costs due to cash inflows or outflows associated with the purchase or sale of Spiders, they do have transaction costs associated with changing their portfolio when the index changes and transaction costs associated with investors directly reinvesting their dividends.[7]

In addition to the cost disadvantages just mentioned, Spiders might underperform the index because of poor replication strategies. It is possible that at every point of time the stocks held by the Spider do not exactly match (in proportion) the stocks in the S&P Index. While at most times composition is very close, if not exact, around the time of a change in the Index purchase and sales might not exactly match the pattern assumed in constructing the Index. The transaction costs of purchase and sale, replication strategy and any inaccuracies in the reported index are considered tracking error, and we will begin our examination of the reasons for underperformance by examining it.

1.1.2 Tracking Error

The difference in performance due to tracking error is easy to estimate. By taking the NAV return, subtracting dividends paid on the underlying stocks and adding back management expenses, we have the return-based entirely on price changes on the Spiders underlying portfolio. This can be directly compared with the *price return* on the S&P index and is free of management expenses and lost revenue due to holding the dividends in a non-interest-bearing account.

When we examine the return on the NAV of a Spider based solely on price changes of its underlying portfolio and compare it with the price return on the standard S&P Index (columns 4 and 5), we find almost no difference (column 7, Section A, Table 1). On average, the NAV price return and the return on the standard S&P index are the same. The range is from -6 basis points to +8 basis points per year, with four years positive and two years negative. It appears that against the S&P Price Index the shortfall is very close to zero. Failure to exactly hold the Index is as likely to lead to superior performance as to inferior performance, and over any period could be

[7] Spiders offer investors a direct reinvestment plan. This plan allows the holders to have the firm that underwrites Spiders hold and reinvest dividends. However, all of these transaction costs should be low, as turnover in the portfolio amounts to only 4 % per year.

plus or minus. The net of transaction costs, any missed capital changes by S&P, and mismatching are quite small, and the total effect of all of these influences leads to virtually no difference.

When we compare the NAV price return with the CRSP S&P price index, we get very different results. The tracking error appears to lead to large underperformance. The average underperformance is 11 basis points per year. Which of these indexes better reflects the Spider performance? It would be surprising that with an average turnover of 4 %, that transaction costs and mismatching could result in an 11 bp underperformance. Thus the standard S&P Index seems the more appropriate benchmark. However, as a further check we investigated the day-to-day tracking performance of the two indexes. We investigated which index better tracked the Spider by regressing the Spider NAV return against each index and the other index orthogonalized to the first. To do so, we first ran a regression using *daily* data of the NAV return on Spiders, excluding dividends and with management expenses added back against the price return on the standard S&P Index, and the CRSP S&P Index with the effect of the standard S&P Index removed (Panel B of Table 2). We then ran a regression of Spider NAV return against the CRSP S&P price Index and the standard S&P price Index with the effect of the CRSP removed (Panel C of Table 2). Note that when the standard S&P Index is used along with the CRSP S&P Index orthogonalized to the S&P Index, the orthogonalized CRSP S&P Index is not statistically significant at the 10 % level. However, when the CRSP S&P Index is used along with the S&P Index orthogonalized to the CRSP S&P Index, the orthogonalized S&P Index is significant at the 1 % level. These results support the fact that Spiders track the standard S&P Index much closer than they track the CRSP Index. As a further test of this we selected the three largest S&P Index funds as of 1999. These were Vanguard, Fidelity Spartan and T. Rowe Price. We collected *daily* return data and ran the same two regressions using the *daily* return on each index fund as the dependent variable. The results for the three funds are also shown in Table 2. Note that like Spiders, the standard S&P Index appears to explain index fund returns better than the CRSP version of the S&P Index. Since the investor can purchase or sell the standard S&P Index by putting money into or taking money out of the S&P Index funds, the standard S&P Index seems to be a better benchmark for Spiders. The difference in return due to tracking error is close to zero when the more appropriate definition of the S&P Index is used.

The following table shows the coefficient of the variable listed at the top of the column when the return of the independent variable is regressed against either the S&P index or the CRSP index and the second of these indexes is orthogonalized to the first. Only one R^2 value is reported since the order of orthogonalization does not impact the overall goodness of fit.

Table 2: Regression of Spider and Index Fund Returns against the S&P 500

Panel A					
Index Fund Return	Intercepts		Standard S&P		R^2
	Coef.	T Value	Coef.	T Value	
Spider	-0.000	-2.341	0.998	2680.82	0.998
Vanguard	0.000	0.1126	1.000	1035.68	0.999
Fidelity	-0.000	-0.592	1.002	558.11	0.995
T Rowe Price	-0.000	-0.401	1.001	326.83	0.986

Panel B							
Index Fund Return	Intercepts		Standard S&P		Orthogonalized CRSP S&P		R^2
	Coef.	T Value	Coef.	T Value	Coef.	T Value	
Spider	-0.000	-2.34	0.998	2680.82	0.008	0.893	1.000
Vanguard	0.000	0.113	1.000	1035.68	0.079	3.244	0.999
Fidelity	-0.000	-0.5932	1.002	558.11	0.126	2.790	0.995
T Rowe Price	-0.000	-0.4009	1.001	326.83	0.090	1.163	0.986

Panel C						
Index Fund Return	Intercepts		Standard S&P		Orthogonalized Standard S&P	
	Coef.	T Value	Coef.	T Value	Coef.	T Value
Spider	-0.000	-4.375	1.002	2678.53	0.990	106.02
Vanguard	0.000	-0.687	1.004	1038.78	0.922	38.20
Fidelity	-0.000	-1.028	1.006	559.04	0.876	19.52
T Rowe Price	-0.000	-0.653	1.005	326.65	0.911	11.87

1.1.3 Other Sources of Underperformance

If tracking error doesn't account for the underperformance of Spiders relative to the standard S&P Index, what does?[8] Of the 28.4 basis points underperformance, clearly 18.45 basis points is due to the expense ratio charged against the return each year. The remaining difference, 9.95 basis points, is due to the return shortfall caused by putting dividends in a non-interest-bearing account. The reasonableness of this number can be seen by examining dividends and returns. The prospectus shows that the dividend yield was about 2.2 % per year. Realizing that dividends are paid once a quarter and that dividends can occur any time over the quarter, the investor loses the market rate of return for an average of 12 months. However, the loss is even greater than this for dividends are not paid to the holders of Spiders for approximately one month after the ex-dividend date. This makes the appropriate loss two and one-half 12ths of the annual return. During the time period of this study the rate of return on the S&P Index was about 22.2 %. Thus the loss due to not reinvesting the dividends on the underlying stock in the index at the time they were received was approximately 10.2 basis points. This is very close to our direct estimate of 9.95 basis points obtained by examining the underperformance of Spiders directly.

As a further check on our statement that the underperformance is due to non-reinvestment of dividends we computed the underperformance each quarter. The amount of underperformance due to not reinvesting the dividends should depend on the performance of the S&P Index in each quarter. In the four quarters where the S&P had negative performance the Spider outperformed the index (since holding dividends in cash rather than reinvesting them is optimal when the market declines). In Table 3, we divide all quarters into 6 groups on the basis of return on the S&P Index (from low to high) and report the return from the Spider minus return on the S&P Index. The higher the return on the S&P Index in any quarter, the worse the relative performance of Spiders in that quarter. As a final check we regressed the difference in performance of the S&P and Spiders on the performance of the S&P Index and the R^2 was .99. The underperformance of Spiders is clearly related to the opportunity cost of not reinvesting dividends.

---

[8] When we subtract out the difference due to tracking error from the total difference in NAV total return, we find the results are virtually identical whether we use the standard S&P Index or the CRSP S&P Index (see column 8 of Table 1).

The table below presents the difference between the Spider return and the return on the S&P index for six groups formed by ranking the 24 quarterly S&P returns form lowest to highest.

Table 3: Excess Return on Spider over S&P as a Function of Reinvestment Return on Dividend

	Group	Spider Returns minus S&P index return (Quarterly Reinvestment in %)
Lowest	1	0.020
	2	-0.011
	3	-0.028
	4	-0.041
	5	-0.062
Highest	6	-0.109

1.2 Deviations of Price from NAV

In the prior section we assumed that all purchases and sales occurred at NAV. However, the Spider price can deviate from NAV and this represents both a cost and opportunity to the investor.

Table 4 shows the distribution using closing prices of both the dollar difference between price and NAV and the percentage difference expressed as the dollar difference divided by the NAV.[9] On average, price lies below NAV by 1.44 or .018 %.[10] In most cases the difference is small. Only about 5 % of the cases have absolute dollar differences greater than 254, and less than 4 % have percentage differences above .35 %. Less than 1 % are above 504 or above .5 %. About 70 % of the time the difference is within 1/8 of a dollar.

---

[9] This difference overstates the true difference because Spiders continue to trade 15 minutes after the New York Stock Exchange closes, and therefore NAV and price differ in time by 15 minutes.

[10] This means on average, price returns are slightly higher than NAV returns. Over the full period this resulted in a 2 bp difference.

While the fact that deviations of price from NAV are small at any moment in time is important, at least of equal significance is the persistence or lack of persistence of these deviations. To investigate this we first defined a variable D_t as the difference between price and NAV expressed in cents at the close of day t. We then regressed the value of D at t+1 against the value of D of t. The results are shown below.

$$D_{t+1} = -1.34 + .0620 D_t \qquad R^2 = .004$$

$$(3.68) \quad (2.39)$$

The results strongly support the fact that deviations of price and NAV disappear in a day. The R^2 and the slope of the regression coefficient are both close to zero. What makes the premium or discount disappear? Differences between NAV and price should signal an arbitrage opportunity and the price pressure associated with the arbitrage should cause the deviation to disappear.

In Section 3 we show that there is a statistically significant relationship between volume and the size of the discount or premium at the close of the previous day. This supports the hypothesis that arbitrage between the Spider and the stocks which back the Spider accounts for the disappearance of the premium on a daily basis. The ability to create and destroy Spiders acts as a very effective mechanism in keeping price close to NAV at any moment in time and assuring that any differences between the two disappear quickly.

Table 4 reports the frequency distribution of 1) the difference between the net asset value of the Spider and the Spider price, and 2) the difference between the net asset value of the Spider and the Spider price as a proportion of the net asset value.

1.3 Comparison to Alternative Vehicles

In addition to the possibility of holding the shares that comprise the S&P Index directly or holding Spiders, investors can approximate the return on an index by holding an index fund or by holding short-term debt instruments and an index future. These alternatives will be examined in turn.

Table 4: Frequency Distribution of Spider Net Asset Value versus Price

NAV-Spider Price			*NAV-Spider Price* NAV		
Difference in Dollars	**Frequency**	**Percentage**	**Difference in Percentage**	**Frequency**	**Percentage**
–2.05 to –1.05	1	.001	–2.05 to –1.05	0	0
–1.05 to –0.55	1	.001	–1.05 to –0.55	3	.002
–0.55 to –0.45	4	.003	–0.55 to –0.45	6	.004
–0.45 to –0.35	8	.005	–0.45 to –0.35	12	.008
–0.35 to –0.25	23	.015	–0.35 to –0.25	47	.031
–0.25 to –0.15	73	.049	–0.25 to –0.15	151	.101
–0.15 to –0.05	255	.170	–0.15 to –0.05	260	.174
–0.05 to 0.05	676	.452	–0.05 to 0.05	439	.293
0.05 to 0.15	304	.203	0.05 to 0.15	312	.208
0.15 to 0.25	79	.053	0.15 to 0.25	154	.103
0.25 to 0.35	33	.022	0.25 to 0.35	56	.037
0.35 to 0.45	19	.013	0.35 to 0.45	25	.017
0.45 to 0.55	11	.007	0.45 to 0.55	15	.010
0.55 to 1.05	10	.007	0.55 to 1.05	17	.011
Average = .014			Average = .018 %		

1.3.1 Index Funds

An individual investor had a wide selection of S&P Index funds from which to choose. Morningstar lists over 100 index funds and over 50 % of these are intended to track the S&P Index. In selecting among these S&P Index funds, there are two considerations: how well the index funds track the S&P, and the amount of the shortfall in return. There is very little difference in tracking error across most open-end S&P index funds with the typical R^2 on the S&P Index above .99. Differences in average performance are primarily related to differences in expenses. Because it has low expenses, we will use the Vanguard Index Fund as a comparison vehicle for Spiders. However, our analysis can be applied to any fund.

Relative performance of an index fund compared to the index itself and Spiders is affected by a number of factors. The first is costs. Mutual funds have a number of costs that reduce performance. An index fund pays management fees and other expenses that lower performance. In the case of Vanguard, the total fees are approximately 18 basis points per year for individuals, and either 6 basis point or 2.5 basis points for institutions depending on the size of the investment. The fees paid by individuals are very close to the annual fees paid by investors in Spiders. In addition, an index fund pays transaction costs every time it buys and sells a stock. Security transactions may be generated when investors place more money with the fund or withdraw money, when the composition of the index is changed or when investors reinvest dividends. This is an area where Spiders have a potential advantage, since new investment or disinvestment is done in kind. In addition, an indirect cost may be borne by the index funds as they need to keep cash on hand to meet withdrawals. This can in part be mitigated by the use of futures, an instrument not available to Spiders. The second factor affecting relative performance is the way index funds adjust their holdings for changes in the composition of the index. They can differ in the way they react to tender offers and other capital changes. Also, they can differ in the timing of adjustments of their portfolio to deal with changes in the S&P 500 Index. The third factor affecting relative performance is security lending. Index funds can, and do, earn extra return by lending their securities for the purpose of short selling, while Spiders do not. The fourth factor affecting relative performance is the treatment of dividends. We know that Spiders underperform the index by about 10 basis points per year because of their requirement to hold dividends received from the underlying stocks in a non-interest-bearing account. In contrast, index funds can reinvest dividends as soon as they are received by the fund.

How do all these influences net out? Over the period 1994 to 1998 the Vanguard Index Fund available to individual investors underperformed the standard S&P Index by 10 basis points per year, but outperformed Spiders by 18.1 basis points.[11] The Vanguard institutional fund performed 12 to 15.5 basis points better than the Vanguard fund available to individuals, depending on the size of the institution's investment and thus the fees it payed. These differences are calculated pre-tax. If we include taxes, there

---

[11] Over time the underperformance of Vanguard relative to the index has been going down. The reader should note that after our sample period the expense ratio on Spiders was lowered to twelve bases points.

is one further possible difference. Capital gains taxes are generated when capital gains are *realized.* Capital gains are *realized* when the index is changed and for index funds potentially if there are net withdrawals. Capital gains generated by net withdrawals should be small, since often they are covered by cash balances and the fund can sell off shares purchased at the highest price. The effect of index changes depends on the average purchase price of the security being sold. Age of fund is probably a reasonable proxy for this. Thus, initially Spiders have an advantage since the shares they hold were purchased more recently.

A major difference between index funds and Spiders is that Spiders can be sold intra-day. What does the prior say about the value of immediacy?

For individual investors the index fund has a performance of pre-tax 18.1 basis points better than Spiders. Thus sophisticated investors in Spiders are valuing immediacy as if it is worth at least 18 basis points per year. We state this as at least because the investors in Spiders incur additional transaction cost associated with buying and selling the Spider, while transactions in the Vanguard index fund are at net asset value without commissions.

1.3.2 Futures

The other alternative to a Spider is holding short-term money market instruments plus S&P futures contracts. If the futures contracts sold for their arbitrage value, then this strategy should generate returns equal to the true S&P return less the transaction costs of purchasing the future. In general, results are better since usually the implicit price of the S&P Index embedded in the future is low relative to the spot price of the Index. We estimate the implicit price of the S&P Index embedded in the futures price using closing prices and *daily* calculation of dividends. The implicit price requires an estimate of the dividend on the index. We assumed perfect forecasting. We took the daily dividends as reported by CRSP as our estimate of the forecasted dividends. We discounted dividends at the commercial paper rate. These resulted in the percentage difference between the S&P 500 Index and price of the S&P implied by the futures price (expressed as a percentage of the S&P Index) of .027 %[12]. If an investor bought futures

---

[12] We used the standard techniques for estimating the implied S&P price from the futures price. For example, see Elton and Gruber (1995), equation 21.3, page 626 . We used the commercial paper rate because this is the rate arbitragers use in valuing futures.

and the associated short-term instrument at the average difference between the futures price and arbitrage price, the result should be an outperformance of the S&P index by this 2.7 basis points. If higher yield short-term instruments were used, this performance could be further increased. If we compare the return from futures with Spiders, futures have an added return of 30.7 basis points per year. However, futures generally involve too large of an investment for individual investors to use these to construct index positions. Furthermore, many institutions cannot own futures or choose not to own futures. The use of futures also involves a certain amount of expertise in forecasting dividends, in estimating correct positions, and in satisfying margin requirements. These reasons explain why the demand for Spiders can continue to grow despite the return advantages of futures.

Before leaving this section, it is worthwhile to examine the relationship of price changes in Spiders to price changes in the S&P Index implicit in futures. To examine this we regressed the change in the Spider price minus accumulations against the change in the implicit value of the S&P index embedded in the futures price. The adjusted R^2 was .98 with a slope coefficient of .99; thus Spiders and futures prices move closely together.

2. Creation / Deletion

As discussed earlier, one of the unique features of Spiders is that they can be created and deleted. It is time to examine this attribute of Spiders more closely. Investors can create Spiders by turning in the shares that comprise the index plus an amount of cash equal to the accumulation unit (accumulated dividends and capital gains, less expenses). The amount of shares and the cash required are based on closing prices and are electronically posted. Orders to create are in minimums of 50,000 Spiders and need to be placed before close. Likewise, Spiders can be deleted by turning in Spiders (with a minimum amount of 50,000 shares) and receiving the stock shares that comprise the index plus an accumulation unit. The process of creation and deletion has meant that as discussed earlier, price and NAV are close.

Table 5 shows data on creation and deletion. Net creations or deletions occur on approximately 15 % of the trading days. The first thing to note is the size of the net trades. On days where there is a net creation, the average size of the net creation is 1,395,430 shares. With prices in the range of \$50 to \$120 per share, average creations are over \$100 million. On days there are net deletions, the average is 1,816,119 shares or a dollar deletion of over $150 million. There are *daily* creations or deletions of over one $1 billion and many over $500 million. Clearly, creations and deletions are being done by large institutions. There is a fixed cost of $3,000 per creation or deletion. On a typical trade of 1,500,000 shares, this is a cost of .2 cents a share. Creations are more common than deletions. There were 158 days with net creations and only 67 with net deletions out of 1,497 trading days in our sample. This has meant that the number of Spiders has grown over time from 150,000 at inception to 131,670,000 on December 31, 1999.[13]

Who is doing the creations and deletions, and why? Discussion with market participants indicates there are two groups: managed accounts (particularly index funds), and market makers. Pension funds or institutional funds on occasion have large transfers. If an institutional fund gains a large customer, it would like to be fully invested very quickly. It might well find it desirable to hold the index and then adjust to a more active posture over time. It can construct an index fund by using futures and money market instruments, it can buy Spiders, or buy company shares directly. Depending on the relative prices, the best strategy may be to buy Spiders, turn them in for shares, and then over time adjust the portfolio. Likewise, an institutional index fund which has lost a large customer might find it cheaper to liquidate by turning in shares and selling the Spiders rather then selling the shares directly. Although the use of futures is generally considered the cheapest way to adjust portfolios, many institutions or funds are prohibited from using futures and there are times where futures prices are very different from their arbitrage value and Spiders are the cheapest instruments.

Market makers and specialists seem to be the major creators and deletors. From trading activities they may find themselves heavily long or short Spiders. The price and NAV may be divergent and they may view that adjusting inventory may require trades so large in magnitude as to adversely move prices, so that creation and deletion is cheaper.[14]

Table 5 reports the frequency distribution of the number of days on which net creations and deletions of different sizes occurred over the sample period. A negative sign indicates deletion. A positive sign indicates creation. Zero indicates neither creation nor deletion.

---

[13] See Prospectus 1999.

[14] It is an industry belief that in times there is such a dearth of shares available for borrowing and shorting that there is a lot of money in Spider lending and the market maker will create shares to profit from this.

Table 5: The Creation and Deletion of Spider Units

Creations and Deletions (in thousands)	Frequency	Percentage Occurrence
–4500 or larger deletion	4	0.27
–4499 to –3000	7	0.47
–2999 to –2000	18	1.20
–1999 to –1500	8	0.53
–1499 to –1000	12	0.80
–999 to –500	13	0.87
–499 to –50	5	0.33
0	1271*	85.96
50 to 499	11	0.73
500 to 999	65	4.34
1000 to 1499	27	1.80
1500 to 1999	18	1.20
2000 to 2999	25	1.67
3000 to 3999	3	0.20
4000 to 4999	6	0.40
5000 or more	3	0.20

Net Average Deletion = 1836.119
Net Average Creation = 1395.43
* Creations and deletions can not occur in the range –49.9 to +49.9

3. Determinants of Volume

Before examining the determinants of volume, it is worthwhile examining volume directly. There is heavy volume in Spiders relative to the outstanding supply. Table 6 shows the average *daily* volume as a percentage of outstanding shares by year. In 1998 over 10 % of the outstanding shares were traded each day. Over the full period on 6 % of the days over 25 % of the outstanding shares were traded. This heavy daily volume is an indication that short-term traders are active participants in the market.

Traditionally, trading volume of a security is thought to be generated by disagreements associated with new information about the security and by liquidity traders. From the earlier discussion it is clear that in the case of Spiders, volume is also heavily influenced by arbitrage and risk control strategies. Short-term traders are likely to use Spiders to hedge their positions to control risk or for short-term speculation.[15] In addition, Spider volume is likely to be affected by arbitrage strategies involving differences in Spider price from NAV. What does this suggest about what factors affect volume? First, market volatility is likely to be a reason able proxy for times when Spider positions are needed for risk control, and also a proxy for occasions when arbitrage opportunities are likely to exist. We measure our first variable market volatility as the high price minus low price divided by the closing price of the S&P Index.

Arbitrage opportunities in the Spider market are also likely to exist when there is a big difference between price and NAV. To control for a time trend in volume and price, we express our second variable as the absolute difference between price and NAV divided by price. Since price differences from NAV are measured at the end of the day, difference should signal arbitrage opportunities the next day so that this variable is lagged.[16] In addition, since differences in either direction indicate arbitrage opportunities, we use the absolute value.

In summary, the regression we ran was

$$Volume_t = a + b_l \left[\frac{High_t - low_t}{close_t} \right] + b_3 \left[\left| \frac{Price_{t-1} - NAV_{t-l}}{NAV_{t-1}} \right| \right] + e_t$$

The results are reported in Table 7. Note, as speculated, the degree of price changes in the market has a large and very highly significant effect on the amount of trading in Spiders. Spiders do seem to be used for risk control and short-term trading strategies. In addition, when the absolute value of the difference between price and NAV is high, arbitragers induce a lot of

15 Part of the appeal of Spiders for short-term trading strategies is that they can be shortsold on a downtick while individual stocks cannot.

16 An alternative explanation for differences is stale prices. Stale prices should occur when trading is low in the securities that comprise the S&P. We examined this by regressing differences in price and NAV on NYSE volume and found no relationship.

trading on the following day. Note that the R^2 is .52, indicating that we have found influences which explain better than 50% of the changes in volume over time. As shown in Table 7, Spider volume increases substantially in times of high market volatility. Futures serve the same hedging role as Spiders do. The issue is in times of turbulence which is the instrument of choice. To examine this we regressed Spider volume divided by future volume against the difference between the S&P high and the S&P low over the S&P close. To examine time trends we performed this regression each year. The results are shown in Table 8. Table 8 shows the growing choice of Spiders as a risk control instrument. In 1993, if either instrument was chosen, it was futures. In the middle years, there was no relationship between market turbulence and relative volume in Spiders compared to futures. However, clearly in the last two years Spiders have become the instrument of choice for managing short term risk. Increased turbulence *leads* to substantial increases in Spider volume relative to futures volume.

Although we do not report the results, we also tested whether volume was affected by a tax postponement strategy and price discrepancies in the futures market. Spiders pay dividends about a month after they go ex-dividend. For example, at the end of the year the Spider goes ex-dividend in December but the dividend is not paid until January. This means that institutions that are on a cash basis (such as most broker dealers) and have a fiscal year that ends in a month when the Spider goes ex dividend can buy before the ex-dividend date and sell before the end of the fiscal year, and take the dividend in the next year. This allows the institution to take the loss associated with the change in price on the ex-dividend date in one year and a gain from receipt of the dividend in the next year, earning the present value of the tax postponement. To check on the possible impact of tax trades around exdividend days on volume we put in a dummy for the ex-dividend day and the following day. These were not significant. We also examined several variables to see if volume in Spiders increased when futures were priced very differently than their arbitrage value. None were significant.

The next table shows the average annual daily volume as a percentage of outstanding shares of the Spider.

Table 7 reports the results of the regression used to explain the daily trading volume of the Spiders. The dependent variable is daily Spider volume. The independent variables are 1) the intercept term, 2) (SP500 intraday high – SP500 intraday low) / SP500 close, and 3) the absolute value of (Spider price – Spider NAV) / Spider price at time t-1.

Table 6: Daily Volume as Percentage of Outstanding Shares

Year	Average Volume
1993	4.53 %
1994	3.90 %
1995	2.67 %
1996	4.49 %
1997	8.53 %
1998	10.65 %

Table 7: Explanations of Daily Spider Volume

	Intercept	*SP500 high – SP500 low* SP500 close	Absolute value of *(SPDR price – SPDR nav)* SPDR price at time t-1	R^2
Coefficient	-0.016	3.228	2.376	0.52
Standard Deviation	0.001	0.085	0.506	
t-statistic	14.152	37.790	4.693	

Table 8: Regression of Relative Volume of Spider against Market Volatility

	Intercept		*SP500 high – SP500 low* SP500 close		R^2
Year	**Coef.**	**T Value**	**Coef.**	**T Value**	
1993	0.00746	0.99	-0.34	-2.74	0.03
1994	0.00478	4.59	0.13	1.15	0.00
1995	0.00467	8.95	-0.03	-0.43	0.00
1996	0.00846	8.74	0.34	3.98	0.06
1997	0.01699	5.74	1.62	8.83	0.23
1998	0.0416	14.49	1.25	8.06	0.20

This table reports the results of the regression used to explain the relative volume of Spider to volume of S&P500 index futures in times of pressure in the market. The regression is done annually. The independent variable is the ration of Spider volume over volume of S&P500 index futures (scaled by 1000). The independent variables are 1) the intercept term, 2) (S&P500 index intraday high-S&P500 index intraday low)/ S&P500 index close.

4. Conclusion

In this paper we examine the characteristics and performance of Spiders. The S&P 500 Spider contract has become an important security in its own right, often being the most highly traded stock with an average *daily* volume in December 1999 of 5.52 million shares. But the instrument is even more important for its organizational form is widely discussed as a prototype for mutual funds of the future. Spiders would seem to offer the benefits of both open- and closed-end mutual funds. The desirable characteristics of Spiders is they trade at close to net asset value and like closed-end funds they offer the ability to transact at market price at any point during the trading day. They avoid the disadvantages of closed-end funds for which prices deviate widely from NAV and the disadvantage of open-end funds of pricing only once a day, and in addition, often having restrictions or minimum limits on sales and purchases.

The principal tool that restricts the deviation of price from NAV is the ability of investors to create or delete Spiders at the end of every trading day by turning in or receiving the physical bundle of securities that stand behind the Spider. When we examine differences in return based on the price of the Spider and return based on its NAV, we find that the difference is less than 1.8 basis points per year on average, and that almost all of the differences disappear within one day.

In addition, we find that the NAV of the Spider, measured before management fees and dividends on the underlying securities, tracks the S&P Index almost exactly.

On the other hand, we show that the holder of a Spider earns a return 18 basis points below the holder of the low cost index funds and below that of futures. Spiders underperform the S&P Index by 28.4 basis points. The two principal causes of the underperformance are the management fee of 18.45 basis points and the loss of return from dividend reinvestment of 9.95 basis points. The loss on dividend reinvestment comes about because the trust form used for Spiders requires all dividends and capital gains received by the Spider to be held in a non-interest-bearing account until paid out. It should be pointed out that this disadvantage has been eliminated in most exchange traded funds (e.g. webs) which were created subsequent to Spiders.

How can the different in return between Spiders and index funds exist? Why do people hold Spiders rather an index funds? We believe the difference is the value investors place on immediacy. Spiders are primarily used as a risk control mechanism and for short-term trading. Evidence of this is easily seen by noting that trading in Spiders increases significantly in times of turbulent stock markets (when prices move a lot).

Spiders also seem to offer a return lower than that which can be earned by holding short term debt and futures. Here immediacy cannot account for the appeal of Spiders. But Spiders have the advantage in that they can be bought and sold in much smaller units than futures, they do not require the active management that futures require (e.g., margin maintenance), and physical delivery can be taken (or supplied).

The success of Spiders would suggest that exchange-traded mutual funds are a viable investment vehicle. Two of their principal disadvantages (inability to earn investment income on dividends and capital gains, and the inability to earn income on security lending) have already been eliminated in most of the second generation of exchange-traded funds. The management fees that Spiders charge have recently been decreased by a third. Despite their bugs, Spiders and other exchange-traded funds which offer immediacy are likely to prosper and reproduce.

5. Bibliography

Elton, Edwin J. and Gruber, Martin J., 1995. Modern portfolio theory and investment analysis. John Wiley & Sons, New York, 5th edition.

Prospectus, Standard & Poors Depository Receipts, 1999.

Xetra Active Funds (XAF) – More than "Just" Index Tracking

Helge Staack

1. Definition: What Are Xetra Active Funds?

"Trading funds like shares" is the philosophy behind these exchange-traded, actively managed mutual funds. Xetra Active Funds combine the merits of investing in a traditional, diversified fund with the advantages of the trading techniques associated with shares. This means that they also have the following characteristics in common with shares:

- they are continuously traded
- efficiently priced
- transparent and liquid
- bought and sold at fair market values
- listed on regulated markets
- traded on Xetra, Deutsche Börse`s electronic platform
- priced on Xetra, supported by designated sponsors

In contrast with passive ETFs, in which the investor can track an index almost 1:1, Xetra Active Funds endeavour to outperform the indices which act as their benchmarks.

Xetra Active Funds were launched in November 2000 and DWS Investments became the world's first investment company to have funds listed in a regulated market segment when its *Typ O* funds (DWS no-load funds) were admitted for trading on Deutsche Börse's exchange. The continuous trading in successful and well-known funds generated considerable interest amongst investors. This pioneering achievement of Deutsche Börse, in collaboration with DWS as issuer and Deutsche Bank as market maker, justifiably attracted a great deal of attention in the international press.

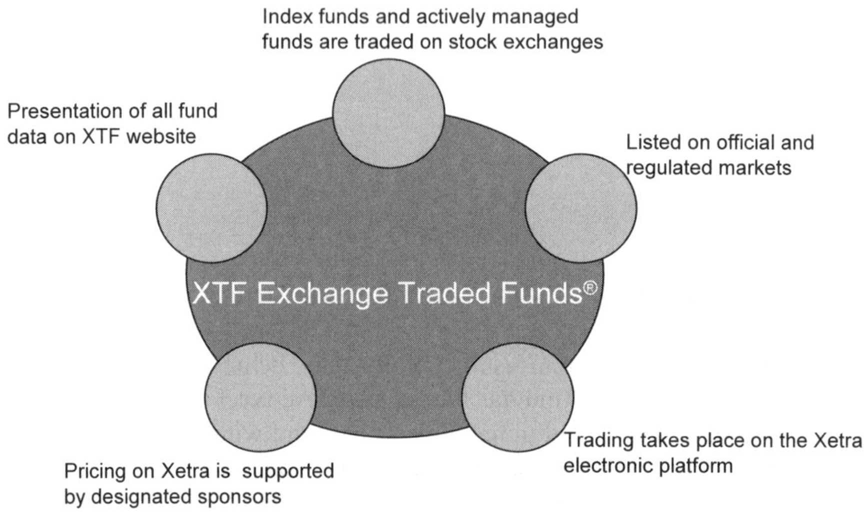

Figure 1: Xetra Active Funds: the segment for exchange-trading of actively managed funds. Source: Deutsche Börse

2. Value Added by Xetra Active Funds – "Active" Comes from "Attractive"

Successful products are particularly striking if they actually involve new characteristics, and are really innovative. This is especially true of actively managed ETFs. They have many strengths deriving from the advantages of continuous price fixing:

- Investors can react quickly to market trends and profit from volatility in the markets. They benefit from maximum flexibility and reliability of pricing. In contrast with the traditional method of placing an order, investors in these funds no longer have to wait for the next official unit price fixing, which takes place once a day, but can trade continuously during trading hours at the prevailing, liquid market price.

- ETFs can be traded in the same way as shares, so there is a wide range of different types of order available (e.g. stop loss orders and limited orders).

- Fund units are traded without the front-end fee, so the investor only has to pay the usual transaction costs charged by banks or direct brokers for buying and selling securities.

- Deutsche Börse's neutral product platform gives investors low-cost, easy access to quality funds, independently of the services offered by their house bank or savings bank. An information pack containing detailed product descriptions is all part of this innovative service.

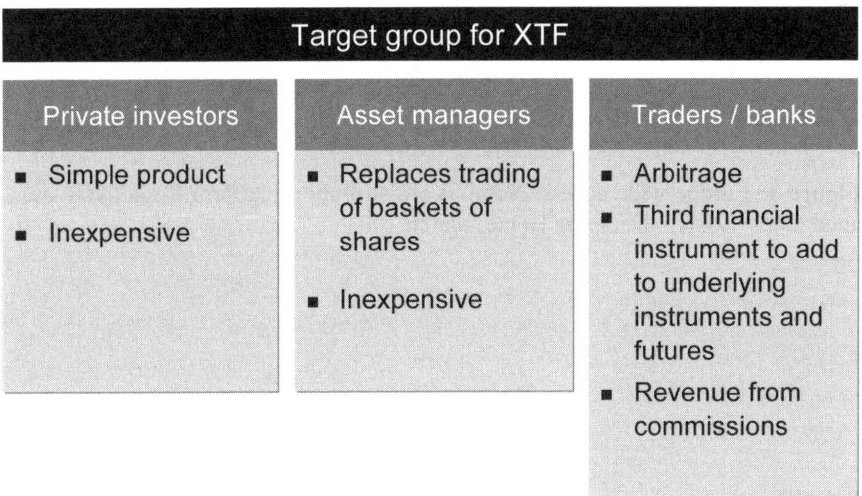

Figure 2: Value added by Xetra Active Funds – investor groups. Source: Deutsche Börse

The specific advantages of actively-managed products lie in the opportunity they offer to outperform their benchmark index. An active manager can avoid the "cluster risks", inherent in many indices that have high individual stock weightings or undesirable country and/or sectoral weightings. Index allocations like these, which may not reflect current market sentiment, can result in a lack of diversification and in unwanted risk/reward combinations. Active management can avoid such "misallocations" by taking into account other factors (timing, sectoral and/or country allocations and currency management) that are outside an index's traditional parameters (market capitalisation, trading volumes, free floating stocks).

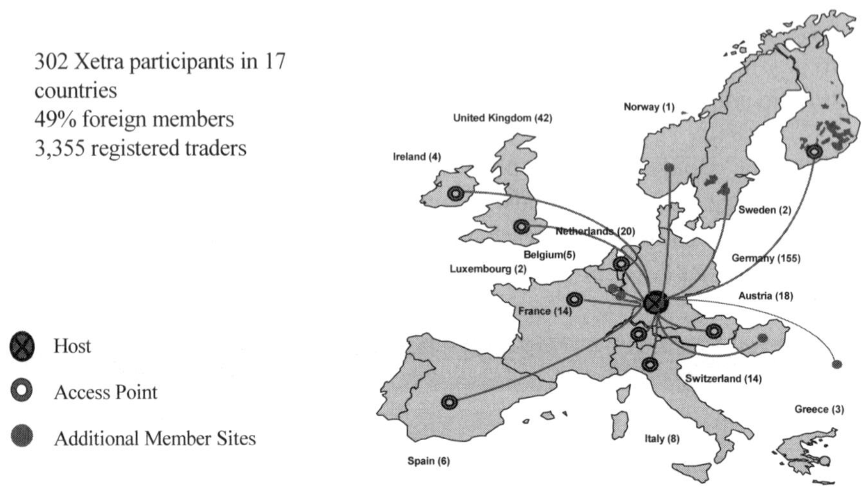

Figure 3: Europe-wide access. Xetra as a distribution platform for actively-managed funds. Source: Deutsche Börse, March 2004

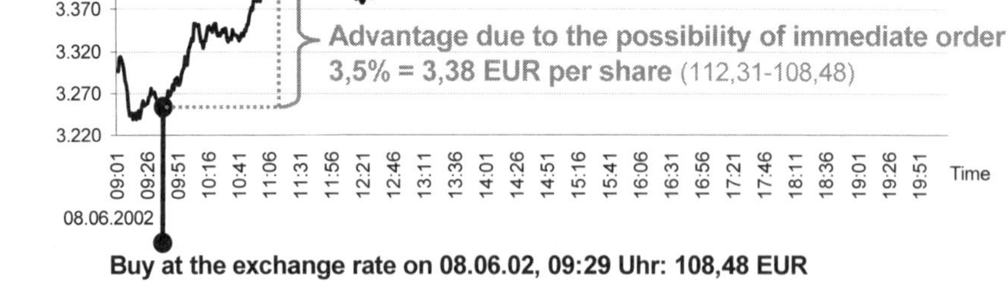

* Registered Trademark of Deutsche Börse AG

Figure 4: Time can be money; e.g. Buying DWS Deutsche Aktien Typ 0 at the exchange price vs. NAV. Source: DWS

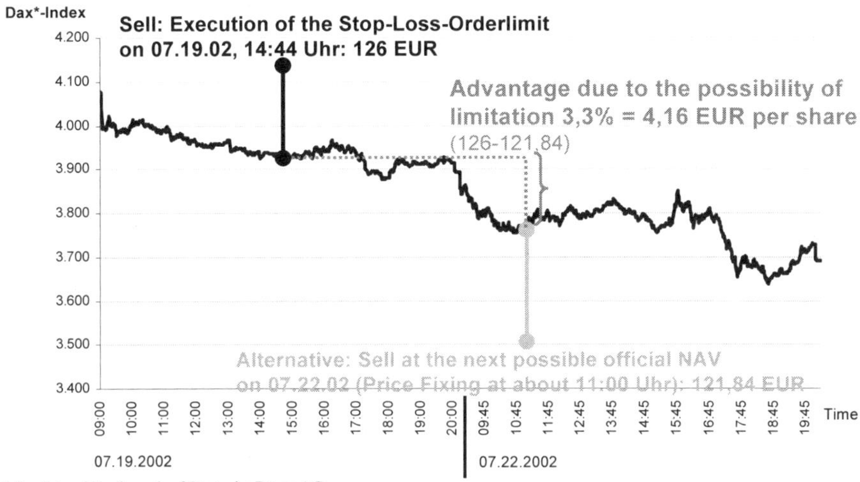

* Registered Trademark of Deutsche Börse AG

Figure 5: Time can be money; e.g. Stop loss limit/selling DWS Deutsche Aktien Typ 0 at the exchange price vs. NAV. Source: DWS

3. Product Design and Mechanics

Deutsche Börse successfully operates what is currently the world's only platform with well-defined rules for the continuous trading of actively-managed funds. XAF is an electronic trading platform which means we have specific advantages in the XTF market segment.

- Europe's largest electronic trading platform,
- Liquidity is supported by designated sponsors and bundled in one central order book for each fund,
- Continuous trading in Xetra Active Funds from 9am to 5.30pm,
- High degree of transparency as a result of binding rules and an open order book,
- Europe-wide network provides access to further customer groups,
- Inexpensive trading and settlement in Xetra,
- Stock exchange as neutral trading and distribution platform.

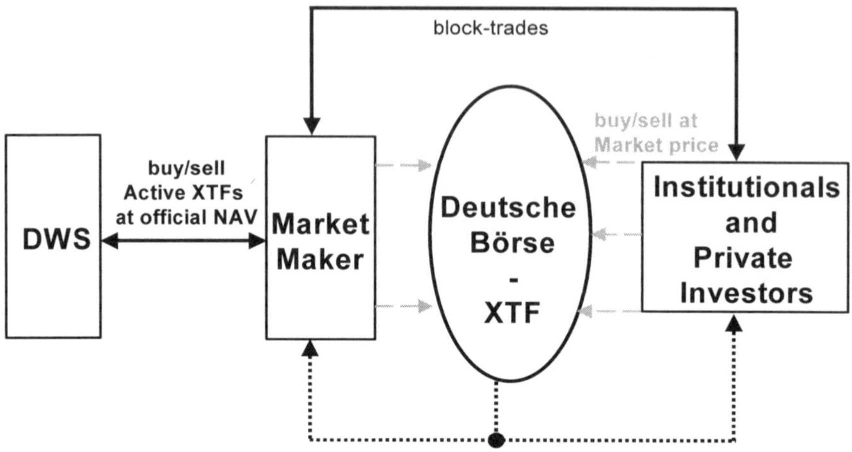

Figure 6: Product designs and –mechanisms. Source: DWS

Segment conditions in Xetra Active Funds ensure market liquidity and transparency:

- Listed on regulated markets,
- Registered for distribution in Germany,
- Publication of semi-annual and monthly reports,
- Monthly publication of the ten largest portfolio positions,
- At least one designated sponsor required,
- Assets under management should exceed €50 million.

There are may differences in the way that Xetra Active Funds and passive ETFs function. The market model for actively-managed funds has to be different from that for passive ETFs, because, unlike the composition of an index, their portfolios cannot be published every day. For this reason, transparency or rather, the reliability of fair pricing and liquidity is of particular importance. Therefore, the Xetra Active Funds segment of the Deutsche Börse lays down, inter alia, the maximum spreads and minimum quotation volumes allowed, to ensure orderly trading of the funds. For example, the maximum spreads for the 14 DWS funds are: 1.5 % for "standard" funds; 2.5 % for sector-based funds with higher risk/reward ratios and 3.5 % for emerging markets funds such as DWS Russia, DWS China and DWS India. The minimum quotation volume is €50,000, whereas the

Xetra platform volumes for market makers are generally many times this amount. Moreover, although intraday volatility in individual market segments is sometimes in double-figures, the spreads at which DWS funds were actually traded are significantly below the maximums allowed, and are evidence that market making is efficient (see section 4 for a comparison of spreads at Deutsche Börse).

3.1 Factors Influencing Prices and Market Making

The continual price fixing process of Xetra Active Funds is based on the market forces of supply and demand. The funds are freely traded on the basis of each fund's Net Asset Value (fund's bid price), which is fixed once a day, and/or the range of their investments plus the general tendency in their underlying market segments. That is the reason why the market prices differ from the official unit prices that are calculated once a day. Secondary market prices also reflect current market data, including expectations that are already priced in. However, the stock exchange price is also influenced by factors originated by the market maker. For example, the liquidity of hedging instruments determines their efficiency as a hedge for open positions, and thus the market maker's spread. The transaction time is also decisive. Because of time-zone differences, the market maker may have greater exposure, for example when the home markets of an underlying fund segment are closed.

Quantitative models based on past fund data help the market maker to manage these risks.

4. Product Review and Quantitative Aspects: Spreads, Trading Volume, Transactions

Who Are the Users of Xetra Active Funds?

10 % of the turnover in Xetra Active Funds is derived from institutional asset managers and 90 % from retail investors.

The turnover figures of Xetra Active Funds are not influenced by arbitrage mechanisms. So, all turnover figures are directly related to AuM (assets under management).

Excellent spread quality
Transparency = fairness = tight bid/ask spread

The following chart shows actual monthly liquidity. These quotation spreads are approximately representative of average values.

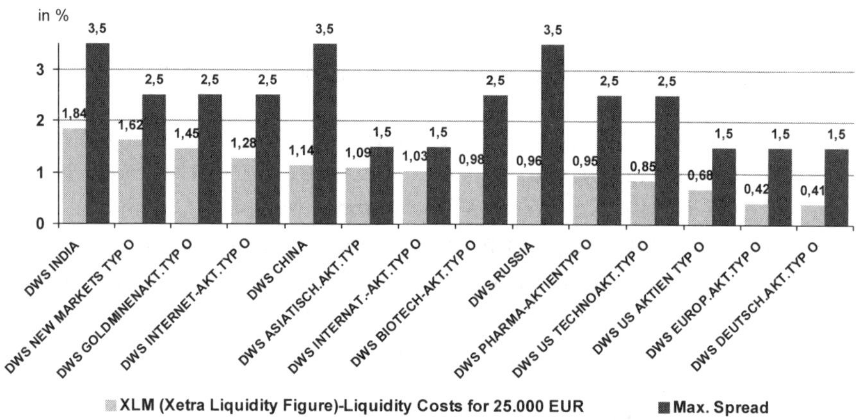

Figure 7: Market maker spreads are far tighter than required by Deutsche Börse (maximum spreads). Source: Deutsche Bank

The following chart shows actual monthly quotation volumes. These quotation volumes are approximately representative of average values.

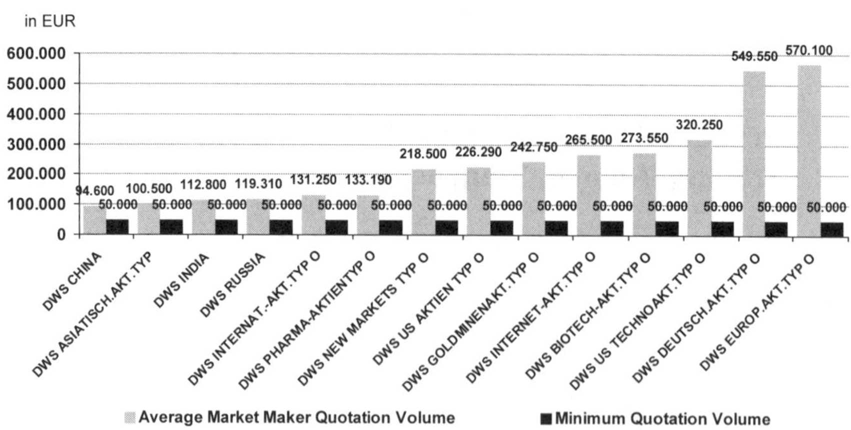

Figure 8: The market makers' quote volume is far better than that required by Deutsche Börse. Source: Deutsche Bank

Table 1: Net cash inflows

	Net cash inflows in € mio.
2001	94
2002	77
2003	100

Source: DWS

The inflow of cash into each fund is strongly influenced by underlying trends in the capital markets and can vary greatly. In 2004, emerging markets funds were of particular interest to investors. The value added in Xetra Active Funds of this type is high, because they are exchange-traded, as there are no suitable passive instruments available in this market segment.

Table 2: XETRA: Xetra Active Funds from DWS

WKN	NAME	
847 428	DWS Deutsche Aktien Typ O	
984 805	DWS New Markets Typ O	
849 082	DWS Europäische Aktien Typ O	Countries / Regions
849 081	DWS US Aktien Typ O	
849 083	DWS Asiatische Aktien Typ O	
984 801	DWS Internationale Aktien Typ O	
976 997	DWS Biotech-Aktien Typ O	
984 800	DWS Internet-Aktien Typ O	
976 985	DWS Pharma-Aktien Typ O	Sectors
976 981	DWS US Technoaktien Typ O	
976 982	DWS Goldminenaktien Typ O	
939 855	DWS Russia	
565 129	DWS China	Emerging Markets
974 879	DWS India	

Source: DWS

5. Future Outlook

The past three years have set a positive pattern for the future, despite difficult market conditions. Both of Deutsche Börse's fund segments, Xetra Active Funds and XTF, managed to increase their inflows of funds by using the stock exchange as a sales channel. This shows that funds trading has been enthusiastically adopted by both private and institutional investors. One factor driving this was undoubtedly increased volatility in the markets and the resulting strong fluctuations in fund values. Since then, investors have been continually demanding more flexibility and better service.

High growth rates are being forecast for passive ETFs in the European market in the next few years. However, we expect to see consolidation of this fragmented market over the course of time. There are currently more than 100 passive ETFs. This has the disadvantage of splitting up the overall market's liquidity which can lead to increased costs for providers, and the size of each fund tends to be small. However, concentrating supply and demand generates the efficiency needed by passive products.

Xetra Active Funds are also on course for growth and this segment seems to be full of retail investors, as evidenced by the large number of individual orders. DWS will continue its pioneering role by further developing this market segment, and is also leading the market by listing new products that include investments in smaller market segments. The most recent innovations were the DWS Russia, DWS China and DWS India funds. Active fund management creates the greatest "value added" in this type of fund, since research has to be more intensive and access to these markets is more restricted. The trend towards exchange-trading of actively-managed funds, along with other innovative products and rising order volumes and fund sizes, is likely to be reflected at other European stock exchanges in the medium term.

Investors benefit from using the stock exchange as a distribution channel because they have a fully-supported means of accessing attractive products that are flexible, liquid and innovative.

The Role of Exchange Traded Funds in the Active vs. Passive Debate

Markus Hübscher

1. Introduction

The first steps in passive investing go back more than 30 years. In the year 1971, the first pioneers at Wells Fargo Bank launched their first passive product. The investment process of the product looks very simple, almost trivial at first glance: the portfolio was invested using an equal weighting approach. The management of the portfolio, however, proofed to be very cumbersome. This is hardly surprising: equally weighted portfolios have to be rebalanced frequently. And remember: neither PCs nor Microsoft did exist at the time and the only computers available were – compared with today's technology – slow and expensive. It took more than five years until this complicated investment process was replaced by the first cap-weighted index mutual fund (launched by Vanguard). This portfolio was fully replicated and owning all the stocks in the index with the same weight as the index. The relatively slow product development did go hand in hand with the development of the assets under management. The IPO of the mutual fund launched by Vanguard was able to attract a mere US$ 11 Mio. The reason for this limited success was most probably the reaction of the investment "experts" to this kind of product. According to John C. Bogle, Founder and Former Chairman of The Vanguard Group, "the fund was greeted by the investment community with derision, dubbed 'Bogle's folly', and described as un-American, inspiring a widely-circulated poster showing Uncle Sam calling on the world to 'Help Stamp Out Index Funds'". As of the end of 1976 less than US$ 100 Mio. were invested in index funds.

Now, how is it possible that such a simple and at first glance uninspiring concept is able to provoke such emotions?

To be able to answer this question, a thorough analysis of the structure of today's fund industry has to be made first. Active fund managers are highly professional and typically have an academic background. Together with their colleagues from research, they try to evaluate companies which are either undervalued or do have an expected earnings growth, which should result in a price performance better than the average company in the market place. On the other hand, index funds do have a completely different approach. They use no company research, buy simply all the securities in the index and don't do any active trading at all! This means that managers of an index fund are only executing transactions when the index changes or the mutual fund does have in- our outflows. This investment strategy is so simple that many investment professionals have problems accepting indexing as an investment strategy at all. While managers of active mutual funds spend a lot of time evaluating companies and investment decisions, passive funds completely ignore any company news at all. Index funds may even have stock holdings in companies, which are reporting a loss or will be reporting a loss, do have financial or other difficulties or – even worse – are about to announce bankruptcy.

One might question – with good reason – whether an index portfolio managed in such a way, is managed diligently. Is it not the responsibility of a fund manager to make sure the customer's portfolio does avoid such securities? This issue becomes even more relevant in the light of the corporate scandals which took place in the last 2 to 3 years in the US. In my view, exactly these arguments were the reason for the heated debate which took place 30 years ago and continues to be controversial today. Even nowadays, index funds are very often not taken seriously and questioned by the community. Managers of index funds are often called "monkey" managers.

However, what is very often forgotten in this controversial debate is the following question: What are the most relevant aspects for a fund manager if awarded with a mandate? In my view, maximising the return for the client is the job of the fund manager. Obviously, there are a number of aspects, which have to be taken into consideration. Some of the aspects have to do with risk awareness, personal financial situation, forecasted expenses and current liabilities of the client etc. Knowing all these aspects, a strategic position has to be defined. This strategic positioning has to be managed in such a way, that the return on behalf of the client is maximised. And even such a simple expression like return can lead to endless discussions. In my view, return should be defined as the return after all fees and taxes.

Such an analysis can be executed relatively simple by comparing the return of the net asset value (NAV) per unit of various mutual funds. The performance calculated in this way does exactly result in the return described above: all the costs which occur managing a mutual fund are typically charged to the fund and lead to a deterioration of the performance of the fund. Tax effects, however, which occur on the individual investor level, cannot be taken into account (capital gains taxes, withholding taxes etc. for the individual investor) and will be ignored. As a rule of thumb, passive funds do create much less capital gains and therefore less capital gains taxes. The reason for this lies in the lower turnover of index funds. To be able to decide which investment strategy leads to a sustainable added value for the investor, the return of these mutual funds can be compared. To increase the quality of the analysis, different time horizons have been compared. In order to avoid distortions, only homogenous groups of mutual funds have been constructed. Therefore, we have grouped the mutual funds according to there strategy (benchmark) and compared the results. The question, which we will be analysing, is: do actively managed mutual funds add value for the investor?

2. Analysis and Facts

In our research, we have done the following analysis: we looked at the percentage of funds, which were able to outperform an index in a certain time span. For this purpose we have created three homogenous groups, these are:

- Equities Switzerland
- Equities Europe
- Equities USA

We concentrated our analysis on equity funds, because most of the indexed money is invested in equities. For Equities Switzerland and Europe, the universe we used to conduct the analysis consisted of all the mutual funds registered for distribution in Switzerland. The universe for Equities USA consisted of all the mutual funds registered for distribution in the USA. The database used was provided by Micropal. In Switzerland, we used the SPI (Swiss Performance Index) as benchmark. We created a homogenous group deleting all the mutual funds which did not fit into our definition (small-cap or capital protected funds etc.). We conducted the analysis for the years 1996-2002 (see Figure 1 on page 74). Looking at the chart, we can see that only in 1996 did the majority of the fund managers (e.g. more than 50 %) achieve an outperformance vs. the benchmark. One year later, only 30 % of the fund managers were able to outperform. However, the funds outperforming in 1997 are not necessarily the same funds, which outperformed in 1996. In other words, a fund, which was able to achieve an outperformance in one year does not necessarily outperform again in the next year. As a matter of fact, only 15 % of all the fund managers were able to outperform in the long run (1996-2002).

It is often argued that index funds do perform better in a bull market environment while they lag in a bear market. The reason for this pattern has to do with the cash holding. Index funds are always fully invested while actively managed mutual funds do typically have a cash holding of 2-3 %. It is therefore very interesting that in the bear market of 99-02 even less than 15 % of the funds were able to outperform the SPI.

There is one important aspect to be mentioned in the context of Swiss equities. The Swiss market is characterised by a high concentration of a few names. For example Novartis and Nestle both have a weighting of almost 20 %. The five biggest companies account for two thirds of the index. But some fund managers do have legal restrictions which do not allow them to weight a single stock with more than 10 % in the fund. This is obviously a huge problem. If some of these heavy index names do outperform the SPI, the fund manager is not able to avoid an underperformance of the index.

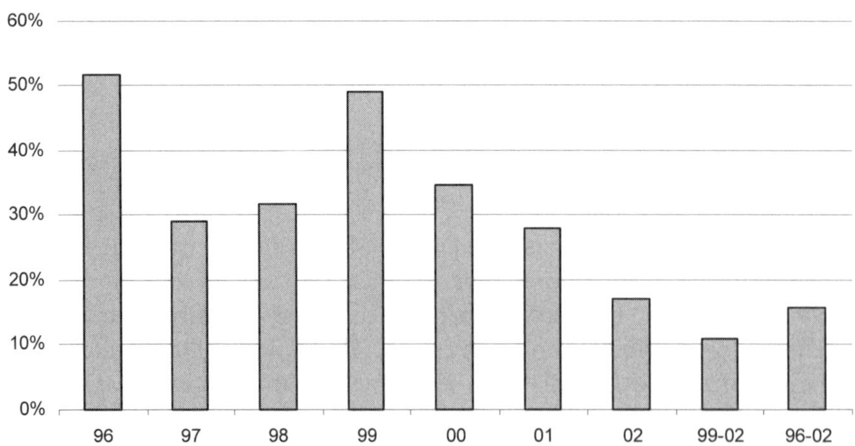

Figure 1: Percentage of funds, which outperformed the SPI. Source: CSAM

This is why we have done the same analysis for European Equities using the MSCI Europe as benchmark. This index is much broader diversified and the problem of not being able to overweight the big names in the index is not applicable here. However, Figure 2 on page 75 clearly shows that the results achieved by European equity fund managers are comparable to the results of the Swiss equity fund managers.

Among the managers of European equities we have a similar pattern: only in 1999 a majority of the fund managers were able to outperform the index. In the long run, a little more than 10 % of the managers did outperform the MSCI Europe. It is interesting that during the bear market of 99-02 the European fund manager did better than the Swiss fund manager.

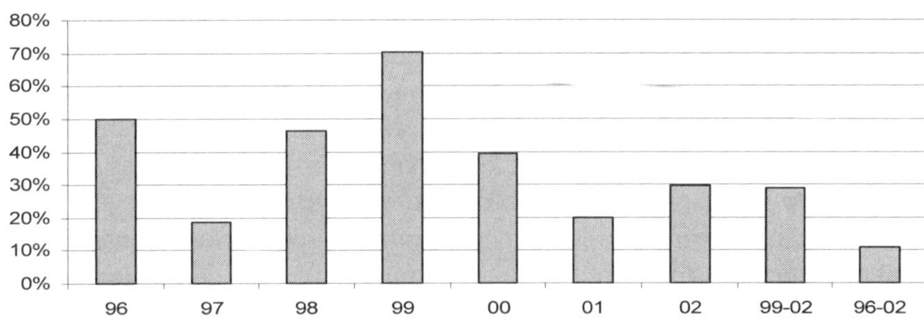

Figure 2: Percentage of funds, which outperformed the MSCI Europe. Source: CSAM

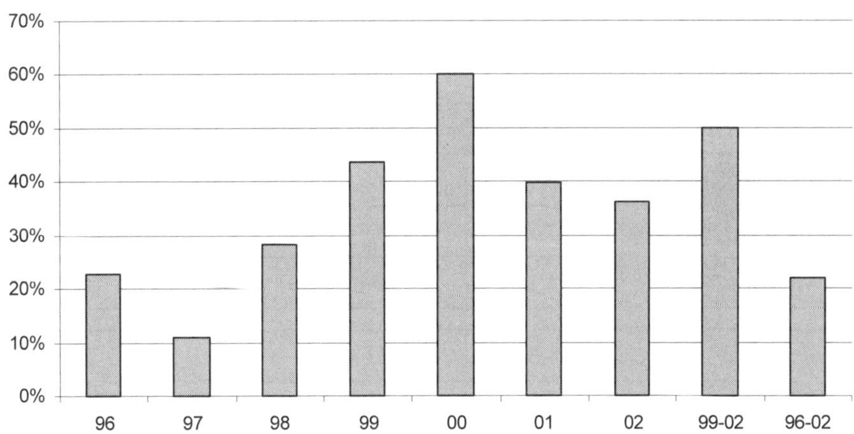

Figure 3: Percentage of funds, which outperformed the S&P 500. Source: CSAM

Now, let's have a look at the US market. The achieved results by the European fund managers have nothing to do with the quality of the people in Europe. In the US we can observe performance figures which can be compared to the results achieved in Europe. Only a minority of the fund managers were able to outperform. The funds were compared against the S&P 500 index.

In the long run, only 20 % of the fund managers were able to outperform the S&P 500. Only in the year 2000, more than 50 % of the fund managers did beat the index. Like their colleagues managing European equities, the US fund managers achieved a better result in the bear market environment of 99-02: 50 % of the managers achieved a performance better than the S%P 500.

One argument, which is often brought forward explaining the rather disappointing result of the fund management industry, is the market efficiency. Market efficiency stipulates that it is almost impossible to have an information advantage about any company. This piece of information would allow a fund manager to achieve an above benchmark performance. At the same time it is argued that the outperformance possibilities in less efficient markets are much bigger. Less efficient markets are typically emerging markets – markets in less developed countries – or markets consisting of smaller companies (mid- and/or small-cap market). S&P conducted a study which analyzed the capabilities of US fund managers in these markets. In the US funds are typically differentiated by style. The analysis was therefore split into value, growth and blend-styles. The results achieved by the US fund managers can be seen in the table below:

Table 1: Percentage of funds outperforming mid- and small-cap indices (in %)

	Last Quarter	1 Year	3 Years	5 Years
Mid Cap Growth	73.91	31.65	17.05	2.84
Mid Cap Blend	77.22	37.65	33.72	13.89
Mid Cap Value	71.15	50.94	28.24	16.67
Small Cap Growth	38.82	9.73	9.27	27.8
Small Cap Blend	71.56	43.88	27.12	39.89
Small Cap Value	88.74	81.37	44.53	58.42

Source: S&P, Data as of March 2003.

The data makes clear, that even in less efficient markets the results do not differ significantly from the results in so called efficient markets. Now why is it so hard to outperform an index? What are the reasons why a relatively small percentage of fund managers are successfully and consistently able to outperform? The next chapter tries to give some answers to these questions.

3. Costs: The Most Important Factor

The most important reason why it is hard for active fund managers to beat the index, are the costs charged to the fund. In the discussion about costs, it is important to distinguish between visible and invisible costs. Visible costs are easy to describe: as a rule of thumb, one can use the management fee. The management fee is the biggest source of visible cost charged to the fund, but there is more! The number which is increasingly used in the mutual fund industry is the total expense ratio (TER). The additional charges, which are not included in the management fee, are usually costs like audit and/or custody fees. A typical TER for an equity fund is – depending on the market and product – between 1 %-2 % p.a. Unfortunately we have only covered the reported costs so far. There are more costs which have to be born by the fund, which are not included in the TER of the fund!

These additional costs can be split into visible and invisible costs. However, they are all related to the fact, that a portfolio manager does actively trade securities. An active fund manager overweights, underweights or even completely drops index stocks in the portfolio depending on his forecast. With changes in his view, the portfolio positioning will change accordingly and transactions are executed. Brokerage fees, domestic and foreign fiscal charges increase the costs charged to the fund in addition to what has been discussed above. Even worse, there is still more! With trading there are invisible costs associated. Bid/Ask spread and "market impact" are costs, which are not visible but do have a performance drag on the mutual fund. Bid/ask spread measures the difference between the prices at which the security can be bought and sold. Depending on the market this spread can be as small as 0.10 % but also as wide as several percentage points. The "market impact" on the other hand describes the process, that the price of a security is influenced by the order of the fund manager. A big buy order may lead – depending on the size of this order – to an increase in the share price of the stock. Because the price of the security has risen from the start of the order until the order is filled the average execution price his higher than when the order was placed. Therefore, some of the expected outperformance of this stock is already lost. It is clear that the effect of this impact depends on the size of the order and the liquidity of the underlying security. It is also clear that this effect applies again selling the stock.

What is the magnitude of the costs resulting from trading? This is obviously a function of the turnover of the fund manager. Typically, active funds do have a turnover between 75-100 % per year. To get a sense of the amount of additional costs lets make a little example which is rather realistic however. We use 100 % turnover as an assumption:

Table 2: Example

	Visible Costs	Invisible Costs	**Total**
Brokerage Fees	20%		
Taxes	10%		
Spread		10%	
Market Impact		20%	
Total			**60%**

With a 100 % turnover, this results in extra costs of 1.20 %. Assuming a TER of 1 %-2 % p.a. an active fund manager does have to outperform the index by 2.20 % – 3.20 % to only achieve a result as good as the index.

Depending on your view, 0.60 % trading costs p.a. may look like a small number to you. But in markets much less liquid, you find brokerage fees and especially spread- and market impact costs significantly higher than that. The invisible costs in these markets may easily exceed 1 %. This is by the way exactly the reason, why – in my opinion – it is pretty hard to outperform the index even in less efficient markets.

Table 1, Percentage of funds outperforming mid- and small-cap indices on page 76, are a clear indication.

The company Plexusgroup in the US has specialised in measuring transaction costs. They have a slightly different view of measuring trading costs. Starting from the implementation shortfall analytics developed by Andre Perold, Plexusgroup has developed an analytical framework which focuses on the chain of communication from sponsor to analyst to manager to trader to broker to exchange. As explained above, many of the costs associated with trading are invisible. This is why Plexusgroup compares trading costs with an iceberg: most of the costs are hidden. Plexusgroup identified four components of trading costs.

These are:

- Commission (payment for broker and exchange services),
- Impact (presence effects of trading in the open marketplace),
- Delay (metering large trades slowly into market liquidity in order to avoid excessive impact),
- Missed Trades (opportunity losses from inability to complete trades at a satisfactory price).

Plexusgroup measures costs from more than 120 manager clients with millions of transactions. A study on the breakdown of the magnitude of leakage confirms that commissions represent the smallest component of trading costs. The research conducted by Plexusgroup showed, that the total transaction costs averaged 1.16 % per year. Applying a 100 % turnover this results in additional cost of 2.32 % p.a. from trading only. Again, if the markets are less efficient and/or the order very big, the costs will rise even more. Plexusgroup has done an analysis in small cap trading and measured costs of 4.5 %, resulting – if 100 % of turnover is applied – in additional costs of 9 % p.a.

Figure 4 clearly shows the magnitude of additional costs, which have to be born by a mutual fund, through trades executed or not executed.

Index funds do minimize trading costs! The turnover – depending on the index – is usually around 10 % p.a. Furthermore, index funds do not need analysts, researchers etc. which allows to reduce the management fee of the fund significantly. Passively managed fund do have therefore cost savings coming from two sources:

1. lower management fees,
2. lower trading costs.

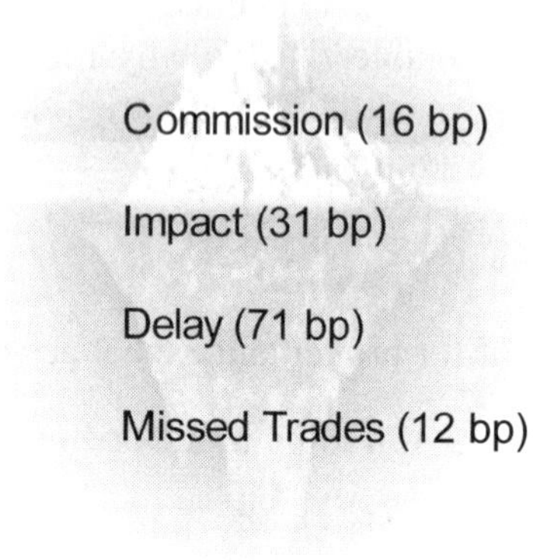

Figure 4: Transaction costs. Source: Plexusgroup

4. ETF: Just One More Investment Vehicle?

How can an investor participate in a passively managed product? In the US passively managed mutual funds were be offered some thirty years ago as described in chapter 1. These investment instruments were used not only by institutional investors but increasingly by retail investors as well. For very large institutional investors, a segregated account is still the cheapest way to get exposure to an index, since a mandate avoids all the extra costs which are part of a mutual fund (administration fee, audit fee etc.).

In Europe on the other hand, passively managed mutual funds have not really been able to achieve a break-through among the investors. During the nineties, so called index certificates became very popular in Europe. Index certificates have – in contrast to a mutual fund – no management fees at all! In order to achieve a profit, the investment, bank typically issuing this sort of product, does retain some of the dividends. This is a smart idea, because in my view, investors have a tendency to focus on minimising costs and completely ignore to maximize the return as well. This is intuitively clear in a little example: who would not prefer a product with 9 % return and no costs to a product with 10 % return but 1 % in costs? What was even more attractive with index certificates was the fact that they traded continuously, while mutual funds are open once a day only. At first glance this advantage of being able to trade intraday seems to be of minor importance for a long term investor. But the psychological importance of being able to trade intraday cannot be underestimated.

Exchange Traded Funds combine the advantages of index certificates (continuous trading) with the advantages of a mutual fund (regulated market, proper and transparent valuation methodology). The table below compares the various passive investment vehicles, which are available to investors:

Table 3: Comparison of Various Index Instruments

Characteristics	ETFs	Index funds	Index certificates	Index Future	Equities (Direct Investment)
Financial instrument	Mutual Fund	Mutual Fund	Bond	Derivative	Equity
Pricing	Continuous	Daily net asset value (forward pricing)	Continuous	Continuous	Continuous
Market liquidity	High	No exchange trading	Medium	High	High
Maturity	None	None	Limited lifespan	Limited lifespan	None
Reinvestment risk	None	None	Yes	Yes	None
Short sales	Yes	No	Yes	Yes	Yes
Costs for purchase/sale	Normal brokerage fees	Front/back-load	Purchase and reinvestment costs	Initial and variation margin payments and rollover costs	Brokerage fees on all index shares
Minimum order size	1 ETF (roughly CHF 60=	1 Fund unit (roughly CHF 100)	1 Certificate (roughly CHF 100)	1 Future (roughly CHF 60'000)	Costs associated with reconstructing the index with individual shares
Dividend payment	As a rule, semi-annual payment	As a rule, annual payment	As a rule, no dividends are paid	Cash settlement at maturity	Annual dividends

Source: CSAM.

Some people argue that ETFs are a speculative investment instrument. Looking at the sometime spectacular volumes, one might get this impression at first glance. Some ETFs do have daily trading volume exceeding 30 % of the fund's asset under management. In my view, there is no reason why an instrument, which is – especially in Europe – on average one third cheaper than a traditional mutual fund, should not be held long term as well. In reality, an ETF is a regular mutual fund with just one additional feature: tradability. To name ETFs a speculative instrument is completely wrong. And investors don't believe this either. This can be seen in the increasing popularity of ETFs around the world.

One question which always comes up in any discussion about ETF is, why most of these products are indexed. Today, there are a few active so called ETFs. However, these products do not have the classical characteristics of an ETF, which are: continuous trading, permanent calculation of intraday NAV and daily distribution of the fund holdings. Exactly these characteristics have helped to increase the liquidity of an ETF at the exchange. Actively managed mutual funds – especially successfully managed mutual funds – do not like this transparency at all. And in my view correctly so! Successful active funds, which are going to publish the fund holdings on a daily basis, run into a risk that free riders will try to follow their investment strategy immediately. A successful fund manager must fear, that the outperformance achieved in the past, may not be repeated anymore. This is why I believe, that successfully managed active mutual funds cannot be launched as ETFs.

5. Summary

If at the end of this article you think that indexing is the only strategy going to survive, you are wrong. In order to keep the financial markets alive, both strategies are needed. I think, there is no other individual who can explain this better than William F. Sharpe STANCO 25 Professor of Finance, Emeritus, Stanford University: "In fact, if everyone indexed, capital markets would cease to provide the relatively efficient security prices that make indexing an attractive strategy for some investors. All the research undertaken by active managers keeps prices closer to values, enabling indexed investors to catch a free ride without paying the costs. Thus there is a fragile equilibrium in which some investors choose to index some or all of their money, while the rest continue to search for mispriced securities." Is this equilibrium already reached? Only the market will tell. But it is interesting to realise, that in continental Europe, indexing as a viable investment strategy has only started to become accepted. This is in contrast to the US, where indexing is popular not only among institutional investors but among retail investors as well. Is there an explanation to this? Financial innovations usually take place in the US and it takes normally a few years until they are introduced in Europe. Not all financial innovations find their way to Europe. For example value and growth investing is still a topic which has not been able to gain attention in Europe. But there is another, I think even more important aspect to be considered. In Europe the financial industry is dominated by universal banks. These banks do have a distribution network and offer asset management services at the same time. Therefore, these banks tend to distribute internally produced products first. As long as open platform architecture is not reality in place, index products do have a hard time gaining the same popularity as we can observe in the US market place. This has to do with the fact that index products tend to have a smaller margin compared to actively managed mutual funds and are therefore not offered actively to retail investors. However, with ETFs finding their way to Europe, this product started to change the mutual fund landscape quite significantly. Firstly, ETFs can be bought and sold like a stock, which makes the existing mutual fund distribution channels obsolete. Secondly, todays ETFs are passively managed, which increases their attractivness even more. However, it is obviously clear that today's distribution channel will continue to favour traditional products as long as possible. This is why investors only slowly learn about this new and attractive financial innovation. This will only slowdown but not stop the breakthrough of ETFs in Europe.

ETFs – Tactical Asset Allocation Tools

Eleanor de Freitas and Catherine Barker

ETFs combine the advantages of both index funds and stocks. They are liquid, easy to use and can be traded in any quantity, just like stocks. At the same time an ETF provides the diversification, market tracking and low expense of an index fund. These characteristics combine to create an investment tool that provides investors with the broad exposure they require, at the level they want; at the moment they need it. As such they have been promoted and branded as an innovative investment opportunity. A claim greatly supported by the accelerated growth in ETFs, which clearly illustrates the appetite for such a product.

The major participants in the ETF market have historically been institutional investors. Some common institutional applications of ETFs include:

- Cash flow equitisation,
- Transition management,
- Core holdings – for smaller segregated accounts,
- Hedging key exposures,
- Asset allocation – global and tactical.

1. Tactical Asset Allocation

Institutional investors will make a strategic asset allocation, broadly between bonds and equities, based on long-term views of market opportunities and risks – this is sometimes called the "policy mix". The decision on how a fund's investments are allocated between stocks, bonds and cash has considerable impact on the performance and risk profile of the portfolio. In fact, the asset allocation decision has been shown to explain over 90 % of the return variability of a multi-asset fund as demonstrated below.

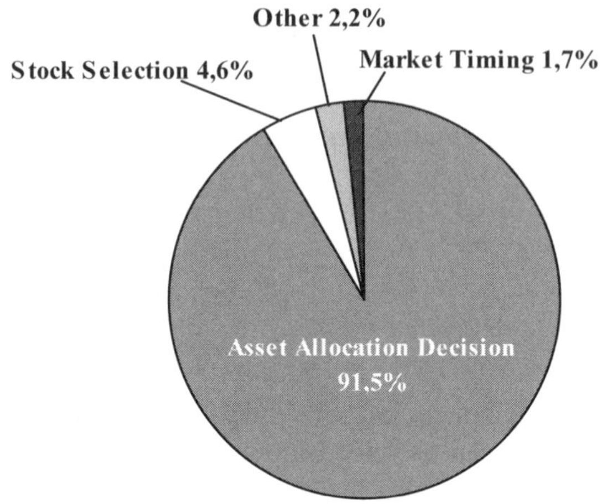

Figure 1: Asset Allocation. Source: Gary P. Brinson, Brian D. Singer and Gilbert L. Beebower, Financial Analysts Journal (May-June 1991)

Tactical asset allocation (TAA) is a quantitatively based investment strategy that maximises the "risk-adjusted return" by identifying and exploiting relative mispricings across asset classes. Although many strategies focus on finding the right mix between domestic stocks, bonds and cash, they can also extend to other asset classes such as real estate and international equities.

TAA complements the strategic asset allocation chosen by constantly reallocating around the portfolio's policy mix. The process assesses the expected return and risk of each asset class and rebalances the portfolio to optimally trade of total portfolio risk and total return. The source of the added return through TAA is attained exclusively through active shifts among the asset classes. The process is dynamic and will respond to changes in expectations and opportunities, adjusting the allocations within a portfolio to take advantage where these deviate from the expectations and opportunities of the strategic mix chosen.

A TAA strategy often implements the desired tilt towards each of the broad asset classes by gaining exposure to highly diversified index portfolios representing the asset class. This is typically achieved by direct investment in the underlying assets, through futures contracts or mutual funds and, over recent years, using ETFs.

2. The Benefits of Indexing

It is widely acknowledged that indexation is an extremely efficient and cost-effective method of gaining diversified exposure to "the market". An index fund offers consistency and reliability in long-term returns, removing surprise factor and "manager risk" from an investment strategy.

„… the return on the average actively managed dollar will equal the return on the average passively managed dollar …"

William Sharpe, "The Arithmetic of Active Management," Financial Analysts Journal, Jan – Feb 1991

In terms of costs, index tracking is certainly the more desirable investment option. An index fund will generally have lower turnover than an actively managed portfolio and, therefore, spends less on trading. An active portfolio manager must also pay for research and other analysis tools. In addition to having lower investment costs, index funds generally come with lower management fees than their more active counterparts. For example, while the average actively managed US equity fund has management fees in excess of 1 %[1]; index funds have a median fee of just 0.44 %.

The broad exposure gained from an investment in an index fund can be achieved through direct investment in the underlying assets or by holding a single entity that provides equivalent exposure. Since direct investment requires the ability to trade, settle and monitor numerous assets and involves daily maintenance, a "one-stop" solution presents a more desirable alternative. Investment tools such as mutual funds, futures contracts and exchange traded funds enable investors to gain exposure to multiple assets with a single investment. In particular, ETFs allow investors to implement asset allocation decisions at every level from the bond/equity mix to sector rotation.

3. Where There's an Index …

One of the key strengths of the ETF as an investment tool is the wide range of products available and the sheer breadth of equity and fixed income benchmarks they track. Over the past nine years, the ETF market has wit-

---

[1] May 1989 to May 1999. Source: Barclays Global Investors Limited analysis of Morningstar data.

nessed dramatic growth in every respect. In 1996 there were just 21 listed ETFs but by the end of September 2003, there were more than 260 different ETFs trading on 28 exchanges around the world. The relatively low level of product overlap between fund advisors means that the variety of ETFs available is quite staggering.

In contrast, futures present limited options in terms of asset or specific index exposure and some investors may be restricted from utilising certain derivative products. For a particular asset class, the tracking risk of using an index other than the one to which you are benchmarked can be high. With some applications such as equitising accruals or small cash flows, the impact of this tracking error may be tolerable. However, for other applications highlighted earlier, the effect of using a product that deviates noticeably from the desired benchmark can be significant.

One such function is asset allocation. The decision to tilt towards a particular asset class or country is, most likely, based upon the risk and return profile of the funds benchmark. If this choice has to be implemented through an instrument that does not track that benchmark, then the fund takes on additional security specific risk. A risk not accounted for in the model that can be exceptionally high and is potentially uncontrollable. The ETFs available cover a far broader range of indices than futures, giving investors more opportunity to action allocation tilts without this risk. In addition, they allow investors to easily gain exposure to a far deeper variety of asset class – fixed income, sectors and additional countries and regions.

Efficient Implementation for Fixed Income Exposure

Fixed income ETFs offer institutional investors a way to implement clean, efficient asset allocation strategies that was previously unavailable. Historically, gaining diversified exposure to fixed income markets required the use of mutual funds. The lack of transparency of these instruments meant that an allocation could be skewed away from the intended tilt, due to the fund's manager taking a different view to that of the end investor.

A large investor might be in a position to purchase individual issues, as long as they had the necessary credit and trading resource. However, for many investors the transaction costs could be prohibitive, especially when trading smaller amounts.

Table 1: European listed ETFs

Asset	Available?
Equity exposure	
European regional	yes
European countries	yes
European sectors	yes
US country	yes
US sector	yes
Japanese equity	yes
Global	yes
Fixed income	
European corporate	yes
German treasury	yes
US corporate	yes

Source: Barclays Global Investors Limited

Fixed income ETFs solve these problems in one trade. Real time intra-day trading allows immediate implementation of a tilt or allocation at spreads that are considerably tighter than those on mutual funds. The size of a trade is not an issue and transaction and administrative costs are limited to one trade. Diversification is immediate and completely transparent – the investor knows exactly what exposure they achieve and the ongoing management of components to match the index is outsourced to the manager of the ETF.

4. Which Instrument? ETFs Versus Futures

In the numerous current and potential applications of ETFs, they most frequently come up against the index future as an alternative investment tool. The decision to use one instrument over the other typically depends upon:

- Investment time horizon,
- Relative richness/cheapness of instrument,
- Desired benchmark,
- Required position size,
- Ability to deliver cash for settlement.

The first two attributes in combination drive the actual costs of holding or transacting in each product to achieve a particular investment objective. For asset allocation purposes it is this assessment of cost, the desired benchmark and, perhaps to a lesser extent, the required position size that are of great importance. In fact, the need to gain exposure to a certain asset class, country or sector through a particular benchmark can far outweigh the additional costs associated with an instrument. The following table summarises some of the key attributes of ETFs and futures that might influence a decision to use each device.

Table 2: Key attributes of futures and ETFs

Future	ETF
Low explicit costs	High explicit costs
Require quarterly rolls with associated costs	No Rolls or special documentation
Need special documentation and accounts	No margin requirements or accounts
Daily margin requirements	A single security - not a derivative
Track a limited number of benchmarks	Track a wide variety of benchmarks
Many with limited liquidity	Pool liquidity from underlying securities
Often traded in larger size	Can be traded in relatively small size

Source: Barclays Global Investors Limited.

5. Futures vs. ETFs: The Costs

An evaluation of futures and ETFs would not be complete without considering the key issues and relative expense involved in holding and trading the two devices. The costs can be broken down into explicit costs that have a definite direction and implicit costs that may impact performance positively or negatively. These implicit costs can be driven by numerous factors and have undesirable performance consequences that far outweigh any explicit transaction or holding costs (See Figure 2).

For both methods of investment, the explicit costs include those incurred upon entry and exit of each position such as commissions, bid/ask spreads and taxes. A future will also incur such costs during the quarterly contract rolls. ETFs have an additional explicit cost in the form of the management fee, which varies between products and regions. There are implicit costs associated with a futures investment as they are subject to contract and calendar roll mispricing and may trade rich or cheap relative to fair value. An ETF carries no such costs, but may experience a degree of mis-tracking due to investment constraints.

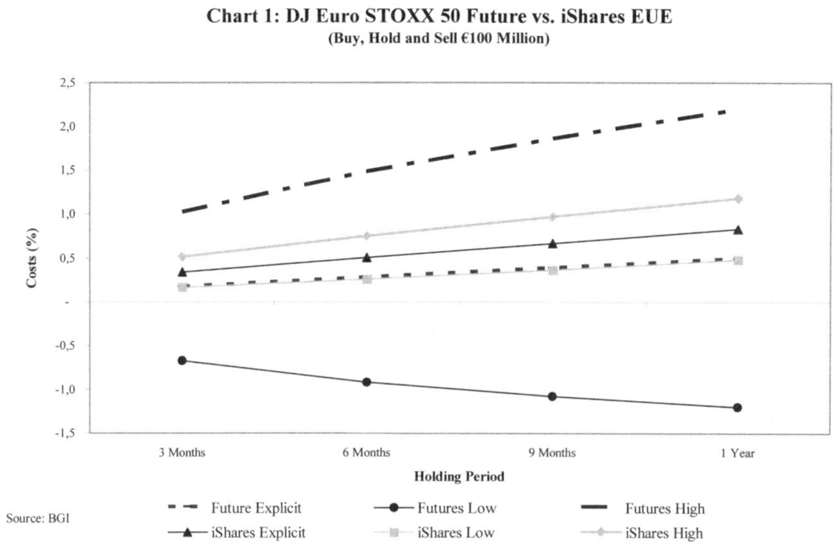

Figure 2: DJ Euro STOXX50 Future vs. iShares EUE (Buy, Hold and Sell €100 Mio.). Source: Barclays Global Investors Limited

In the US, there are much lower overall costs connected with holding ETFs versus the equivalent future. This is partly a consequence of the small management fees of US equity ETFs, but also a result of the comparatively higher cost of holding/trading US futures. The annual roll costs of an S&P 500 contract have risen remarkably in recent years, with the contracts currently rolling at a consistent premium to fair value. The picture is slightly different in Europe where some (but not all) index futures have witnessed a steady decrease in the annual cost of rolls. This, coupled with the larger management fees due on European listed ETFs, often makes futures the cheaper option.

It is, however, worth pointing out that some of the conclusions surrounding costs alluded to above do not hold in the short term. Some studies would suggest that, even in Europe, ETFs have a more desirable cost structure in the short term. This is mainly a result of the proportionally lower impact of management fees, which are drawn on a daily basis.

Improved Access to International Exposure

Some markets impose limits on the access available to foreign investors. For example, in Taiwan, investors must comply with Qualifying Foreign

Institutional Investor rules, which can be onerous to achieve and maintain. Even those that qualify to invest must be resourced to research and trade the stocks in that specific market. An ETF, such as the MSCI Taiwan iShare, offers a simple solution to institutional investors – listed on the American Stock Exchange, one trade in the ETF provides indexed exposure to the Taiwanese market without administrative complications or requiring special licences.

6. The "Right" Index

The heightened interest in index investing over the past ten years has seen an explosion of benchmark choice across many asset classes. For example, an investor desiring Pan-European equity exposure is presented with more than 15 index options. As mentioned earlier, when implementing an asset allocation strategy using the "right" index for a particular asset class is important. An allocation decision is based on the risk and return profile of a certain benchmark and so executing that strategy by gaining exposure to a different index brings additional tracking risk – this can be high.

Table 3: Historic tracking error[2] of local equity indices

Country / region	Local index	Tracking vs. MSCI Standard Index Series	Tracking vs. FTSE All-World Index Series
Eurobloc	DJ EuroSTOXX 50	Feb 91	Feb 48
UK	FTSE 100	Jan 41	Jan 67
France	CAC 40	Feb 99	Feb 15
Germany	DAX	Feb 99	Feb 49
Switzerland	SMI	Jan 16	Jan 58
Netherlands	AEX	Apr 13	05. Mrz
Italy	MIB 30	Feb 51	Mrz 79
Spain	IBEX 35	Apr 23	Apr 70
US	S&P 500	0.73	01. Jan
Canada	S&P/TSE 60	Feb 79	Jan 92
Japan	Topix	Feb 60	Mrz 62
Australia	S&P/ASX 200	Mrz 43	Feb 42
Hong Kong	Hang Seng	Mai 99	Sep 89

Source: Barclays Global Investors Limited analysis of Datastream data

[2] Annualised standard deviation of the difference in monthly price returns (local currency) from January 2000 to September 2003.

When it comes to asset allocation strategies the impact on performance of any benchmark mis-match can be noticeable. In the past, investors looking to gain broad asset exposure through a single entity have been limited to a few asset classes and very specific indices. The wider range of asset classes and indices for which an ETF product is available has gone a long way to reduce this issue. For example, where equity index futures are limited to local market indices, there are ETFs tracking global benchmarks such as MSCI and FTSE. It can be far easier to track fully global benchmarks such as these with a basket of ETFs than with a basket of futures.

Not All ETFs Track Perfectly

It is important to note that not all ETFs are based on full replication and so will not necessarily track their benchmark perfectly. For the ETF to maintain many of its desirable qualities it may have to compromise on tracking error to some degree. For example, to ensure tax efficiency the funds must often adhere to certain concentration constraints dictated by legislation i.e. '40 Act (US) or UCITS (UK). If a benchmark is heavily concentrated and does not satisfy such rules (often the case for many single country indices) it becomes difficult for an ETF to track perfectly. In most cases even those ETFs that hold an optimised basket of securities offer a superior option in terms of tracking to many of the futures.

7. Conclusions: The Complete Solution?

The pace of innovation and expansion in the ETF marketplace has clearly opened up new and unique alternatives for fund management. ETFs can present opportunities for cost savings, improved tracking, efficiency and simplicity. For investors attempting to implement asset allocation tilts, this improvement in tracking is essential, particularly for investors benchmarked to a global series like MSCI or FTSE. The breadth of indices covered by ETFs allows investors to easily and simply gain exposure to a whole host of additional "asset classes" from fixed income to specific equity market sectors, industries, size segments and styles. Either in isolation, or in combination with futures, ETFs can be used in numerous ways to improve and enhance the investment management process.

The global equity investor benchmarked to the MSCI index series is presented, through ETFs, with a very comprehensive set of tools for country level equity asset allocation. The iShares suite covers the main MSCI regional indices but also more than 15 individual "developed market" countries. There are also six individual "emerging markets" represented and a broad MSCI EMF iShare. This provides a comprehensive set of tools to implement a broad range of country tilts simply, easily and with a minimal amount of tracking risk.

Exchange Traded Funds from a Lawyer's Perspective – The Case of Germany

Ute Brunner-Reumann

1. Overview

Exchange traded funds ("**ETFs**") from a lawyer's perspective provide for a myriad of legal and regulatory issues. Each of the member states of the European Economic Area ("**EEA**") and the other countries in Europe have their own distinct regulatory regimes. Although certain EEA legislation was introduced to harmonise aspects of those regimes, it was not done to facilitate the easy establishment of ETFs, since ETFs did not exist at that time in Europe or just started to gain some popularity. Rather, ETFs must use whatever harmonising European legislation they can, albeit subject to modification where that legislation has been implemented in each EEA member state.

1.1 Structure of an ETF

ETFs are undertakings for collective investments (i.e. funds) offering investors the investment performance of a designated index (an "**Index**") by the acquisition of shares or units of the ETF listed and traded on stock exchanges.

ETFs can be structured as open-ended investment companies or as alternative vehicles issuing shares, interest or units. In this article, unless stated otherwise, the interests in an ETF, irrespective of its legal form are referred to as "units".

The legal structure of an ETF usually is as follows: subscription and redemption of a minimum number of units (e.g. having a value of at least Euro 1 million) on an in-kind basis at the level of the ETF (the "**Primary**

Market") are reserved to institutional investors, so-called "**Authorised Participants**". The Authorised Participants are typically large investment banks or brokerage businesses. Authorised Participants will have concluded a participation agreement with the ETF setting out the conditions and procedures which allow the Authorised Participant to subscribe and redeem units of the ETF on an in-kind basis. The participation agreement may also cover issues such as how the Authorised Participant will market the units of the ETF. The Authorised Participants act as whole-sellers of the ETF's units. Those Authorised Participants may also act–as market makers for the distribution of the units of the ETF on various stock exchanges, on which other investors are allowed to buy and sell units in accordance with the rules and regulations of those stock exchanges (the "**Secondary Market**").

One key feature, touched upon above, which distinguishes ETFs from traditional funds, is that the constitutional documents of the ETF provide that its units are created in predetermined multiples of units, the "Creation Units" and that the subscription price of those units is paid in kind (or, depending on regulatory requirements, in a way as near as possible to an in-kind solution) by a basket of component securities of the respective Index plus or minus a balancing cash component reflecting the net asset value of the ETF unit.

Similarly, the units can only be redeemed by the Authorised Participants in predetermined multiples of units, the "Redemption Units", against payment in-kind (or, depending on regulatory requirements, in a way as near as possible to an "in-kind solution") by the ETF of a basket of component securities of the Index plus or minus a balancing cash component reflecting the relevant net asset value.

A key benefit is that the in-kind contribution and redemption of component securities eliminates transaction fees to be borne by the ETF as the portfolio manager does generally not need to buy and sell component securities of the Index within the portfolio of the ETF. Another advantage is that ETFs can then provide an attractive fee structure. Mostly, they do not provide for subscription and redemption fees and provide capped all-in-fees of a maximum of around 50 basis points on the net assets of the ETF. For some ETFs their capped all-in-fees are around 20 basis points.

Price transparency for investors on the Secondary Market is ensured by publication at the stock exchange of the so-called iNAV (indicative intra-day net asset value), which is calculated even by the relevant stock exchange or a service provider of the ETF and disclosed regularly during the trading day. The Deutsche Börse AG ("**DBAG**") as operator of the Frankfurter Wertpapierbörse ("**FWB**") publishes it every minute, for certain indices even every 15 seconds).[1] This iNAV permits to investors on the Secondary Market to assess the proposed bid and offer prices on the stock exchange and help to ensure that the Authorised Participants and other market makers in the ETF units maintain bid and offer prices close to the iNAV.

Graphically, the structure of an ETF could be described as follows:

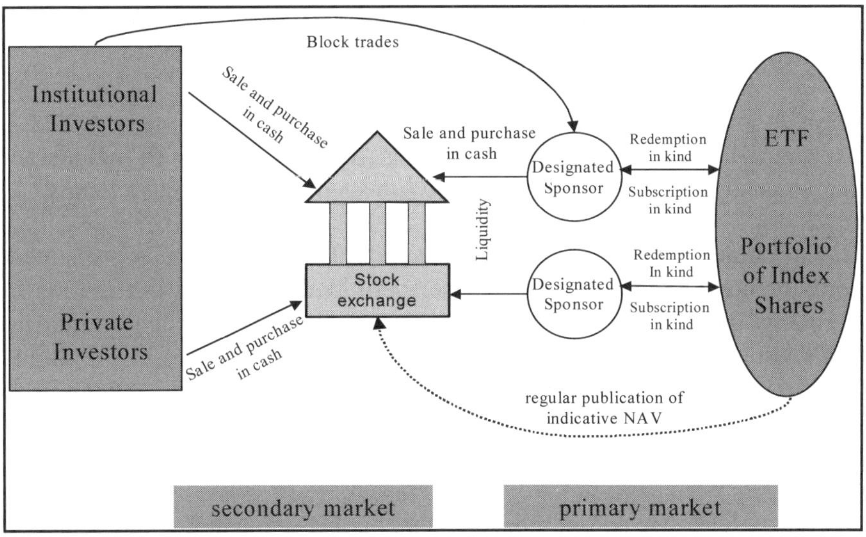

Figure 1: Structure of an ETF

1.2 The Market Place for ETFs in Germany

ETFs are not entirely new products, and have first appeared in the United States. In October 2003 approximately 117 ETFs were distributed within the American market, representing a total amount of US$ 129.375 billion assets under management. In Europe there were 98 ETFs with 168 listings representing US$ 17.33 billion at the same period.[2]

1 See www.deutsche-boerse.com

2 Debora Fuhr, ETFs: into orbit; FOW January 2004 pages 12 et seq.

But also the European market has developed substantially over the last years. In particular, the market for ETFs in Germany has grown rapidly since, in April 2000, DBAG, which runs the FWB, established a specific market platform for ETFs, the market segment XTF (now: Xetra Funds).

The market segment Xetra Funds does not only contain the typical, i.e. passively managed ETF but also provides for actively managed ETFs to be listed. The fund management of the latter mentioned ETFs competes with the performance of a benchmark given in order to obtain a higher yield. Therefore, the fund management deliberately deviates from the index chosen by over- or underweighting of specific single stocks according to market research results. The listing rules for the market segment Xetra Funds differentiate between those passively and actively managed ETFs.

Passively managed investment funds are included in the sub-segment XTF – Exchange Traded Funds whereas there is also a possibility to include actively managed investment funds in the sub-segment Xetra Active Funds.

The investment funds currently listed at Xetra Funds are German investment funds or non-German UCITS that are permitted for public distribution in Germany. Participants at Xetra Funds are, for example, German investment funds issued by Indexchange Investment AG and DWS Investment GmbH (which has listed actively managed investment funds), and non-German UCITS as UBS Exchange Traded Funds, a Luxembourg SICAV, or the European Exchange Traded Fund Company plc.

Of course, ETFs are not only listed at this market segment but may rather be listed on any German stock exchange but the market segment Xetra Funds at Frankfurt stock exchange is the largest market place for ETFs in Germany, even in Europe.[3] Another established market place for ETFs in Germany is the EUWAX segment at the Stuttgart stock exchange.

1.3 Summary of Listing Requirements

In essence, an ETF to be listed in the market segment Xetra Funds must be at the same time listed either at the Official Trading (*Amtlicher Handel*) or

[3] According to the DBAG's website information, around 50,25 % of the European ETF turnover has being processed in DBAG's XTF segment in December 2004 (see www. Deutsche-boerse.com).

Regulated Market (*Geregelter Markt*) segments of the FWB. All listing requirements for such market have to be fulfilled.

Additionally, the ETF must meet the requirements of the Conditions for Participation (*Teilnahmebedingungen*) at Xetra Funds. It must, in particular, be permitted for public distribution in Germany. Furthermore, at least one Designated Sponsor needs to be appointed. Designated Sponsors must provide for higher liquidity by quoting binding prices for buying and selling ETF units.

Actively managed investment funds need to comply with further requirements. They need to have an index as a benchmark and a minimum size. The volume of an actively managed ETF shall be at least 50 mill. Euro.

2. Establishment of an ETF – Regulatory Impacts

2.1 German ETFs

ETFs are usually open-ended investment funds. In order to ease distribution throughout Europe, it is advantageous for them to comply with the UCITS- regime[4], although this is not necessary. Under German law an ETF would be established as an investment fund under the new investment

---

[4] The UCITS-regime (i.e. the Directive 85/611/EEC, the „**UCITS Directive**" of 20 December 1985 of the European Council, now modified by Directive 2001/107/EC and the Directive 2001/108/EC of 21 January 2002 of the European Parliament and the Council (the **„UCITS III Directives"**) provides a framework of the minimum standard that a fund suitable for offering to the public across Europe must comply with. On the basis that an ETF complies with these standards and is therefore an Undertaking for Collective Investment in Transferable Securities (i.e. the ETF is a „**UCITS**") then the home regulatory authorities in the EEA member state in which it is established will authorise it for public distribution in that state and issue a UCITS certificate. With its UCITS certificate the UCITS can apply for registration with the relevant regulatory authorities in other EEA member states to permit the units of the ETF to be publicly marketed. The UCITS may commence marketing in that state after a maximum waiting period of two months, unless the regulatory authorities in that state give a reasoned decision to the contrary. Under the UCITS regime the regulatory authorities in those other EEA member states must accept the UCITS certificate issued by the EEA member state in which the UCITS is established.

fund regime, in particular the German Investment Act (*Investmentgesetz* – "**InvG**").[5]

There are two alternatives for establishing a German investment fund. On the one hand, one could make use of a capital investment company (*Kapitalanlagegesellschaft,* "**KAG**") which would manage and administer such investment fund. On the other hand one could make use of the newly introduced investment stock corporation with variable capital (*Investmentaktiengesellschaft mit veränderlichem Kapital* – "**InvAG**").

KAGs are credit institutions which may, as their sole principal banking activity, conduct the management of investment funds. KAGs qualify as credit institutions and are, thus, subject to the provisions of both the Banking Act (*Kreditwesengesetz* – "**KWG**") and the InvG which has replaced the Investment Companies Act (*Gesetz über Kapitalanlagegesellschaften* – "**KAGG**"). KAGs are supervised by the German Federal Financial Supervisory Authority (*Bundesanstalt für Finanzdienstleistungsaufsicht* – "**BaFin**").

KAGs must be established in the form of either limited liability companies or stock corporations. In practice, KAGs are predominantly limited liability companies. The statutory minimum paid-in share capital must amount to EUR 730,000. If the assets under management exceed EUR 3 billion, a surcharge of at least 0.02 % of the asset value exceeding EUR 3 billion (in total not to exceed EUR 10 million) will be added to the minimum initial capital.

Two trustworthy and qualified managers have to be appointed by a KAG. The BaFin decides whether the applicants have sufficient experience and the required qualifications in managing investment funds.

---

[5] The Investment Modernisation Act (*Investmentmodernisierungsgesetz*) merged the provisions of the KAGG with those of the Foreign Investment Act (*Auslandinvestmentgesetz*), implemented the UCITS III Directives into German law and entered into force on 1 January 2004. The Investment Modernisation Act consists of the InvG and the Investment Tax Act *(Investmentsteuergesetz* – „**InvStG**"). For a transitional period an existing KAG may, until 13 February 2007, continue to apply the provisions of the KAGG to funds existing on 1 January 2004.

As credit institutions, KAGs are fully supervised by the BaFin and have to comply with most of the restrictions and provisions applicable to banks, i.e. organisational, reporting and own capital requirements under the KWG.

A German KAG may set up one or more investment funds. Each such investment fund must be approved by the BaFin as competent regulator. Such investment fund established by a KAG does not constitute an own legal entity separate from the KAG. Rather, the legal basis of an investment fund managed by a KAG is contractual, i.e. an investment fund is established by the KAG and the unit-holders agreeing on the fund rules of such investment fund which have to comply with the general and specific restrictions as to investment policy etc., depending, inter alia, on the category of the investment fund being set up (e.g. special restrictions for "index funds"). The German Association of Investment Funds (*Bundesverband Investment and Asset Management e.V.* – "**BVI**") has produced sample fund rules and even sample prospectuses already co-ordinated with the BaFin.[6]

The assets of the KAG are separated into several categories, KAG's own assets and investment fund assets. The investment fund assets are not "liable" for the KAG's obligations, even if those obligations derive from the proper management of the investment fund. No action can be brought against such an investment fund. An investment fund cannot be the subject of bankruptcy or composition proceedings.

Units may be issued in the form of registered or bearer certificates. However, when establishing an ETF bearer certificates will be chosen which will be held in collective safe custody by Clearstream Banking AG as book-entry securities to facilitate bookings. The units issued by a KAG qualify as securities, however they are not considered to be shares (*Aktien*). This has an impact on the listing requirements.

---

6 These have been initially produced in cooperation with the Federal Banking Authority (*Bundesaufsichtsamt für das Kreditwesen,*) which has been merged with the Federal Insurance Authority *(Bundesaufsichtsamt für das Versicherungswesen)* and the Federal Securities Trading Supervisory Authority (*Bundesaufsichtsamt für Wertpapierhandel)* to one single supervisory body, the BaFin as of 1 May 2002. Given the changes under the new InvG these templates are currently updated. Samples are available at the BVI's website www.bvi.de.

Under the new InvG, investment funds may be established also with different classes of units.

Since 1 January 2004 there is also an attractive corporate structure available under the InvG in order to establish an investment fund, the so-called InvAG being a stock corporation with variable capital. The InvAG does not administer separate investment funds (*Sondervermögen*) as a contractual structure like a KAG, rather it constitutes itself the investment fund (comparable to a Luxembourg SICAV). Being a stock corporation under the German Stock Corporation Act (*Aktiengesetz*), the provisions of this Act apply, however with substantial modifications, for example as it issues and redeems shares on a regular basis on facilitated conditions.

Furthermore, the InvAG does not qualify as credit institution but is comparable to a financial services provider under the KWG, also being subject to the BaFin's supervision. However, its regulatory obligations are limited. Also, as a minimum, an initial capital of EUR 300,000 only is required.

Nevertheless, as the structure is quite new several issues remain unresolved. For example, it is not foreseen that an InvAG establishes several sub-funds. Furthermore, details about the redemption process are not regulated. Once these issues are resolved, the InvAG may be an attractive alternative to the establishment of a KAG. In particular, the listing of InvAGs is explicitly foreseen in the InvG. But also here, the law does not foresee any harmonisation rules as regards listing documentation.

There are currently several German investment funds marketed publicly in Germany as ETFs. These are "common" German investment funds managed by a German KAG whose units are listed on the FWB in the market segment Xetra Funds and which are either actively or passively managed.

2.2 Foreign ETFs

In the German market, also a lot of foreign ETFs are offered. The market segment Xetra Funds of Deutsche Börse AG does contain several foreign ETFs.

Under German law, any ETF qualifies as an investment fund, thus, being subject to the investment fund regime. One of the most important preconditions for a listing at Xetra Funds is that the ETF to be listed at Xetra Funds must be approved by the BaFin for public distribution in Germany in accordance with the InvG. The mere listing on a German stock exchange does not automatically permit the public distribution of a non-German investment fund in Germany under the InvG. As rules are not harmonised, the regime applicable to investment funds (i.e. the InvG) and the rules governing the listing of securities (in case of SICAVs for example, of shares) apply both.

Thus, before being distributed publicly (including any public marketing activities), the foreign ETF must be notified/registered for public distribution in Germany with the BaFin. The public distribution or marketing of non-German ETFs is only permissible after either a two months period (for UCITS) or after a three months period (for non-UCITS) following the filing of the notification has elapsed, provided that the BaFin does not prohibit the public distribution of the ETF.

2.2.1 Non-UCITS-Funds

The requirements concerning the marketing of foreign investment units that are non-EU investment units has in fact been largely maintained unchanged under the new InvG and still follows similar rules as under the KAGG.

It is *inter alia* necessary that a foreign investment company is subject to an effective public supervision and that the competent supervisory body is in the experience of the BaFin prepared to cooperate satisfactorily. A certificate of this must be given by the foreign supervisor which may cause problems in some foreign jurisdictions. All relevant documents concerning the investment fund need to be filed and are subject to review by BaFin which requires a level of protection for investors comparable to the position of investors in a German investment fund by requiring similar structures (for example as regards the investment fund's custodian bank etc.).

2.2.2 UCITS-Funds

Most ETFs targeted towards European investors are launched within the regime of the UCITS Directive and are therefore able to be "passported" for public distribution in Europe.[7]

---

[7] The UCITS Directive 85/611/EC has been amended by the Directive 2001/107/EC and the Directive 2001/108/EC of 21 January 2002 of the European Parliament and the Council (the **„UCITS III Directives"**). For the passporting process see above footnote 4.

In order to be UCITS compliant the ETF has to comply with the following conditions:

1. have the sole object of collective investment in transferable securities and eligible assets as specified in the UCITS Directive (as modified),
2. have capital raised from the public,
3. operate on the principle of risk spreading and
4. have its shares repurchased or redeemed, directly or indirectly, out of its assets at the request of holders.

Similar restrictions as listed under (2) to (4) apply to a certain extent for German KAGs anyway.

2.3 Risk Diversification

Under the investment fund regime prior to 2004, in particular under the original UCITS –Directive 85/611/EC, strict risk diversification rules needed to be complied with. This raises problems where an ETF is to replicate an Index which is not sufficiently diversified. In the past, it was difficult for UCITS funds to replicate such an Index and it still is as the old provisions do continue to apply for a lot of investment funds which have not yet changed their investment policy to comply with the new applicable UCITS regime.[8]

The original UCITS Directive 85/611/EC provided that a UCITS may not invest more than 5 % of its assets in transferable securities issued by the same issuer. The UCITS Directive 85/611/EC, however, allowed each EEA member state to raise this limit to 10 % (and this is the case in Germany, Luxembourg and Ireland). However the UCITS Directive 85/611/EC provided that the total value of the transferable securities held by a UCITS in the issuing bodies in which it invests more than 5 % of its assets must not then in aggregate exceed 40 % of the value of its assets (the „5/10/40

[8] In Germany, for example, because making use of the provisions available under the UCITS III Directives and the InvG would also result in the requirement to comply with new obligations, e.g. with regard to derivatives following the restrictions set out in the new „*Derivateverordnung*".

Rule"). The 5/10/40 Rule is an issue for investment managers who are asked to track an Index where certain constituent securities in that Index exceed 5 % weightings and together exceed in total 40 % of the value of the Index and/or individual constituent securities have weightings in excess of 10 %. This is often the case for indices which have fewer than 50 constituent securities or follow niche economic sectors.

Under the UCITS III Directives, the concept of index funds has been introduced on an EU-wide level and the restrictions have been lowered. The UCITS III Directives now permit that Member States may raise the 5 % and 10 % limit respectively to a maximum of 20 % for investment in shares and/ or debt securities issued by the same body, when according to the fund rules or instruments of incorporation, the aim of the UCITS′ investment policy is to replicate the composition of a certain stock or debt securities index which is recognised by the competent authorities. Member States may raise the limit laid down above for one single issuer to a maximum of 35 % where that proves to be justified by exceptional market conditions in particular in regulated markets where certain transferable securities or money market instruments are highly dominant.

For German ETFs this concept has been implemented into section 63 of the German InvG. Under the current InvG, the German legislator made use of option to raise the limits concerning transferable securities issued by the same issuer to 20 % and 35 % respectively. German investment funds which track a specific index and are in compliance with these provisions can receive a UCITS certificate.

Beyond that, a KAG may exceed even these limits for securities index funds if according to the contractual terms and conditions the selection of securities to be acquired for a mixed fund is aimed at tracking a specific securities index which is recognised generally and by the BaFin, by observing an appropriate level of risk diversification. Such German investment funds, however, do not qualify as UCITS funds any more.

2.4 Cash Window

A further issue for ETFs is the redemption of units by investors parallel to the trading at the Secondary Market.

2.4.1 General Requirement to Redeem in Cash

German investment funds must allow the investors to redeem their units/shares in cash. This restriction applies also to foreign investment funds as soon as public distribution in Germany is sought (which is necessary for listing at Xetra Funds). The BaFin does neither accept that units in an ETF may only be redeemed "in kind" nor merely through repurchase companies or via the secondary market at a stock exchange. This restriction generally applies also for both types of foreign investment funds, non-UCITS and UCITS funds.

In case of non-UCITS, the BaFin will ensure that this is provided for in the fund documentation and a derogation will usually not be given.

Also under the UCITS regime (in which case the BaFin does not have the competence to supervise the foreign investment fund's structure) there is no suitable solution. Generally the UCITS regime provides that a UCITS must repurchase or redeem its units at the request of any unitholder or shareholder.

The UCITS regime does, however, recognise that where a UCITS is listed then action taken by a UCITS to ensure that the exchange value of its units does not significantly vary from the net asset value is to be regarded by way of derogation as equivalent to the right of repurchase or redemption.[9] However, the terms of this derogation are difficult for ETFs to comply with. One major difficulty is that this derogation also requires the UCITS to intervene on the market to prevent the stock exchange value of its units from deviating by more than 5 % of their net asset value. This is of itself problematic, bearing in mind that to ensure minimisation of tracking error the ETF will be holding very small amounts of cash, if any, and the dealing costs that would be incurred in raising cash. The ETF would also need to reduce the amounts of securities held from each line of constituent securities it held to avoid any tracking error. It is almost unknown for a UCITS to seek this derogation.

9 See Article 1 (2) of the UCITS Directive (as modified). This provision has, however, not been directly taken over into the InvG.

2.4.2 Problems for ETFs

For an ETF the concept of permitting cash redemptions via a so-called "cash window" is problematic. The pricing efficiencies generated from only permitting in-kind subscriptions and redemptions for the ETF units can be undermined if individual unitholders, Authorised Participants or others who have purchased units in that ETF in the Secondary Market, have the right for their units to be redeemed by the ETF for cash.

This requirement to provide a "cash window" to holders of the units in the ETF puts the ETF in the position of being a continuous market maker offering Authorised Participants and any Secondary Market unitholders a price which is always at the net asset value even though the redemption price will be calculated on a forward priced basis.

One could argue that because of the natural arbitrage opportunities which Authorised Participants will seek with an ETF and the requirements imposed by some exchanges on market makers of the units in an ETF, that investors in the Secondary Market who purchase units in an ETF do not need to have the right to redeem out of the ETF's assets for cash. The unitholders will always be able to sell in the Secondary Market at the close to the net asset value.

While this argument might be accepted in the future if an efficient and liquid market in units of ETF develops, it does not satisfy the minimum standards requirements of the UCITS regime or the concerns of some EEA regulators.

The current solution to this situation is to permit a cash window but to require the redeeming unitholder to pay a punitive charge to the extent permissible under regulatory law. Combined with redemptions always being on a forward priced basis this should reduce the use of the cash window.

Additionally, it is also important to ensure that the amount of cash redemptions which can occur is managed effectively. Bearing in mind that the ETF will not usually have any cash available to meet such redemptions and that dealing charges will cause tracking errors, then there needs to be a restriction on the amount of units in an ETF that may be redeemed for cash at one time.

3. Trading the ETF at Xetra Funds

As already mentioned above, the most relevant market for trading ETFs in Germany is the FWB (operated by DBAG) and its market segment Xetra Funds. The most liquid ETFs are listed there. An ETF must be listed either in the Official Trading (*Amtlicher Handel*) or Regulated Market (*Geregelter Markt*) segment of FWB to be permitted for this market segment.

The German legislation (and as well EEA legislation which endeavoured to harmonise the marketing of investments in Europe) has for historic reasons been split into two distinct regimes. The first regime covers the offering of investment funds to the public as described above. The second regime covers listing particulars when offering listed securities to the public (and EEA-wide harmonisation of this for multiple listings). The first does not take account of the second as historically it was not envisaged that investment funds being offered to the public would be listed. Accordingly, the legislation to be complied with when listing an ETF is quite complex and in particular, exemptions or eased processes are hardly available.[10]

3.1 Listing Process

However, in order to give some guidance, the DBAG has published guidelines on the listing process of securities and in particular, ETFs and its preparation.[11] In addition it recommends, as a first step, an informal meeting with the competent department which answers questions on the market segment and admission requirements.

Existing investment funds can be admitted to the Official Trading or Regulated Market segments within 15 trading days. The application must be filed together with a lead-manager, admitted to trading on a German exchange. One or more "Designated Sponsors" must be appointed for each of the investment funds.

---

[10] The new Prospectus Directive Implementation Act (*Prospektrichtlinie-Umsetzungsgesetz*) entering into force mid 2005 which seeks further harmonisation in the area of listing and processes does not change this situation substantially as it is not applicable to investment funds.

[11] The documents are available at the website http://deutsche-boerse.com/dbag/dispatch/de/kir/gdb_navigation/home.

3.1.1 Documentation

Of primary importance for the listing at the FWB is the investment fund's documentation, i.e. the listing prospectus for admissions at the Official Trading (*Amtlicher Handel*) or the business report for admissions at the Regulated Market (*Geregelter Markt*). As the exchange rules and investment fund provisions have not been harmonised, the sales prospectus under the investment fund regime will not be automatically accepted by the FWB for the purpose as the listing prospectus/business report for listing at the exchange. Rather a separate document following the requirements of the German Exchange Act (*Börsengesetz*), the Exchange Rules for the Frankfurt Stock Exchange (*Börsenordnung für die Frankfurter Wertpapierbörse*) and the Exchange Admissions Regulation (*Börsenzulassungsverordnung*) has to be prepared.

This document should in any event comply with the legal requirements but also the FWB's and market standards in order to be sufficiently transparent. An informal preliminary examination of the prospectus by DBAG's listing department can accelerate the admission process.

The document to be prepared may be a combined document serving as sales prospectus for public distribution under the investment fund regime and as basis of the for the listing prospectus/business report provided that it contains all necessary information for both purposes.

Preparing a combined document or very closely related documents is also of advantage as the listing prospectus/business report is the basis for the listing, according to the investment fund regime, however, any public distribution of the investment fund, i.e. any marketing activities, requires that the sales prospectus is mentioned as relevant document for information of the investor.

However, preparing a combined document raises several issues: Although the main requirements regarding the content of a sales prospectus under the InvG on the one hand and the contents of a listing prospectus/business report under the Exchange Admissions Regulation on the other hand match to a large extent, there are also decisive differences which have to be taken into consideration. In this context it has to be considered that the documents (sales prospectus for public distribution under the investment fund regime and the listing prospectus/business report) serve two different purposes. Whereas the sales prospectus provides continuously information for each investor when purchasing the units, the listing prospectus/business report is prepared for the listing and provides information on the ETF at that specific time of listing. In contrast to the sales prospectus, it is not updated continuously.

Preparing the document for the listing, specific information will be required to be added into the document which is usually not contained in a standard sales prospectus for investment funds as for example financial statements which are usually only incorporated by reference or the exact composition of the index.

Furthermore, the content of the sales prospectus and its amendments are subject to the review and consent of the relevant investment fund regulator. In particular, foreign regulators may have concerns as regards specific German listing language.

Thus, a combined document often may not be a suitable solution.

3.2 Cross Listing

Another provision providing for relief in relation to listing, from which, however, only limited use is made in relation to ETFs, is the cross-listing of units in the ETF.[12] Under the German Exchange Act there are certain possibilities for an issuer of securities to ease international listing processes by benefiting from simplifications of a cross listing within the EEA. However, the cross listing of an ETF might require modifications in the documentation in order to comply with various exchanges' requirements.

If listing of securities is intended (virtually) simultaneously with an exchange in an EEA-state and with DBAG, DBAG may generally waive the requirement that the issuer has to prepare a new prospectus for the listing in Germany.

This does not mean, however, that one document is sufficient for all stock exchanges under this simplified process. Rather, additional information for German investors may be required (for example taxation). Also, DBAG has a right to require the issuer to add information customarily required for a prospectus should the exchange in the other EEA-state have waived such

[12] Given the size and importance of the FWB's Xetra Fund segment, the possibility of a cross-listing often is not required.

requirement. Consequently, the exemption although being a relief under certain circumstances does not provide for an automatic recognition of a foreign listing document.

Furthermore, the exchanges interpret the term "simultaneously" or "virtually simultaneously" very restrictive. Also, difficulties may arise as regards settlement and safe custody of the global certificates given the fact that new securities are constantly issued and/or redeemed and cancelled.

4. Prospectus Liability

The problem that different documents for the purpose of public distribution and for the listing have to be prepared continues when it comes to statutory liability for the content of these documents. Also here, two regimes apply to the relevant documentation.

It is in the discretion of the issuer to achieve conformity between the ways of presenting the required information in the prospectuses in order to limit the drafting expenses. However, conformity between the two documents is also important in order to reduce the risk of being liable for the content (or omissions) of one or both documents. Liability issues can arise if information contained in the documents is incorrect, incomplete or misleading.

4.1 Prospectus Liability According to the InvG

Under the investment fund regime, if information contained in the sales prospectus which is of "material importance" for an evaluation of the units is incorrect or incomplete, a person who has purchased units on the basis of the sales prospectus may demand from

1. the management company of the ETF,

2. the person having sold such units in his own name, and

3. under certain circumstances, the broker of investment units

as joint and several debtors to take over the units against reimbursement of the amount paid by the purchase. If the investor is no longer the holder of the unit at the time he becomes aware of such incorrectness or incompleteness of the sales prospectuses, he may demand payment of the amount by which the amount paid by him exceeds the repurchase price of the unit at the time of disposal.

Such claim becomes time-barred one year after the investor has received knowledge of the false or missing information, in any event three years after the purchase.

The sales prospectus must be correct at the time at which an investor purchases a unit or applies for such purchase. Accordingly, there is an ongoing requirement to update the sales prospectus in use for public distribution. This is usually done by constantly updating the document.

The InvG explicitly determines (and restricts) the term "information of material importance" as it refers to the list of information statutorily required as minimum content of a sales prospectus.

4.2 Prospectus Liability According to the German Exchange Act

A similar provision on prospectus liability exists for the listing prospectus/business report under the German Exchange Act. Purchasers of securities (i.e. the units in the ETF) which have been admitted to exchange trading on the basis of a listing prospectus/business report containing incorrect or incomplete statements which are material to the assessment of the value of such securities have (under certain circumstances) a claim against

1. the persons who assumed liability for the prospectus and
2. the persons who initiated the issue of the prospectus on a joint and several basis.

The purchaser may claim surrender of the securities against reimbursement of both the purchase price and the costs customarily involved in the purchase of securities if the purchase price does not exceed the initial issue price. If the purchaser is no longer the holder of the securities, he or she may claim payment of the difference between the purchase price, to the extent that said price does not exceed the initial issue price, and the selling price of the securities together with the costs customarily involved in the purchase of securities.

Precondition is that the transaction was concluded after the publication of the listing prospectus or business report and within six months of the commencement of quotation of the securities.

Different from a sales prospectus, a listing prospectus or business report will not be updated. Rather, there exists an obligation to publish an addendum for changes having occurred between approval of the listing prospectus and the offering of securities. After the offering has started, the majority in legal literature does not consider the publication of further updates being required because the issuer has an ongoing reporting obligation (see below item 5.2.2). Given the prospectus liability, it is obviously within the issuer's interest to publish required corrections.

The scope of liability under the Exchange Act is, despite being more limited in time, different (and to a certain extent wider) than the scope of liability under the InvG. Under the Exchange Act, also the sponsor of an ETF could be held liable as well as any other person being responsible for contents of the listing document. Furthermore, the term "material statements" is not defined by law, thus, subject to the interpretation by German courts.

However, the Exchange Act also provides for an exclusion of liability where the securities have not been purchased on the basis of the listing document. Accordingly, prospectus liability under the InvG and under the Exchange Act should apply alternatively.

4.2.1 General Prospectus Liability

Apart from the special statutory provisions on prospectus liability with its relatively short periods of limitation, German courts have developed a case law on general (civil law) prospectus liability. According to German courts, any written selling or marketing material which is provided to an actual or potential customer and contains information on an investment can qualify as sales prospectus which leads to a general prospectus liability in Germany.

The question, which information material qualifies as prospectus within the meaning of this civil law prospectus liability is considered by German courts taking into consideration the view of an average investor. Typically, most market material given to an investor will be covered by such liability.

Furthermore, liability for false or misleading advice may arise under general statutory law.

5. Ongoing Reporting Requirements

Obligations do not only arise in the form of preparing the relevant documentation in context of listing and admission for public distribution. Rather, from the fact that an ETF is listed at an exchange or distributed publicly in Germany, additional ongoing obligations arise. In particular, there are numerous reporting and notification requirements for an ETF under both areas of law.

5.1 Reporting Requirements Under the Investment Fund Regime

As an ETF is subject to both, the investment fund provisions and the exchange provisions, specific care has to be taken as regards its ongoing reporting duties under the applicable provisions.

Generally under the InvG, an ETF in the form of a German KAG or InvAG must in particular transfer a list of assets for any of its investment funds to the BaFin on a regular basis by means of remote data transmission. The information shall, regarding the individual investment assets and liabilities, be structured in such a way that compliance with the investment limits applicable to each investment fund is apparent. Further details have to be provided as regards exchange-traded securities and derivatives including options to the extent that the KAG concludes such transaction in the name of one of its funds.

Also under the KWG, the usual reporting requirements applicable to credit institutions and financial services providers apply.

Furthermore, the KAG or InvAG must publish, among others, the issue and redemption prices (usually on a daily basis), details on dividends and financial statements.

This publication requirements as regards issue and redemption prices, details on dividends and financial statements also applies to foreign ETFs registered for public distribution in Germany in particular under taxation aspects. Furthermore, German investors have to be informed accordingly if a statutory publication requirement for investors in the ETF's home state applies.

5.2 Reporting Requirements According to Exchange Laws

5.2.1 Reporting Requirements for Listed Investment Funds

Being listed at FWB and in the market segment Xetra Funds, further specific reporting requirements *vis-à-vis* the FWB apply.

These ongoing reporting requirements concern primarily any changes in the ETF's main documents as for example any changes in the listing prospectus/company report, the current annual and semi-annual reports. Furthermore, changes in the contractual structure that constitutes the basis of the investment fund and the investment fund's assets have to be reported. Also amendments in the Index composition and the list of Authorised Participants need to be reported to the FWB.

The ETF is also obliged to do a monthly reporting of the Index composition to which the ETF's fund units, which are included in the Xetra Funds, are linked. Any change in the composition shall be reported immediately.

Moreover, there are daily reporting requirements for the ETF. The ETF must submit the Index closing quotation on a daily basis and information on a daily basis prior to the start of trading such as, inter alia, the investment fund's volume in Euro, the net asset value on last trading day, the cash component of the ETF and any amendments in the composition of the Index compared to the previous trading day.

The reporting may be done on an electronic basis to DBAG.

5.2.2 Ad-hoc Publicity

Besides these reporting requirements which are specific for ETFs listed in the market segment Xetra Funds at FWB, the exchange and security trading provisions provide for general publication and reporting requirements. In particular, the ETF is obliged to publish and disclose price-sensitive information. Such information must be given to the FWB, to any stock exchange on which derivatives on the ETF units are traded and to the BaFin in advance.

In case of an ETF which replicates a recognised Index, such obligation is, however, of lower importance than for other (corporate) issuers of securities. The value of the units in the ETF primarily depends on the value of the securities contained in the Index replicated. Price sensitive information about these securities is not primarily information the ETF regularly receives before the information becomes public. Thus, the publication requirement is often restricted to important information about the ETF structure.

However, under the new Investor Protection Improvement Act (*Anlegerschutzverbesserungsgesetz*)[13] the definition of "inside information" which needs to be published (i.e. information which would have the ability to materially influence the price of the securities, as determined by a prudent investor), is much broader than formerly. Under some circumstances, issuers may receive information which directly concerns them, but which may much more closely be connected to another company. This may in particular be relevant for the business of ETFs. The language of the Investor Protection Improvement Act implies that the issuer has the duty to disclose inside information, even about other companies, including competitors, as long as it also directly concerns the issuer or its business. The Investor Protection Improvement Act does not require that the information arise from the issuer's own sphere of activity, as under the formerly existing rules. This may broaden the scope of application of the provision also for ETFs. It remains to be seen how the Investor Protection Improvement Act is interpreted in this aspect and whether such publication obligation may eventually become relevant for ETFs. The BaFin is currently working on an Issuer's Guideline (*Emittentenleitfaden*) providing more detailed interpretation.

6. Summary

ETFs, since their appearance on the European market a couple of years ago, have now become a well established investment with a great market share successfully competing with other index-related products such as index certificates and derivatives. Due to their cost efficient structure they are attractive investments for institutional but also retail investors.

Nevertheless, the legal framework for ETFs in Germany is not harmonised yet and the regulations for listed investment funds are still twofold which

[13] This Act is part of a „Ten Point Program" initiated by the German government to strengthen German financial markets within the European Union and internationally and serves to implement the European Parliament and Council Directive2003/6/EC (dated 28 January 2003) on insider dealing and market manipulation (market abuse). It has (largely) entered into force on 1 January 2005.

causes additional care, work and, of course, costs. Given the still increasing market appearance of ETFs and their increasing importance also for the stock exchanges, further developments also in the legislative area may be desirable. The extended possibilities to replicate indices under the UCITS regime as well as introduction of new vehicles as the German InvAG are positive signs for the further development of this market.

Liquidity and Innovation – Nothing Else Matters

Rainer Riess[1]

1. Introduction

As little as five years ago, at best only a small group of experts in Europe knew what the abbreviation ETF stood for. In fact, anyone wanting to invest in ETFs – exchange-traded funds – had to do it in the United States; there was simply no such product in Europe. The situation has since changed dramatically, and over the past three years ETFs have become an established investment vehicle in Europe. And it is without doubt that Deutsche Börse AG was the pioneer and co-founder of the European ETF market.

As has often been the case in investment history, the idea for exchange-traded funds came from the United States, where they were invented about ten years ago. In a relatively short period of time ETFs have succeeded in establishing themselves as an indispensable investment category. It is with good cause that Deborah Fuhr of Morgan Stanley has termed them the "financial innovation of the last decade". Their unbeatable advantage is that, for the first time, two highly traditional, self-sufficient and completely separate branches of the investing world, namely fund investing and exchange trading, are combined in a single product. What is more, they are enticingly simple, for by means of ETFs investors can commit resources to exchange indices – and thus with one product cover entire markets, sectors and regions.

A glance at the figures soon reveals their significance in terms of worldwide asset allocation. At the end of the third quarter 2004, more than €200

---

[1] My particular thanks go to Candice Adam and Stephan Kraus for their professional support as well as to Heiner Seidel for his principal role in the drafting and production of this article.

billion was entrusted to a total of 318 funds. By virtue of the fact that the product is cost-effective and easy to trade, the volume invested worldwide and the number of existing funds has increased exponentially in recent years.

In the 1993-2000 period, ETFs first became all the rage on the US market. The American Stock Exchange AMEX was the trailblazer in this regard. One of the very first funds was the Spider (SPDR), which tracks the S&P 500 Index. Today, this fund rates as one of the most heavily traded funds in the world, with some US$37.1 billion in assets under management. Other well-known funds soon followed, among them the Diamonds (Dow Jones Industrial Average Index) and the Cubes (Nasdaq 100 Index). In total, the number of exchange-listed funds in the United States surged from one in 1993 to 148 at the end of the third quarter 2004, and assets under management grew from €0.4 billion to €146 billion.

Trading segments for exchange-traded funds were first introduced in Europe in 2000. Deutsche Börse launched its XTF® segment in April 2000, and it has since emerged as the single most important trading platform for ETFs in Europe, significantly contributing to the success of this investment vehicle throughout Europe. Other ETF segments have emerged on Euronext, the London Stock Exchange, SWX Swiss Exchange and other exchanges. In Europe, the exchange operating companies do not act as issuers but simply supply the legal and organizational framework.

Specifically in Europe, the ETF market is booming. The number of ETFs in Europe has reached levels similar to those in the United States, with more than 100 funds listed in Europe at the end of Q3/2004. Assets under management increased by more than 60 percent over the last 12 month, reaching €21 billion in Europe at the end of Q3/2004 – yet still only a fraction of the US figure of €146 billion.

2. The XTF Platform: Europe's First ETF Segment

On 11 April 2000, Deutsche Börse launched its ETF segment XTF Exchange Traded Funds®. Right from the start, the vast majority of trading has taken place through the fully electronic Xetra® trading system. XTF started out with two index funds floated by European ETF Company plc, a subsidiary of Merrill Lynch. The indices tracked were the Dow Jones STOXX 50℠ and Dow Jones EURO STOXX 50℠. In the months that followed, the number of funds listed increased steadily. In 2001, ETFs were also introduced on the DAX®, MDAX®, SMI and NEMAX® 50 indices. In 2002, issuers then offered funds which tracked entire index families such as DJ STOXX 600 and MSCI Europe. In addition, index funds on large well-known indices such as the Dow Jones Industrial Average, the MSCI World and FTSE 100 were listed. At present, there are also ETFs available on the S&P 500, not to mention a number of DJ Country Titans indices. And, early in 2003, XTF was the very first segment to introduce fixed-income ETFs, namely eb.rexx® and iBoxx®. At the end of Q3/2004, a total of 56 ETFs were listed on XTF.

Despite the low equity market volatility in 2004, trading volumes in ETFs were only slightly affected. At the end of third quarter 2004, average monthly turnover came to more than €2.7 billion, with the daily volume averaging approximately €130 million. Total trading volume in 2003 came to €37 billion, an increase of 17 percent on 2002 (approx. €32 billion) and of 68 percent on 2001 (approx. €22 billion).

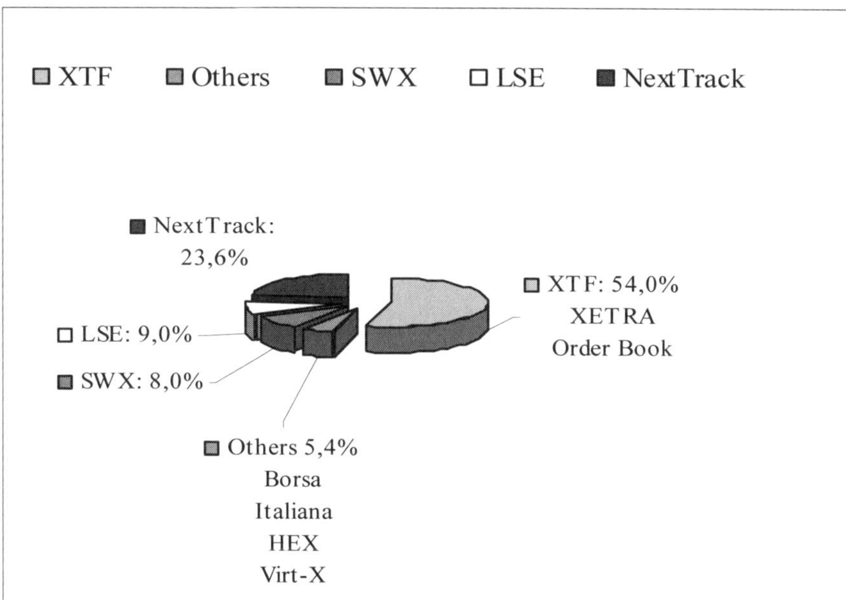

Figure 1: XTF – Europe's leading ETF platform. Total European Turnover Q1/2004-Q3/2004 €45.5 billion. Market Shares Q1/2004-Q3/2004, based on on-exchange turnover data. Source: Deutsche Börse, SWX, virt-X, Bloomberg, 2004, Stockholmsbörsen excluded due to unavailability of separate on-exchange turnover data

In comparison with other European ETF segments, XTF is the most liquid segment. More than half of the total trading volume in ETFs in Europe is generated in this segment. At the end of third quarter 2004, XTF accounted for a 54% market share in European ETF trading.

Assets under management committed to the ETFs listed in the XTF segment have increased considerably. At the end of Q3/2004, they ran at €14 billion, as compared with €10 billion at year-end 2003, €5 billion at year-end 2002 and €2.7 billion at the end of 2001.

Based on this development, Deutsche Börse was voted the "most innovative exchange" for ETFs in 2003 by market participants as part of International Fund Investment Magazine's second annual European ETF Award. Deutsche Börse also won awards in the categories "Largest exchange for ETFs in Europe" and "Exchange with the largest number of listed ETFs in Europe".

In addition to the XTF segment for exchange-traded funds, Deutsche Börse offers another segment, made up entirely of actively managed investment funds. Both segments are part of "Xetra Funds". On 20 November 2000 – just six months after XTF kicked off – DWS Investment GmbH decided to list 11 trading funds without front-end load charges on Deutsche Börse. Xavex soon followed suit with eight funds. Xetra Active Funds offers investors a broad range of actively managed funds covering asset classes not yet available in Europe in the form of ETFs. These new funds cover a variety of different investment focuses, including gold shares and emerging market regions or those which pursue value and growth strategies. All in all, 23 actively managed funds are now listed in Xetra Active Funds.

3. The Structure of an ETF

The experts agree that the structure of ETFs is the prime reason for their success. ETFs are as straightforward as normal investment funds, with the difference that by virtue of being listed on an exchange they are fungible at all times and at extremely low costs. Further, illegal business practices such as market timing, as were seen in 2003 in the US fund sector, are not possible with ETFs.

Before the first ETFs were launched in 1993, exchange trading and fund investing were two completely separate domains that came into contact at best through a complex and partly inefficient web of brokerage relationships and OTC deals. Investors were only able to trade baskets outside the organized markets, resulting in higher implicit risk, higher trading costs, slower execution times, and overall inefficiencies in trade management. With the invention of ETFs, these inefficiencies were erased forever, and investors can now trade a diversified basket, gain exposure to an entire market, and hedge these products easily and cost-effectively by relying on a family of related derivatives.

In Germany, ETFs are subject to strict statutory regulation. Indeed, in order to qualify for a listing on the XTF segment, a fund must first be admitted to Deutsche Börse's first- or second-tier trading segments. In addition, public sale of the fund units must be approved by BaFin, the German Federal Financial Supervisory Office. Issuers are obliged to publish annual and six-monthly reports and disclose net asset values (NAV) on a daily basis. In addition, every ETF must post a continuously updated indicative net asset value (iNAV®). Furthermore, every ETF is required to have at least one Designated Sponsor[2].

So how exactly is an ETF structured?

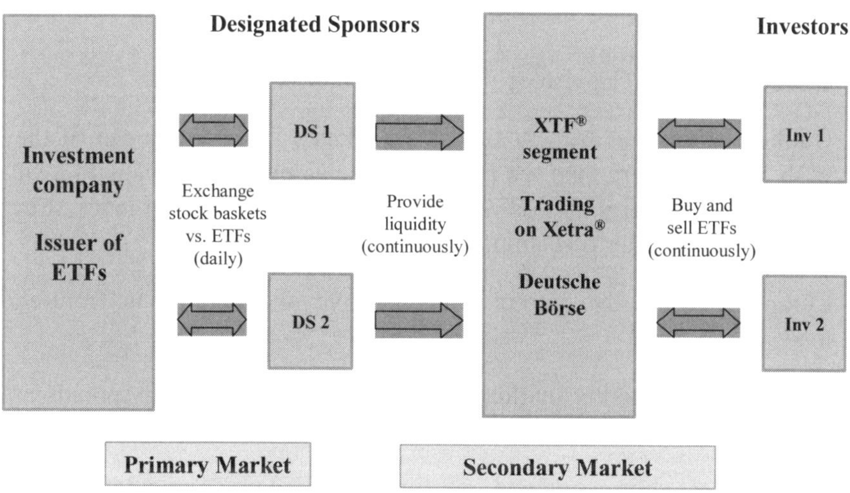

Figure 2: Creation/redemption process ensures liquidity in ETFs. Source: Deutsche Börse

---

[2] Designated Sponsors support specific shares and other securities such as ETFs in Xetra by acting as market maker for them. By posting binding bid and offer prices for the security in question, they assure its liquidity.

All ETFs in the XTF segment (see figure) make use of a creation-redemption model. To track an index, the Designated Sponsor assembles a basket of equities, the composition of which mirrors the index. He passes this equities basket on to the issuer and in return receives unit shares in the fund from the issuer corresponding to the value of the equities basket. The Designated Sponsor can then sell these shares on the market (creation). By the same token, he can also return the fund units to the issuer, in which case he receives the equities basket (redemption). Thanks to this mechanism, the Designated Sponsor assumes the trading risk from the issuer while being able to hedge his own position through continuous tracking.

The Designated Sponsor ensures the fairest price by reducing price inefficiencies between the fund itself and the underlying index. The market price can be monitored and assessed at any time thanks to the indicative net asset value (iNAV) calculated on a continuous basis by Deutsche Börse (or alternatively by another service provider on behalf of the issuer). Moreover, the issuer and Deutsche Börse together specify exactly how high the Sponsor's maximum spread for a product can be; as a rule, the spread lies far below the maximum permitted.

Deutsche Börse's ETFs also exhibit other attractive features:

- Unlike classical investment funds, most ETFs in Germany can, if they wish, commit more than ten percent of the assets they manage to a single stock or security. In this way, they are able to mirror an index structure with far greater precision.

- Commissions are also extremely competitive, and there are no front-end loads.

- The use of competing market makers means that bid/offer spreads are very tight and, for the most liquid ETFs, even lower than in the US.

- Prices are set continuously in real-time. The ongoing computation of an iNAV serves as the indication for the respective fund's fair value. By contrast, with a conventional investment fund the price of unit shares is only set once a day. In other words, ETFs offer investors greater scope in deciding when to buy or sell the fund.

- Further, ETFs are structured and designed around an efficient arbitrage mechanism that helps them closely track their net asset value. This transparency allows arbitrageurs to determine the value of an ETF portfolio relative to the value of the shares in it, and permits investors to take advantage of arbitrage opportunities.

Things are somewhat different in the case of the actively managed funds traded in the Xetra Active Funds sub-segment. Given the fact that the portfolio positions of these funds are not known, there is no creation and redemption process "in kind". Fund units are instead exchanged for cash and delivered to the market maker, who then places them in the Xetra order book. The investor can also buy and sell unit shares in the fund directly from the fund issuer at the NAV price.

4. Xetra – A Liquid Trading Platform for ETFs

Unlike in the United States, where ETFs still mainly tend to be traded on the floor in the traditional manner, in Europe the lion's share of trading takes place using electronic platforms. About 98 percent of total XTF turnover is handled through Xetra. Three key factors have fueled the success of the electronic order books, namely liquidity, international accessibility and transparency.

Xetra meets all these criteria. It is an exceptionally liquid, pan-European open trading platform. The system brings together continuous trading in securities with auctions, processes a wide variety of order types and has a minimum trading lot size of one. It handles in excess of 260,000 orders a day. The order book posts real-time buy and sell data on each and every fungible security, making for a completely transparent market, as all the participants trade at the same fair conditions. Some 300 participants from 18 different countries can access a total of some 6,000 shares – and ETFs. And the Xetra participants can access their system from anywhere in the world. This pooling of orders also fosters high liquidity in the order book – as do the Designated Sponsors in securities where the market is tight.

The advantages Xetra delivers also apply to the funds listed on the system: continuous trading with no front-end load. In other words, investors only bear the customary transaction costs. The presence of Designated Sponsors keeps liquidity costs low measured in terms of the XLM (the Xetra Liquidity Measure).

XLM measures order-book liquidity in three dimensions: immediacy, breadth and depth. To this end, XLM first calculates market impact, that is to say the costs of direct demand for liquidity in an open order book. Market impact consists of two components: the liquidity premium, as it is known, and the adverse price movement. The liquidity premium, which reflects the breadth of the order book, is half the bid/offer spread; the adverse price movement, which gauges the depth of the order book, is the adverse price effect in the case of an order being executed across several limits in the order-book depth.

In fact, it is two ETFs, namely DAX EX and eb.rexx Government Germany EX, that are the most liquid securities traded on Xetra. ETFs based on the pan-European DJ EURO STOXX 50 are among the 30 most heavily traded equities on the Xetra trading platform, contradicting the theory that multiple listings of ETFs based on the same index will inevitably lead to a detrimental split in liquidity. The same beneficial phenomenon is to be observed for funds that are cross-listed on a number of different European exchanges. As a point of fact, of all the cross-listed products in Deutsche Börse's XTF segment, most of the total European trading volume in these products is actually generated within XTF itself.

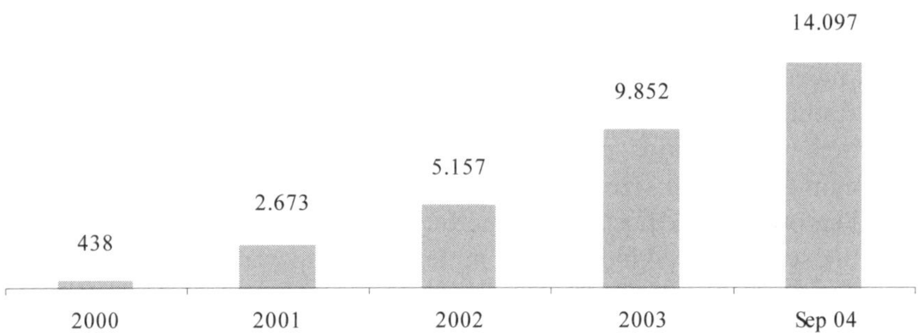

Figure 3: XTF – from a financial innovation to an established capital market product. Assets under management of all ETFs listed in XTF (€ million). Source: Deutsche Börse, 2004

5. Main Users and Usage of ETFs

In Europe, initially it was primarily the institutional investors who engaged in trading ETFs, but more recently an increasing number of private investors have preferred the tool – a trend that is also to be observed in the United States.

This is borne out by the XTF trading volume: whereas three years ago only 15 percent of orders were placed by private investors, today almost half of them are. Like their institutional counterparts, retail investors evidently appreciate the flexibility offered by exchange-based trading and the very low transaction costs.

A further reason for the success: ETFs provide a simple and cost-effective instrument allowing institutional investors to enjoy passive asset management. The group of investors who actively use ETFs includes asset managers, hedge funds, insurance and investment companies, pension funds and trading houses.

The most frequent applications for which institutional investors use ETFs are:

- Cash management/equitization: Investors can manage their daily cash inflow and outflow, specifically through funds, which are also a good alternative or complement to a reliance on futures.
- Asset allocation: Investors can establish a basic investment portfolio by choosing a broad pan-European ETF and then overweight or underweight sectors, countries and regions by additionally buying or short selling the corresponding ETF.
- Arbitrage: The potential here is to exploit temporary price differences between ETFs and the cash and futures markets.
- Hedging existing portfolios: ETFs may offer more trading opportunities than derivatives because there is a wide range of sector ETFs available. Investors can hedge exposure to all or parts of their portfolios.

A good example of the benefits of ETFs is the arbitrage mechanism between them and underlying equities. While ETFs are pegged to a basket of underlying stocks, the trading of an ETF is theoretically not related in any way to the actual equities pooled in it. That said, the ETF is in fact interchangeable with the securities in it. Arbitrageurs will therefore buy or sell an ETF, trading at a discount or at a premium, and establish an offsetting position by creating or redeeming the underlying stocks. As a consequence, ETF shares generally trade close to their indicative NAV. The creation/redemption functionality assures that most price gaps are temporary and limited. If the arbitrage costs are lower then in general, then so is the deviation from the indicative NAV of an ETF.

The arbitrage process is quite simple: if an ETF starts to trade at a discount (that is, at a price less than the iNAV), arbitrageurs can buy the ETF and, after accumulating enough shares to equal a creation unit, redeem them from the ETF at the NAV. They will eventually acquire the more valuable securities in the redemption basket. At the same time, by buying the ETF shares they increase market demand for the shares, which may in turn raise the market price to a level closer to NAV. The procedure is similar for the reverse case. In both scenarios, the possibility of creation/redemption typically leads to price movement within a band close to the NAV of an ETF.

6. EXTF – Expanding ETF Trading via Eurex

Another key factor underlying the XTF success story is the close links to Eurex, the world's largest futures market and a joint venture of Deutsche Börse AG and SWX Swiss Exchange. As a supplement to the successful Eurex product line, on 18 November 2002 the futures exchange listed floated options and futures on ETFs for the first time. In other words, it was the European trailblazer for options as well as the very first futures exchange worldwide to develop futures on ETFs. During the first three quarters of 2004, a total of more than 127,000 contracts had been traded on the EXTF options and futures. The greatest turnover was seen in the derivatives on the DJ EURO STOXX 50 EX, the DAX EX and the XMTCH on SMI.

Table 1: EXTF Products

EXTF Products
DAX EX Future and Option
Dow Jones EURO STOXX 50 EX Future and Option
iShares Dow Jones EURO STOXX 50 Future and Option
XMTCH on SMI Future and Option

There are some decisive differences between the ETF derivatives on Eurex and the other Eurex index products. For example, unlike stock index derivatives, ETF derivatives are settled by physical delivery of securities. On maturity, the investor accordingly accepts or delivers the ETF shares serving as the underlying. Owing to the ETF redemption process (for more on the creation-redemption model, see figure 4), the investor may have direct access to the underlying basket of shares. Since the latter is structured in line with the American-style principle, they can be bought/sold at any time.

Moreover, contract sizes for ETF futures are smaller than those for established stock index products. In other words, they also appeal to players who have lower risk positions, as more precise hedging is possible. By way of example: a futures contract on the DAX ETF has a nominal value of €1 per index point, i.e. the nominal contract value derives from the current index level of the DAX in euros. Compared with this, a DAX future is based on a contract value of €25 per index point, which at present spells a nominal value of more than €100,000.

In terms of their features, the EXTF options resemble other Eurex stock options. Both the futures and the options contracts refer to 100 fund unit shares. The minimum price change amounts in both cases to €0.01. Liquidity is secured by active market making. Market makers adhere to maximum spreads, as they are known, and accordingly post pre-defined minimum bid/offer quotes in the order book. EXTFs are traded on Eurex from 9 a.m. through 8 p.m.

A glance at the US market, where options on ETFs are exceedingly popular, highlights the potential EXTFs clearly have. More than 100,000 contracts on the Cubes change hands every day.

7. Trading Strategies with ETF Derivatives

Essentially, ETFs and ETF derivatives can be used to pursue similar investment strategies; EXTFs have a complementary character. They afford investors even greater scope in the choice of trading strategy. Several criteria are decisive when choosing the right instruments: planned investment duration, risk preference and scale of financial resources. Whereas ETFs have no maturity or expiry dates in the cash market, the corresponding derivatives are traded on the basis of a three-month cycle. The cash market products are thus more suitable for "buy-and-hold" strategies with a longer focus, as no rollover into the respective next maturity period is required.

The most conventional forms of meaningfully using ETF derivatives as part of the investment process are:

- for hedging purposes,
- as a substitute for ETF investments (for long strategies),
- as an arbitrage instrument,
- for asset management purposes.

Traditional hedging strategies, for example, serve to protect an equity portfolio against expected price falls. In such a case, the portfolio holdings can be hedged by buying put options on ETFs or selling futures, without the funds themselves having to be sold.

Similarly, by means of EXTFs, new long positions can easily be established – particularly in times of extreme market volatility. An investor might be of the opinion that a market has fallen sufficiently far and instead of buying into numerous different individual equities then buys ETF derivatives, thus re-entering the market with a single transaction.

Arbitrage transactions play a vital role. Although both unit shares in ETFs and individual ETF derivatives involve almost negligible tracking error, deviation can never be completely excluded. For example, should the Dow Jones EURO STOXX 50 ETF be quoted below its NAV and the ETF future above it, then there is an edge for arbitrageurs. The difference may arise because the dividend forecasts (prior to actual disbursement) are already factored into the price of the future – as opposed to the ETFs.

Last but not least, there are strategies that enable investors to augment the effective return on the assets managed. The most customary methods include selling "covered" call options that are out of the money and are underwritten by corresponding holdings in the underlying – this is also referred to as "covered-call writing". Traders make use of this tool whenever market trends are rated neutrally or pessimistically and the risk entailed is relatively minor. In such cases, the strike price for the option is higher than the current level of the market. Should prices fall or remain unchanged, which is what the asset managers are counting on, then the fund benefits by collecting the option premium. Should the market buck expectations and rise, with the option therefore being exercised, the fund manager can rely as a fallback on his holdings of the underlying to fulfill his delivery obligation. Similar strategies are conceivable using put options or a combination of different calls and/or put options.

To summarize: ETF derivatives thus enable asset managers to control outflows and inflows into their funds with great precision, to hedge their portfolios and to boost the earnings made with the assets they manage.

8. Conclusions: Advantages of Deutsche Börse's Integrated Markets

Investors can lock into a vast array of new opportunities through the unique combination of ETFs, derivatives on ETFs (EXTF), index futures and an efficient cash market – and this places Deutsche Börse right at the forefront of things. Moreover, its carefully fine-tuned and coordinated infrastructure delivers smooth links between the different markets. And in the form of its Clearstream subsidiary – a leading international settlement and custody house – settlement is offered from a single source. No other exchange operator can boast more efficient straight-through processing (STP).

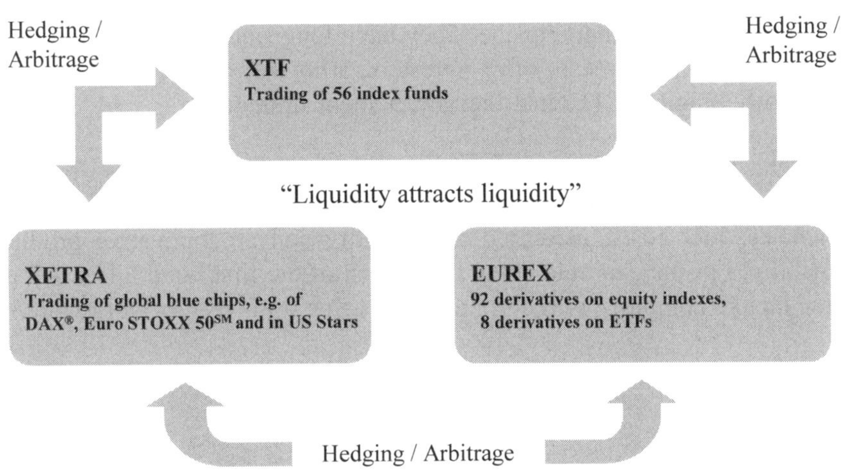

Figure 4: The XTF advantage: Deutsche Börse's integrated offering

Specifically hedge funds and arbitrageurs have been availing themselves of the unique combination of three-way pricing relationships. After all, it spells possible arbitrage transactions in the following areas:

1. between ETFs and the stocks/bonds contained in the index,

2. between index options/futures and the corresponding ETFs,

3. between ETFs and derivatives on ETFs,

4. between the same ETFs on the same or on different exchanges.

There is a pleasant side to exploiting these differences: the real spreads stay low – even with ETFs that see low trading volume. At the same time, it compensates for price differences between the markets, meaning that the price quality as a whole rises.

At the end of the day, ETF trading always translates into cost savings for investors. After all, the prime price quality and liquidity ensure that transaction costs remain low. ETF issuers, vendors and Deutsche Börse all benefit here from economies of scale, which allow them to offer efficient trading at the lowest cost. In addition, thanks to the highly efficient STP infrastructure, it assures low transaction costs.

With around €20 billion currently in assets, European ETFs still have a long way to go before they reach the €6 trillion in assets managed by the open-end fund industry worldwide. ETF sponsors will continue to bring new products to the marketplace. They have long since understood the advantages such instruments offer investors, who will persist in integrating the readily fungible ETFs into their investment strategies.

Deutsche Börse AG will continue to play a pivotal role in this development going forward, as the company's strategy is to offer clear trading efficiencies, low costs, increased accessibility and an innovative product portfolio (a prime example being the launch of the first bond ETF). All of these factors combined will definitely add value for investors worldwide.

The Gateway to International Islamic Investing

Andrew Broadley

1. Seeking New Opportunities in Islamic Investing

Over the past ten years, investors have sought quantitative equity strategies to enhance their returns and diversify their portfolios. However, Islamic investors were limited in their choices and were unable to take advantage of these new opportunities. The challenge was to find a diversified quantitative equity strategy that can achieve above market returns without compromising on Islamic principles. In 2003 a solution was made available by The National Commercial Bank and Deutsche Bank when they proudly introduced the Islamic EquityBuilder Certificates™, one of the first Islamic products that uses a quantitative strategy to provide diversification, transparency, liquidity and flexibility.

1.1 Powerful Partnerships, with Character and Judgement

The National Commercial Bank, with its expertise in Islamic investing, and Deutsche Bank, with its years of portfolio product experience, joined forces to provide an unparalleled opportunity for investors. The Islamic EquityBuilder Certificates™ are four new Islamic equity products approved by The National Commercial Bank's highly regarded and esteemed Shariah Board. The Certificates enable innovation with attention to performance and respect for values.

1.2 A Strategy for Adding Value

The Islamic EquityBuilder Certificates™ reflect the Islamic Equity Builder Portfolios™, which implement a rigorous quantitative model that selects stocks with the most improved earnings outlook. These stocks tend to perform significantly better than those with a weakened earnings outlook. The purpose of the strategy is to identify stocks with a high probability of performing better than the market.

Quantitative portfolio strategies can sometimes add risk. The Islamic Equity-Builder Certificates™ offer opportunities for superior returns while maintaining a reasonable risk profile, in full conformity with Shariah principles.

2. Innovation, Performance, and Principles

2.1 Building a Portfolio

Investors can use the four Islamic EquityBuilder Certificates™ as portfolio building blocks. Three of the Certificates invest in geographic regions – Europe, Asia Pacific and the United States.The fourth, the Global Certificate, is a combination of the three regional Certificates. Investors can choose either a single region or a combination of regions on an ongoing basis to create and manage a tailored equity portfolio.

2.2 Monitoring for Shariah Compliance

The National Commercial Bank's highly regarded and esteemed Shariah Board approved the product for Shariah compliance. The National Commercial Bank monitors the product for compliance on a quarterly basis.

2.3 Quantitative, Transparent Portfolio Strategy

The Islamic EquityBuilder Portfolios™, developed by Deutsche Bank's quantitative structured products team, are clearly defined and objective. The process for selecting the stocks in the Portfolios is fully disclosed and freely available.

2.4 Superior Performance

The Islamic EquityBuilder Portfolios™ have shown good performance since inception on 31 January 2003, with the worst performance (being Europe) delivering a return to investors after fees of 17.3 % and the best performance (from Asia Pacific) delivering a return of 47.2 % (see Table below).

2.5 Quarterly Rebalancing

The Portfolios are rebalanced and re-weighted on a quarterly basis, ensuring that they remain fully invested in equities at all times. There is no charge to the Certificate holder for this turnover and therefore no adverse impact on returns.

Table 1: Performance comparisons from 31 January 2003 to 31 May 2004

	Cumulative Percentage Return			
	Global	Europe	Asia Pacific	US
Islamic EquityBuilder Portfolios™	38.3	17.3	47.2	-36.0
Dow Jones Islamic Index™	-35.6	-22.7	-35.1	-33.0
Excess Return vs:				
Islamic Benchmark	-2.7	-(5.4)	-12.1	-3.0

Source: Deutsche Bank, Dow Jones. Only EquityBuilder Certificate returns include dividends. All returns are in USD except for Europe, which is in Euros.

2.6 Efficient Pricing

The total cost of the Certificates is an annual management fee of 1.25 %. For this fee, investors receive portfolio-trading capability, wholesale cash execution, continuous liquidity, diversification, a quantitative portfolio strategy and Shariah compliance.

3. Adding Value – The Portfolio Strategy

3.1 The Theory Behind the Portfolio Strategy

- The Islamic EquityBuilder Portfolios™ utilize a strategy that seeks out companies with the greatest number of recent upgrades in earnings estimates. The share price of these companies tends to increase following the upgrades, reflecting the expectation of higher dividends and returns to investors. The earnings outlook is represented by consensus earnings estimates for a company's current fiscal year. The market closely monitors revisions to these estimates and tends to react rapidly to them.
- The strategy considers both the direction and breadth of analysts' estimate revisions:

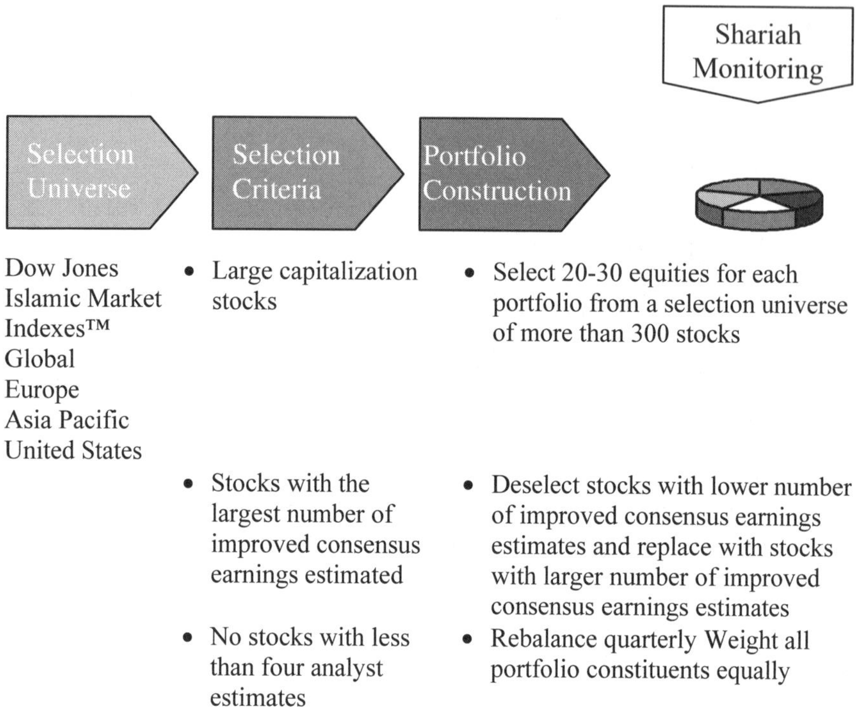

Figure 1: The investment process. Source: Deutsche Bank

Table 2: Portfolios as of May 2004

Europe	Asia Pacific	US
Air Liquide	BHP Billiton	Accenture
Aventis SA	Bluescope steel	Apache
BASF AG	Citic Pacific	Avon Products
Beiersdorf AG	Denway Motors	Bed, Bath & Beyond
Electrabel	Funai Electric	Boston Scientific
ENI	Global Bio-Chem	Chevron Texaco
Gas Natural	Keyence Corp	Coca-Cola
Henkel	Matsushita	Dell
Hennes & Mauritz	Murata	Du Pont De Nemours
Inditex	Omron	Exxon Mobil
L'Oreal	Rinker Group	Fedex
Novo-Nordisk	Sankyo	Gap
Philips Electrical	Shimano	Genentech
Sanofi	Shiseido	Harley Davidson

Table 2 (continued)

SAP	Singapore Airlines	Honeywell
Schneider Electric	Techtronic Industries	Johnson & Johnson
Siemens	Trend Micro	Kimberly-Clark
Statoil	Wesfarmers	Limited Brands
T I M	Woodside Petroleum	Newmont Mining
Total	Yamato Transport	Nike
		Occidental Petroleum
		Paychex
		Pepsico
		Starbucks
		Symantec
		Target
		Texas Instruments
		TJX Companies
		United Health
		Zimmer Holdings

Source: Deutsche Bank

All constituents in each of the Portfolios shown above are equally weighted. The Global Certificate comprises the constituents of the three regional Certificates weighted on the rebalancing date at US 50 %, Europe 33.33 % and Asia Pacific 16.67 %. The regional portions reflect the Dow Jones Islamic Market Index regional weightings.

Direction: The number of estimates upgraded compared to the number of estimates downgraded.

Breadth: The net number of upgrades or downgrades as a percentage of the total number of earnings estimates. This indicates the strength of the estimates' agreement.

- This analysis determines the portfolio constituents on each quarterly rebalancing date.

3.2 The Current Portfolios: Stocks with the Most Improved Outlook

Table 2 shows the constituents of the Islamic EquityBuilder Portfolios as of May 2004. It represents stocks which have had the greatest recent improvement in their earnings outlook.

4. Quality Selection Leads to Quality Performance

4.1 Numbers That Speak for Themselves

The following graphs demonstrate the historical strength of the Islamic EquityBuilder Portfolios™ compared to their respective Islamic and conventional market benchmarks. All return figures shown include the reinvestment of net dividends.

5. Benefits at a Glance

- Collaboration of experts: Represents a combination of The National Commercial Bank's expertise in Islamic investing with Deutsche Bank's experience in portfolio products.
- Shariah compliance: The Islamic EquityBuilder Certificates™ have been approved by The National Commercial Bank's Shariah Board.
- Portfolio building blocks: Opportunity to invest in a single geographic region – Europe, Asia Pacific, United States or globally on an ongoing basis to create and manage a tailored equity portfolio.
- Quantitative portfolio strategy: A clearly defined and objective portfolio strategy selects the stocks in the Portfolios. This process is fully disclosed and freely available.
- Superior returns after fees: The Islamic EquityBuilder Certificates™ outperform comparable indices on a historical basis.
- Exchange listing: Liquidity is provided via a listing on the Frankfurt Stock Exchange. Deutsche Bank also makes a market in the Certificates.
- Efficient pricing: Annual management fee of 1.25 % with no other costs. Investors receive portfolio-trading capability, wholesale cash execution, continuous liquidity, diversification, a quantitative portfolio strategy and Shariah compliance.

6. Conclusions

Investors who wish to combine the important aspects of their Islamic faith with the way that they invest their savings for capital growth now have a set of world-class investment solutions to invest in. Wherever such investors may live in the world, these investments can be easily bought and sold because they are listed on a recognized stock-market, Frankfurt.

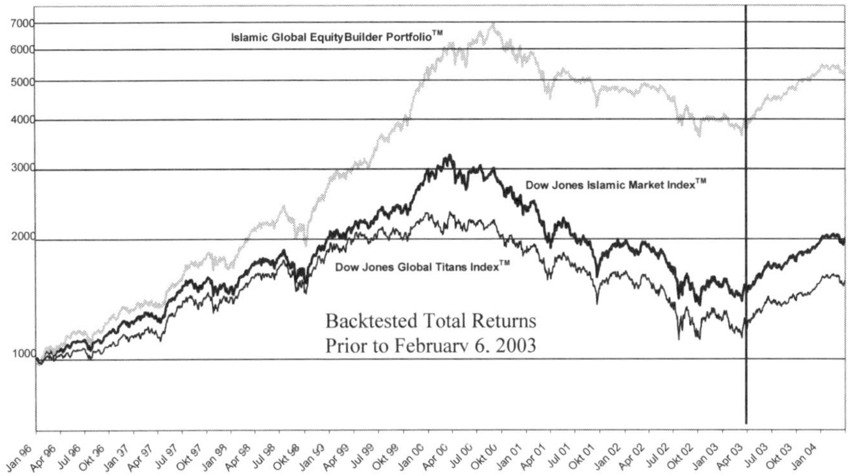

Figure 2: Performance of Islamic Global EquityBuilder Portfolio™ compared to Islamic and conventional benchmarks (January 1996 – January 2004); Returns are Log scale. Source: Deutsche Bank, Dow Jones

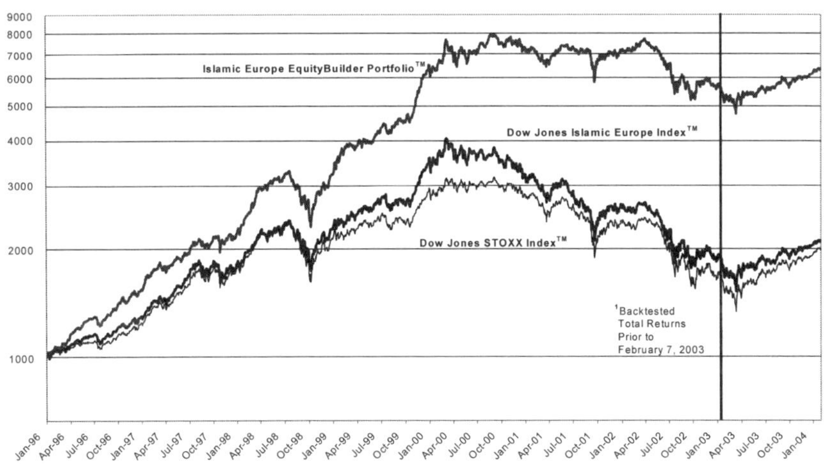

Figure 3: Performance of Islamic Europe EquityBuilder Portfolio™ compared to Islamic and conventional benchmarks (January 1996 – January 2004); Returns are Log scale. Source: Deutsche Bank, Dow Jones

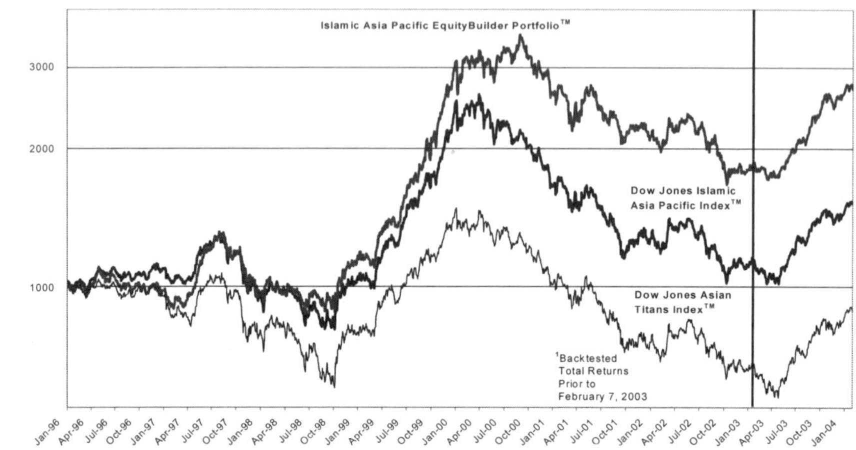

Figure 4: Performance of Islamic Asia Pacific EquityBuilder Portfolio™ compared to Islamic and conventional benchmarks (January 1996 – January 2004); Returns are Log scale. Source: Deutsche Bank, Dow Jones

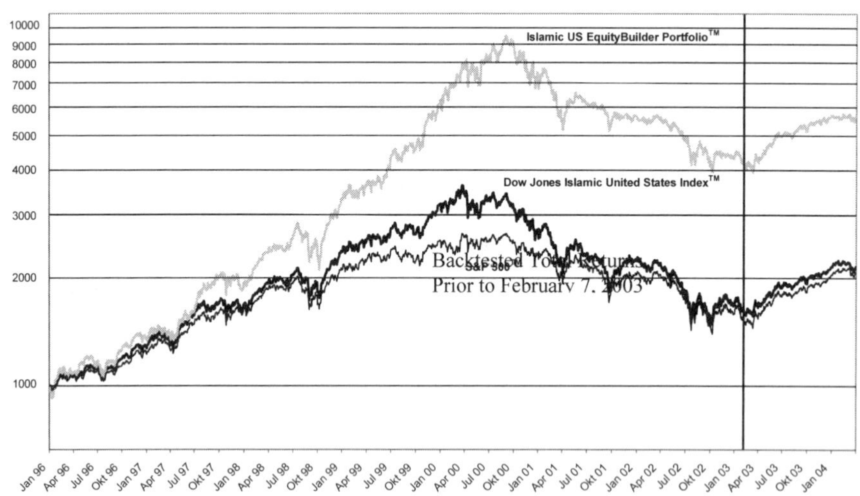

Figure 5: Performance of Islamic US EquityBuilder Portfolio™ compared to Islamic and conventional benchmarks (January 1996 – January 2004); Returns are Log scale. Source: Deutsche Bank, Dow Jones

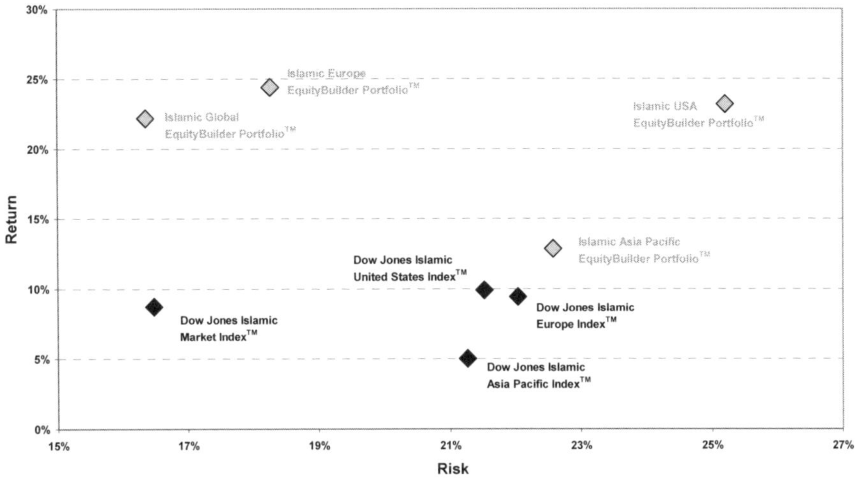

Figure 6: Risk return comparisons. Source: Deutsche Bank, Dow Jones

Review: Facts & Figures on ETFs

Elisabeth Hehn

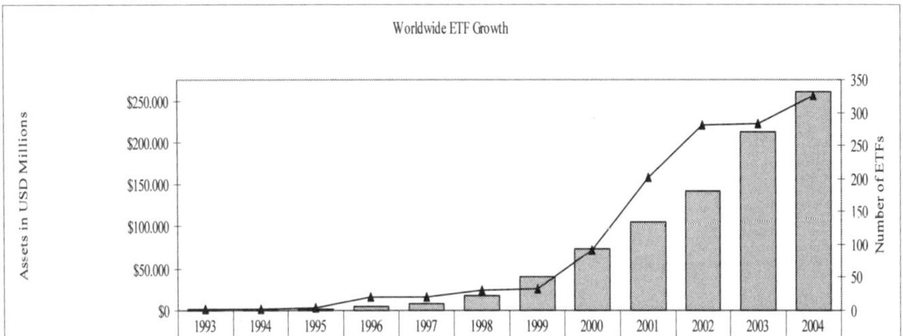

	1993	1994	1995	1996	1997	1998	1999	2000	2001	2002	2003	2004
Assets USD Millions	$811	$1.121	$2.302	$5.258	$8.234	$17.596	$39.605	$74.337	$104.800	$141.621	$212.018	$260.348
Number of ETFs	3	3	4	21	21	31	33	92	202	280	282	326

Figure 1: Worldwide Listed ETF Growth. Source: Morgan Stanley ETF Strategies, Bloomberg, ETF Worldwide Guidebook, Global Summary as of October 29, 2004

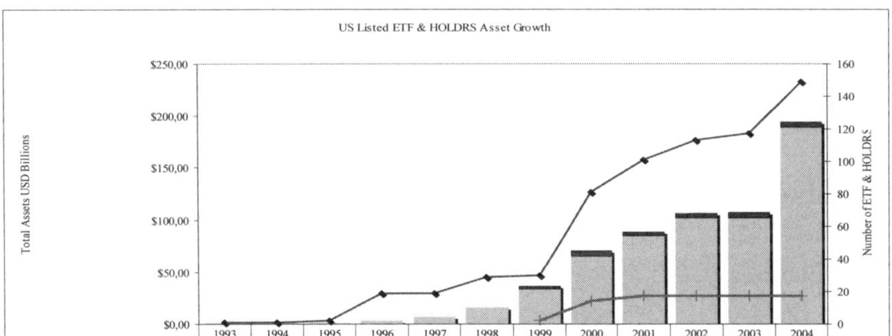

	1993	1994	1995	1996	1997	1998	1999	2000	2001	2002	2003	2004
HOLDRS Assets USD Billions							$1,98	$5,02	$3,80	$4,00	$4,45	$5,29
ETF Assets USD Billions	$0,46	$0,42	$1,05	$2,40	$6,70	$15,56	$33,86	$65,59	$84,60	$102,28	$102,28	$188,67
HOLDRS							2	14	17	17	17	17
ETFs	1	1	2	19	19	29	30	81	101	113	117	149

Figure 2: US Listed ETF Growth. Source: Morgan Stanley ETF Strategies, Bloomberg, ETF Worldwide Guidebook, Global Summary as of October 29, 2004

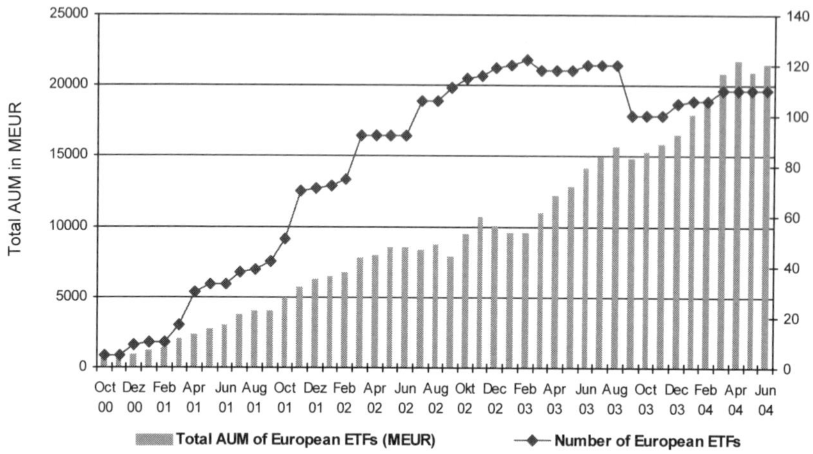

Figure 3: Total AUM / Number of European ETFs. Source: STOXX Ltd.

Table 1: European ETFs by underlying Indexes (% of AUM)

Name	% of AUM
STOXX	34,9 %
STOXX Sectors	3,9 %
Dow Jones	3,6 %
Dow Jones Sectors	0,4 %
FTSE	3,6 %
MSCI	5,9 %
MSCI Sectors	1,4 %
DBAG (DAX)	7,3 %
DBAG Bond	6,9 %
EN Paris (CAC)	9,1 %
SWX	6,8 %
SWX Bond	0,2 %
S&P	3,8 %
S&P Europe	3,0 %
iBoxx Bond	2,2 %
SSX (OMX,SBX)	3,7 %
Goldman Sachs Bond	0,5 %
EuroMTS	0,9 %
Others	1,7 %

Source: STOXX Ltd.

Table 2: European ETFs by Index Character (% of AUM)

	June 2003	June 2004
Europe	10,2 %	8,8 %
European Sector	3,8 %	3,4 %
Eurozone Bond	0	0,9 %
European Bond	5,6 %	2,2 %
Eurozone	31,8 %	36,0 %
Eurozone Sector	2,0 %	1,7 %
Global	1,0 %	1,2 %
Global Sectors	0,8 %	0,1 %
Global Bond	2,4 %	0,5 %
National	40,3 %	37,6 %
National Sectors	0,8 %	0,5 %
National Bond	1,4 %	7,1 %

Source: STOXX Ltd.

Table 3: European ETFs by Product/Issuer (% in AUM) 03/04 vs. 06/04

Name	March 2004	June 2004
Index Change (HVB)	26,9 %	27,2 %
iShares (BGI)	24,0 %	22,2 %
Easy ETF (AXA)	2,0 %	2,0 %
Master Unit (Lyxor)	19,6 %	22,5 %
StreetTRACKS (SsgA)	4,8 %	4,5 %
XMTCH (CS)	8,6 %	8,5 %
XACT Fonder	3,8 %	3,9 %
FRESCO (UBS Asset M.)	4,0 %	3,9 %
SPDR (CL)	2,0 %	3,0 %
Seligson	0,3 %	0,3 %
UNICO (DZ Bank)	0,8 %	0,8 %
Beta1 ETFand Plc	0,8 %	0,9 %
EQQQ (Nasdaq)	0,4 %	0,4 %
TrackinDex (Dexia)	0,1 %	0,2 %

Source: STOXX Ltd. In June 2004 there were 14 issuers with 110 products.

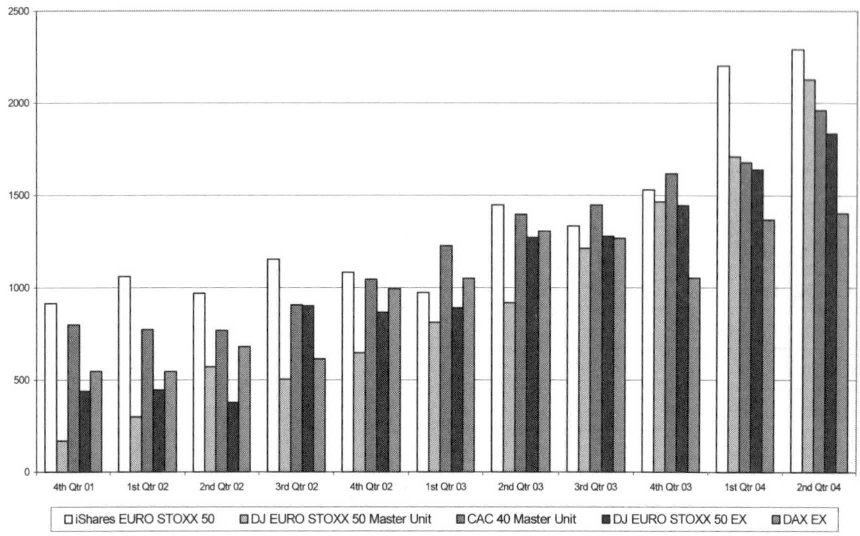

Figure 4: Top 5 European Products by AUM. Source: STOXX Ltd.

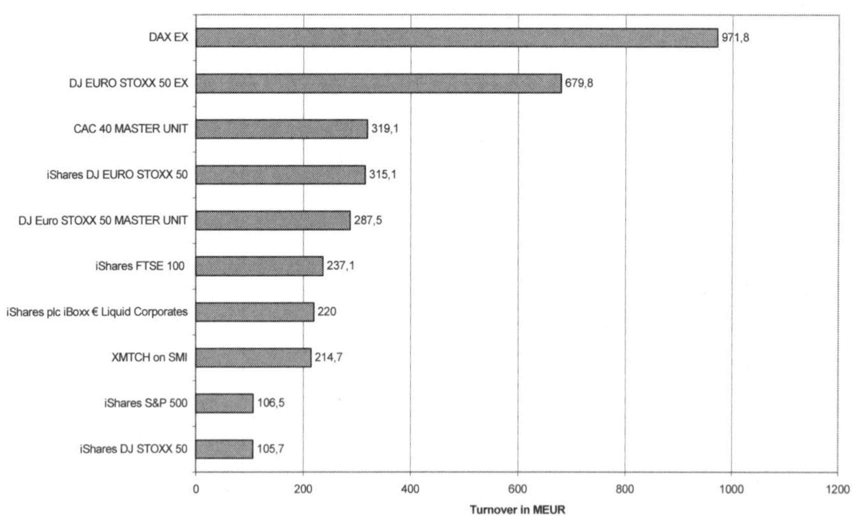

Figure 5: Top Ten European ETFs by Turnover (in MEUR, 05/04). Source: STOXX Ltd. Top Ten European ETF: 70.8 % of total European turnover (5/04) (XACT OMX and XACT SBX n. incl.)

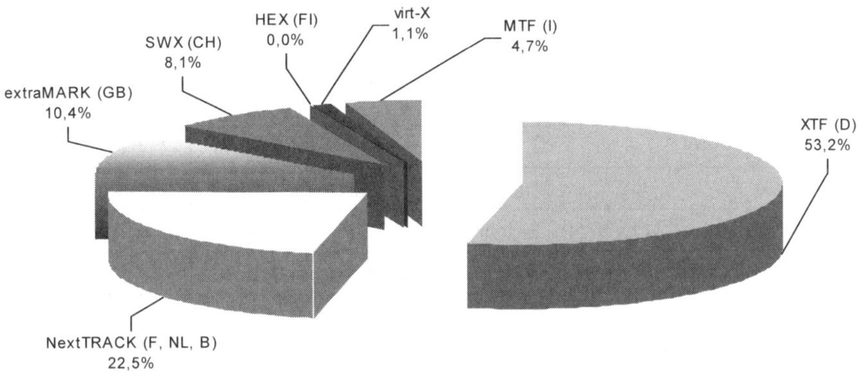

Figure 6: Turnover by exchange (in MEUR, 06/04). Source: STOXX Ltd. Total turnover of European ETFs: 4'880 MEUR (XACT OMX and XACT SBX n. incl.)

The next two tables will show the Top 10 / Top 15 European listed ETFs – the first one in March 2004 and the second one in July 2002. In each case it is a daily average volume over past month.

Table 4: Top 10 European Listed ETFs by volume – March 2004

ETF Name	Issuer / Domicile	TER	Daily Avg. Vol. (MEUR)
DAX EX	Indexchange / Ger	0,50 %	66,59
DJ Euro STOXX 50 Ex	Indexchange / Ger	0,40 %	26,19
CAC 40 Master Unit	Lyxor / Fra	0,30 %	16,56
iShares DJ Euro STOXX 50	BGI / Ire	0,35 %	11,96
XMTCH on SMI	Credit Suisse / Swit	0,40 %	11,87
DJ Euro STOXX 50 Master Unit	Lyxor / Fra	0,40 %	11,03
iShares iFTSE 100	BGI / Ire	0,40 %	8,82
DJ STOXX 50 EX	Indexchange / Ger	0,50 %	3,64
Fresco DJ Japan Titans 100	Fresco – UBS / Lux	0,75 %	3,01
XACT SBX	Xact Fonder / Swed	0,30 %	2,53

Source: Deutsche Bank

Table 5: Top 15 European Listed ETFs by volume – July 2002

ETF Name	Issuer / Domicile	Fee	Daily Avg. Vol. (MEUR)
Master CAC 40	Lyxor / Fra	0,30 %	60,53
DAX EX	Indexchange / Ger	0,50 %	41,03
Master DJ Euro STOXX 50	Lyxor / Fra	0,40 %	40,09
DJ Euro STOXX 50 EX	Indexchanche / Ger	0,40 %	22,71
DJ Euro STOXX 50 LDRS	Merrill Lynch / Ire	0,50 %	18,04
iShares iFTSE 100	BGI / Ire	0,35 %	9,13
SPDR Europe 350	Credit Lyonnais / Ire	0,35 %	8,26
SPDR Euro	Credit Lyonnais / Ire	0,35 %	7.99
XMTCH on SMI	Credit Suisse / Swit	0,35 %	7,70
DJ Euro STOXX 50 LDRS	Merrill Lynch / Ire	0,50 %	7,46
Master DJIA	Lyxor / Fra	0,50 %	5,04
DJ Euro STOXX 50 EX	Indexchange / Ger	0,40 %	3,79
DJ Euro STOXX 50 LDRS	Merrill Lynch / Ire	0,50 %	3,53
DJ STOXX 50 LDRS	Merrill Lynch / Ire	0,50 %	3,44
Fresco Euro STOXX 50	Fresco – UBS / Lux	0,50 %	2,99

Source: Deutsche Bank

Table 6: Comparison between various financial instruments

Characteristics	ETFs	Index Certificates	Equity Funds (Index Funds)	Futures	Shares
Financial Instrument	Stock indices	Bonds	Equity funds	Derivatives	Shares
Pricing	Continuous	Continuous	Daily net asset value (forward Pricing)	Continuous	Continuous
Market Liquidity	Very High	Medium	No exchange trading	High	High
Maturity	None	As a rule, limited lifespan	None	Limited lifespan	None
Reinvestment Risk	None	Yes	None	Yes	Normally, none
Short Sales	Yes	No	No	Yes	Yes

Table 6 (continued)

Characteristics	ETFs	Index Certificates	Equity Funds (Index Funds)	Futures	Shares
Cost for Purchase / Sale	Normal exchange fees	Purchase and reinvestment costs	Issuance and redemption commissions	Initial and variation margin payments and rollover costs	Exchange fees for all FTSE 100 based shares
Minimum Order Size	1 ETF (ca.£30)	1 certificate (ca. £50)	No minimum	£10 x index (ca. £50,000)	Cost associated with reconstructing the FTSE 100 with individual share positions
Dividend Payment	As a rule, semi-annual payment	As a rule, dividends are not paid out to investors	As a rule, annual payment	Cash settlement at maturity	Annual dividend payment

Source: Virt-x .

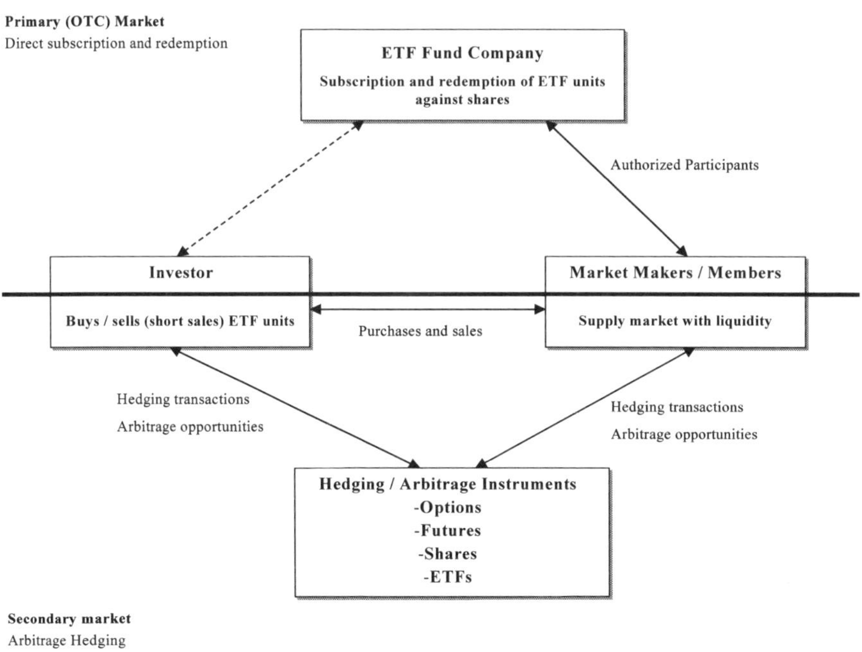

Figure 7: Origination and Trading. Source: Virt-x

"The origination of ETFs takes place according to a special mechanism. In the issuance of fund shares, two transactions take place in the primary market, whereby the exchange of ETF shares versus stocks takes place. This is the function of creation and redemption (see graph).

On each trading day, investors can subscribe to or redeem ETFs at their net asset value directly with the issuer. Through the creation of new ETFs or redemption of existing ones in the primary market, it can be ensured that ETFs are traded at a price that is closely in line with the net asset value as reflected in the secondary market. As a result, the leeway for an agio (premium) or disagio (discount) is removed.

The current market value (traded price) of an ETF can vary slightly from its intrinsic value (NAV). However, should the ETF trade at a considerable disagio or agio, that differential should be eliminated by an arbitrage mechanism carried out by professional market participants. For example, if an ETF is currently trading at a premium to NAV, a market maker will attempt to purchase the securities that underlie the ETF for what amounts to its indicative price, which is calculated and published every 15 seconds during trading hours, and then swap those securities for the premium-priced ETF shares. If, on the other hand, a discount to the current market price exists, the market maker will purchase the „low-priced" ETF shares and then exchange them for the corresponding stocks." *Ref.: www.virt-x.com.*

Table 7: Key Points of the European ETF Market (06/04)

Product	AUM MEUR	AUM Change MoM	AUM Change YoY	Market share AUM	Market share Change MoM	No. of ETF	No. of ETF Change MoM
Total European ETF	**21.504,0**	2,8%	50,9%	100%	-	110	0
Non STOXX ETF	13.146,8	2,1%	43,4%	61,4%	-0,7%	68	0
STOXX ETF	8.357,3	3,9%	64,4%	38,9%	1,0%	42	0
Total global sector	18,2	1,1%	-84,2%	0,08%	-1,7%	3	0
Total European sector ETF	1.095,9	5,1%	33,7%	5,1%	-1,7%	42	0
STOXX sector ETF	843,8	-0,5%	65,5%	3,9%	-3,2%	32	0

Source: STOXX Ltd.

Table 8: Key Points of the European ETF Market (05/04)

Product	AUM MEUR	AUM Change MoM	AUM Change YoY	Market share AUM	Market share Change MoM	No. of ETF	No. of ETF Change MoM
Total European ETF	20.730,7	-4,8%	60,7 %	100%	–	110	0
Non STOXX ETF	13.084,2	-4,6%	58,7 %	63,1%	0,2 %	68	0
STOXX ETF	7.646,5	-5,1%	64,2 %	36,9%	-0,3 %	42	0
Total global sector	18,4	0,8%	-87,8%	0,09%	5,8 %	3	0
Total European sector ETF	1062,6	-4,6%	44,3%	5,1%	0,2 %	42	0
STOXX sector ETF	841,8	-3,1 %	81,1 %	4,1 %	1,8 %	32	0

Source: STOXX Ltd.

The tables above show the changes between Month on Month as well as Year on Year concerning the Asset under Management, Market share and Number of ETFs. As can be seen, the values can differ a lot between single months or years. The MoM value for STOXX ETFs for example changed from April to May –5.1% while the difference from May to June was 3.9%. Source: Deutsche Bank

Exchange-Traded Funds Glossary[1]

Closed-end fund

A type of mutual fund. Like ETFs, closed-end funds differ from open-end mutual funds in that they trade throughout the day over an exchange. Unlike ETFs, however, they have no mechanism to prevent them from trading at substantial premiums or discounts to their net asset values.

Commission

The fee you pay a broker to buy or sell a security, such as a stock or an ETF, for your account. The charge is typically assessed on a per-trade basis. You do not need to pay a commission to buy or sell no-load, open-end mutual funds, giving them a cost-advantage over ETFs for investors who plan to invest regular sums of money or who trade frequently.

Creation Unit

The smallest block of ETF shares that can be bought or sold from the fund company at net asset value, usually 50,000. These are only bought and sold "in-kind." For example, when you sell one, you receive a portfolio of securities that approximates the ETF's holdings, not cash. Creation units' size means that only market makers and institutions can afford to buy or sell them. All other investors can buy or sell ETF shares in any size lot at the market price, rather than at NAV, over an exchange.

DIAMONDs

Shares in an ETF, Diamonds Trust Series I, that track the Dow Jones Industrial Average. The fund is structured as a unit investment trust.

Discount to NAV

Unlike regular open-end mutual funds, which are bought and sold directly from the fund company at the net asset value (NAV) of their portfolio se-

---

[1] Morningstar; www.morningstar.com/etfglossary/ETFGlossary.html

curities, ETFs and closed-end funds trade at prices determined by the market forces of supply and demand. A fund that trades at a price less than its NAV is said to trade at a discount to its NAV.

Exchange-traded fund (ETF)

The broad class of funds, excluding closed-end funds, which trade throughout the day over an exchange. ETFs have low annual expenses, but you must pay commissions to trade them. ETFs do not redeem shares for cash, and thus do not need to sell securities (possibly realizing capital gains) to pay investors who redeem their shares. They are typically more tax-efficient than mutual funds. Unlike closed-end funds, ETFs market prices usually closely track their NAVs. Most ETFs are index funds.

Expense ratio

The annual fee that all funds or ETFs charge their shareholders, expressed as a percentage of the fund's average daily net assets. This ratio includes such items as the management fee, trustee's fee, license fee, and 12b-1 fee, among others. It does not include the commissions you must pay to buy and sell ETF shares, or the costs incurred by the fund in trading its securities. HOLDRs do not express their fees as expense ratios, but instead charge a flat quarterly fee per 100 shares.

iShares

A group of ETFs advised and marketed by Barclays Global Investors. iShares are structured as open-end mutual funds.

HOLDRs

Holding company depository receipts, a type of ETF marketed by Merrill Lynch. Unlike other ETFs, HOLDRs can only be bought and sold in 100-share increments. HOLDRs do not have creation units like other ETFs, but investors may exchange 100 shares of a HOLDR for its underlying stocks at any time. Existing HOLDRs focus on narrow industry groups. Each initially owns 20 stocks, but they are unmanaged, and so can become more concentrated due to mergers, or the disparate performance of their holdings.

Market return

The total return of an ETF based on its market price at the beginning and end of the holding period. This may be different from the ETF's NAV return. The market return is the return actually earned by ETF investors, except for those who hold creation units.

Market price

The price of an ETF as determined by the market forces of supply and demand. Unlike regular open-end mutual funds, which are always bought and sold at NAV, the market price may differ from NAV. Most ETFs typically trade at market prices near their NAVs.

Net asset value (NAV)

The value of each share of a fund as determined by the value of its underlying holdings, including any cash in the portfolio. NAV is calculated by dividing a fund's total net assets by its number of shares outstanding. Shares in regular open-end mutual funds are bought and sold at NAV, but shares in ETFs (with the exception of creation units) are bought and sold at the market price, which can differ from NAV.

NAV return

The total return of an ETF, based on its NAV at the beginning and end of the holding period. This may be different from the ETF's market return. The market return, not the NAV return, is the return actually earned by ETF investors, except for those who hold creation units.

Open-end fund

The typical mutual-fund structure, and one used by several groups of ETFs, including iShares and Select Sector Spiders. This structure allows the funds to reinvest their dividends immediately, which could permit them to hold slightly less cash than ETFs that are structured as unit investment trusts.

Premium to NAV

Unlike regular open-end mutual funds, which are bought and sold directly from the fund company at the net asset value (NAV) of their portfolio securities, ETFs and closed-end funds trade at prices determined by the market forces of supply and demand. A fund that trades at a price higher than its NAV is said to trade at a premium to its NAV.

Qubes (QQQ)

The Nasdaq-100 tracking stock, an ETF that tracks the technology-laden Nasdaq-100 index. The popular name, Qubes, derives from the ETF's ticker symbol, QQQ. Qubes are structured as unit investment trusts. Qubes are by far the most heavily traded ETF.

Spiders

SPDRs, or Standard & Poors' Depository Receipts. A group of ETFs that track a variety of Standard & Poors' indexes. SPDR Trust, Series 1, usually referred to as "Spiders," tracks the S&P 500 index. Select Sector SPDRs track various sector indices that carve up the S&P 500 index into separate industry groups. SPDR Trust, Series 1 is structured as a unit investment trust, but Select Sector SPDRs are open-end funds.

Street Tracks

A group of ETFs managed by State Street Global Advisors. These ETFs track various indexes, including Dow Jones style-specific and global indexes, technology indexes from Morgan Stanley Dean Witter, and the Wilshire REIT index. StreetTracks are open-end funds, not unit investment trusts, and trade on the American Stock Exchange.

Unit investment trust

A structure used by some ETFs. One important difference between this format and the open-end fund format is that the latter allows ETFs to reinvest dividends immediately, while the former does not. This could result in ETFs that use the unit investment trust structure having a slight cash drag on their performance.

VIPERs

Vanguard Index Participation Receipts ETF versions of several Vanguard index funds. VIPERs are structured as share classes of existing open-end funds. The only VIPER currently available is the Vanguard Total Stock Market VIPER, but Vanguard plans to launch others.

Source: www.morningstar.com/etfglossary/ETFGlossary.html.

Appendix A: ETFs – Global Tracking Monitor[1]

ETFs are designed to track the performance of specific indexes as well as to minimize the tracking error. Due to fees, costs, dividend payments and index adjustments, the performance of an ETF may deviate from that of its underlying index. The following tables contain detailed information of that deviation between ETF and relevant index.

---

1 Morgan Stanley Quantitative and Derivative Strategies. Industry Overview Exchange Traded Funds – Global Tracking Monitor, November 24, 2004.

Table 1: European: streetTRACKS MSCI Europe Sector ETFs vs. MSCI Europe

ETF	Index	No. of Names in ETF	No. of Names in Index
streetTRACKS MSCI Europe Consumer Discretionary [STV]	MSCI Europe (Consumer Discretionary)	109	109
streetTRACKS MSCI Europe Consumer Staples [STS]	MSCI Europe (Consumer Staples)	43	43
streetTRACKS MSCI Europe Energy [STN]	MSCI Europe (Energy)	17	17
streetTRACKS MSCI Europe Financials [STZ]	MSCI Europe (Financials)	109	109
streetTRACKS MSCI Europe Healthcare [STW]	MSCI Europe (Health Care)	36	36
streetTRACKS MSCI Europe Industrials [STQ]	MSCI Europe (Industrials)	111	111
streetTRACKS MSCI Europe Information Technology [STK]	MSCI Europe (Information Technology)	35	35
streetTRACKS MSCI Europe Materials [STP]	MSCI Europe (Materials)	51	51
streetTRACKS MSCI Europe Telecommunicaiton Services [STT]	MSCI Europe (Telecommunication Services)	24	24
streetTRACKS MSCI Europe Utilities [STU]	MSCI Europe (Utilities)	28	28

Tracking Risk	Correlation	ETF Liquidity (10 Mn)	ETF % Bid-Ask Spread	ETF Hist. Volatility	Index Hist. Volatility	Index Basket Return (21d)
0.10%	100.00	0.31%	0.19%	15.20%	15.20%	3.90%
0.10%	99.99%	0.46%	0.13%	12.30%	12.40%	6.40%
0.20%	99.99%	0.33%	0.12%	15.20%	15.30%	1.60%
0.20%	99.99%	0.17%	0.50%	14.50%	14.50%	5.00%
0.30%	99.98	0.54%	0.17%	14.00%	14.00%	3.80%
0.10%	100.00	0.48%	0.88%	14.90%	14.90%	4.20%
0.00%	100.00	0.46%	0.21%	27.00%	27.00%	6.80%
0.40%	99.97	0.68%	0.88%	15.10%	15.10%	2.50%
0.00%	100.00	0.41%	0.16%	16.80%	16.80%	6.70%
0.00%	100.00	0.62%	0.60%	13.30%	13.30%	9.00%

Table 2: European: streetTRACKS MSCI Europe Sector ETFs vs. FTSE Europe

ETF	Index	No. of Names in ETF	No. of Names in Index
streetTRACKS MSCI Europe Consumer Discretionary [STV]	FTSE Europe (Cyclical Consumer Goods)	109	22
streetTRACKS MSCI Europe Consumer Staples [STS]	FTSE Europe (Non-Cyclical Consumer Goods / Cyclical Services)	43	165
streetTRACKS MSCI Europe Energy [STN]	FTSE Europe (Resources / Non-Cyclical Services)	17	51
streetTRACKS MSCI Europe Financials [STZ]	FTSE Europe (Financials)	109	136
streetTRACKS MSCI Europe Healthcare [STW]	FTSE Europe (Pharma-ceuticals)	36	17
streetTRACKS MSCI Europe Industrials [STQ]	FTSE Europe (General Industrials)	111	39
streetTRACKS MSCI Europe Information Technology [STK]	FTSE Europe (Information Technology)	35	17
streetTRACKS MSCI Europe Materials [STP]	FTSE Europe (Chemicals)	51	18
streetTRACKS MSCI Europe Telecommunicaiton Services [STT]	FTSE Europe (Telecommu-nication Services / Con-structions & Materials)	24	48
streetTRACKS MSCI Europe Utilities [STU]	FTSE Europe (Utilities)	28	29

Tracking Risk	Correlation	ETF Liquidity (10 Mn)	ETF % Bid-Ask Spread	ETF Hist. Volatility	Index Hist. Volatility	Index Basket Return (21d)
6.90%	92.21%	0.31%	0.19%	15.20%	17.70%	1.70%
5.30%	90.74%	0.46%	0.13%	12.30%	12.00%	5.10%
7.90%	85.60%	0.33%	0.12%	15.20%	14.00%	3.40%
0.50%	99.94%	0.17%	0.50%	14.50%	14.40%	5.10%
1.10%	99.72%	0.54%	0.17%	14.00%	14.20%	4.10%
5.90%	95.90%	0.48%	0.88%	14.90%	18.50%	3.10%
1.50%	99.89%	0.46%	0.21%	27.00%	27.80%	7.20%
5.60%	93.44%	0.68%	0.88%	15.10%	15.70%	4.70%
2.10%	99.27%	0.41%	0.16%	16.80%	16.10%	6.30%
0.50%	99.93%	0.62%	0.60%	13.30%	13.30%	9.00%

Table 3: European: IndEXchange DJ STOXX 600 Sector ETFs vs. Dow Jones STOXX

ETF	Index	No. of Names in ETF	No. of Names in Index
IndEXchange DJ STOXX 600 Dow Jones STOXX Automobiles & Parts [SXAPEX]	Dow Jones STOXX (Automobile)	14	13
IndEXchange DJ STOXX 600 Dow Jones STOXX Banks [SBANK]	Dow Jones STOXX (Banks)	70	70
IndEXchange DJ STOXX 600 Dow Jones STOXX Basic Resources [SXPPEX]	Dow Jones STOXX (Basic Resources)	19	20
IndEXchange DJ STOXX 600 Chemicals [SX4PEX]	Dow Jones STOXX (Chemicals)	18	17
IndEXchange DJ STOXX 600 Construction & Materials [SXOPEX]	Dow Jones STOXX (Construction)	29	29
IndEXchange DJ STOXX 600 Dow Jones STOXX Financial Services [SXFPEX]	Dow Jones STOXX (Financial Services)	41	36
IndEXchange DJ STOXX 600 Dow Jones STOXX Food Food & Beverage [SX3PEX]	Dow Jones STOXX (Food & Beverages)	28	28
IndEXchange DJ STOXX 600 Health Care [SHEL]	Dow Jones STOXX (Helthcare)	33	31
IndEXchange DJ STOXX 600 Industrial Goods & Services [SXNPEX]	Dow Jones STOXX (Industrial Goods & Services)	81	84
IndEXchange DJ STOXX 600 Insurance [SXIPEX]	Dow Jones STOXX (Insurance)	38	38

Tracking Risk	Correlation	ETF Liquidity (10 Mn)	ETF % Bid-Ask Spread	ETF Hist. Volatility	Index Hist. Volatility	Index Basket Return (21d)
0.60%	99.96%	1.18%	0.11%	18.30%	18.60%	1.00%
0.20%	99.98%	0.24%	0.67%	14.10%	14.10%	5.50%
1.20%	99.82%	1.08%	1.12%	19.50%	19.60%	-1.90%
0.60%	99.94%	1.59%	0.14%	15.80%	15.60%	4.80%
1.30%	99.65%	1.95%	2.12%	15.20%	15.10%	4.50%
1.20%	99.53%	3.11%	0.33%	12.60%	12.60%	6.20%
0.10%	100.00%	0.84%	0.16%	12.90%	12.90%	6.90%
0.40%	99.96%	0.54%	0.19%	14.00%	14.00%	3.90%
0.80%	99.86%	0.57%	0.27%	15.20%	15.30%	3.50%
0.20%	100.00%	0.53%	0.17%	18.00%	18.00%	3.50%

Table 3 (continued)

ETF	Index	No. of Names in ETF	No. of Names in Index
IndEXchange DJ STOXX 600 Media [SXMPEX]	Dow Jones STOXX (Media)	38	36
IndEXchange DJ STOXX 600 Oil & Gas [SXEPEX]	Dow Jones STOXX (Energy)	17	15
IndEXchange DJ STOXX 600 Personal & Household Goods [SXHPEX]	Dow Jones STOXX (Non-cyclical Goods & Services)	35	28
IndEXchange DJ STOXX 600 Retail [SX1PEX]	Dow Jones STOXX (Retail)	29	21
IndEXchange DJ STOXX 600 Technology [STECH]	Dow Jones STOXX (Technology)	27	27
IndEXchange DJ STOXX 600 Telecommunications [STEL]	Dow Jones STOXX (Telecommunications)	25	25
IndEXchange DJ STOXX 600 Travel & Leisure [SX2PEX]	Dow Jones STOXX (Cyclical Goods & Services)	29	42
IndEXchange DJ STOXX 600 Utilities [SX6PEX]	Dow Jones STOXX (Utilities)	29	30

Tracking Risk	Correlation	ETF Liquidity (10 Mn)	ETF % Bid-Ask Spread	ETF Hist. Volatility	Index Hist. Volatility	Index Basket Return (21d)
0.40%	99.99%	0.96%	0.18%	17.10%	17.40%	5.60%
0.20%	99.99%	0.33%	0.09%	15.20%	15.20%	1.70%
6.70%	88.06%	1.11%	0.15%	14.10%	12.70%	5.80%
6.00%	90.66%	0.88%	0.17%	13.70%	13.90%	4.50%
1.00%	99.94%	0.47%	0.21%	27.40%	27.60%	6.60%
0.00%	100.00%	0.40%	0.17%	17.00%	17.00%	6.80%
7.10%	89.96%	1.34%	0.22%	14.90%	16.20%	4.60%
0.40%	99.95%	0.64%	0.13%	13.40%	13.40%	8.80%

Table 4: European: IndEXchange DJ STOXX 600 Sector ETFs vs. MSCI Europe

ETF	Index	No. of Names in ETF	No. of Names in Index
IndEXchange DJ STOXX 600 Dow Jones STOXX Automo-biles & Parts [SXAPEX]	MSCI Europe (Automobiles & Components)	14	14
IndEXchange DJ STOXX 600 Dow Jones STOXX Banks [SBANK]	MSCI Europe (Banks)	70	46
IndEXchange DJ STOXX 600 Dow Jones STOXX Basic Resources [SXPPEX]	MSCI Europe (Materials)	19	51
IndEXchange DJ STOXX 600 Chemicals [SX4PEX]	MSCI Europe (Materials)	18	51
IndEXchange DJ STOXX 600 Construction & Materials [SXOPEX]	MSCI Europe (Capital Go-ods)	29	67
IndEXchange DJ STOXX 600 Dow Jones STOXX Financial Services [SXFPEX]	MSCI Europe (Diversified Financials)	41	24
IndEXchange DJ STOXX 600 Dow Jones STOXX Food Food & Beverage [SX3PEX]	MSCI Europe (Food Bever-age & Tobacco)	28	25
IndEXchange DJ STOXX 600 Health Care [SHEL]	MSCI Europe (Health Care)	33	36
IndEXchange DJ STOXX 600 Industrial Goods & Services [SXNPEX]	MSCI Europe (Industrials)	81	111
IndEXchange DJ STOXX 600 Insurance [SXIPEX]	MSCI Europe (Insurance)	38	22

Tracking Risk	Correlation	ETF Liquidity (10 Mn)	ETF % Bid-Ask Spread	ETF Hist. Volatility	Index Hist. Volatility	Index Basket Return (21d)
1.80%	99.53%	1.18%	0.11%	18.30%	18.40%	1.50%
1.80%	99.15%	0.24%	0.67%	14.10%	13.90%	5.20%
9.90%	86.62%	1.08%	1.12%	19.50%	15.10%	2.50%
5.70%	93.14%	1.59%	0.14%	15.80%	15.10%	2.50%
7.30%	89.39%	1.95%	2.12%	15.20%	16.30%	4.20%
10.60%	78.55%	3.11%	0.33%	12.60%	17.00%	5.50%
1.70%	99.11%	0.84%	0.16%	12.90%	12.60%	7.20%
0.50%	99.92%	0.54%	0.19%	14.00%	14.00%	3.80%
1.50%	99.55%	0.57%	0.27%	15.20%	14.90%	4.20%
2.00%	99.40%	0.53%	0.17%	18.00%	18.20%	3.30%

Table 4 (continued)

ETF	Index	No. of Names in ETF	No. of Names in Index
IndEXchange DJ STOXX 600 Media [SXMPEX]	MSCI Europe (Media)	38	34
IndEXchange DJ STOXX 600 Oil & Gas [SXEPEX]	MSCI Europe (Energy)	17	17
IndEXchange DJ STOXX 600 Personal & Household Goods [SXHPEX]	MSCI Europe (Consumer Staples)	35	43
IndEXchange DJ STOXX 600 Retail [SX1PEX]	MSCI Europe (Retailing)	29	19
IndEXchange DJ STOXX 600 Technology [STECH]	MSCI Europe (Information Technology)	27	35
IndEXchange DJ STOXX 600 Telecommunications [STEL]	MSCI Europe (Telecommunication Services)	25	24
IndEXchange DJ STOXX 600 Travel & Leisure [SX2PEX]	MSCI Europe (Consumer Durables & Apparel)	29	24
IndEXchange DJ STOXX 600 Utilities [SX6PEX]	MSCI Europe (Utilities)	29	28

Tracking Risk	Correlation	ETF Liquidity (10 Mn)	ETF % Bid-Ask Spread	ETF Hist. Volatility	Index Hist. Volatility	Index Basket Return (21d)
1.00%	99.89%	0.96%	0.18%	17.10%	17.60%	5.70%
0.50%	99.95%	0.33%	0.09%	15.20%	15.30%	1.60%
7.40%	85.01%	1.11%	0.15%	14.10%	12.40%	6.40%
6.60%	89.39%	0.88%	0.17%	13.70%	14.50%	3.60%
0.80%	99.97%	0.47%	0.21%	27.40%	27.00%	6.80%
1.00%	99.84%	0.40%	0.17%	17.00%	16.80%	6.70%
12.00%	75.87%	1.34%	0.22%	14.90%	18.40%	2.60%
0.70%	99.86%	0.64%	0.13%	13.40%	13.30%	9.00%

Table 5: European: EasyETF EuroStoxx Sector ETFs vs. Dow Jones Euro STOXX

ETF	Index	No. of Names in ETF	No. of Names in Index
EasyETF EuroStoxx Automobile [SYA]	Dow Jones Euro STOXX (Automobile)	10	10
EasyETF EuroStoxx Banks [SYB]	Dow Jones Euro STOXX (Banks)	48	48
EasyETF EuroStoxx Construction [SYC]	Dow Jones Euro STOXX (Energy)	17	18
EasyETF EuroStoxx Energy [SYE]	Dow Jones Euro STOXX (Energy)	11	10
EasyETF EuroStoxx Healthcare [SYH]	Dow Jones Euro STOXX (Healthcare)	12	12
EasyETF EuroStoxx Insurance [SYI]	Dow Jones Euro STOXX (Insurance)	19	19
EasyETF EuroStoxx Media [SYM]	Dow Jones Euro STOXX (Media)	21	19
EasyETF EuroStoxx Technology [SYQ]	Dow Jones Euro STOXX (Technology)	17	16
EasyETF EuroStoxx Telecomm [SYT]	Dow Jones Euro STOXX (Telecommunications)	16	16
EasyETF EuroStoxx Utilities [SYU]	Dow Jones Euro STOXX (Utilities)	17	18

Tracking Risk	Correlation	ETF Liquidity (10 Mn)	ETF % Bid-Ask Spread	ETF Hist. Volatility	Index Hist. Volatility	Index Basket Return (21d)
0.00%	100.00%	1,31%	0,09%	18,80%	18,80%	0,80%
0,50%	99,95%	0,47%	1,41%	16,00%	16,10%	6,90%
1,40%	99,64%	3,27%	2,97%	16,00%	15,90%	4,80%
0,30%	99,98%	0,63%	0,07%	15,60%	15,70%	2,40%
1,50%	99,72%	2,97%	0,25%	19,40%	19,40%	3,10%
0,20%	99,99%	0,84%	0,12%	19,10%	19,10%	4,20%
0,80%	99,97%	2,24%	0,16%	18,20%	18,80%	5,00%
1,30%	99,90%	0,68%	0,11%	27,00%	27,40%	9,60%
0,10%	100,00%	0,55%	0,15%	17,10%	17,10%	7,10%
0,60%	99,92%	0,95%	0,11%	15,30%	15,30%	9,70%

Table 6: European: EasyETF EuroStoxx Sector ETFs vs. MSCI Europe

ETF	Index	No. of Names in ETF	No. of Names in Index
EasyETF EuroStoxx Automobile [SYA]	MSCI Europe (Automobiles & Components)	10	14
EasyETF EuroStoxx Banks [SYB]	MSCI Europe (Banks)	48	46
EasyETF EuroStoxx Construction [SYC]	MSCI Europe (Construction & Engineering)	17	12
EasyETF EuroStoxx Energy [SYE]	MSCI Europe (Energy)	11	17
EasyETF EuroStoxx Healthcare [SYH]	MSCI Europe (Health Care)	12	36
EasyETF EuroStoxx Insurance [SYI]	MSCI Europe (Insurance)	19	22
EasyETF EuroStoxx Media [SYM]	MSCI Europe (Media)	21	34
EasyETF EuroStoxx Technology [SYQ]	MSCI Europe (Information Technology)	17	35
EasyETF EuroStoxx Telecom [SYT]	MSCI Europe (Telecommunication Services)	16	24
EasyETF EuroStoxx Utilities [SYU]	MSCI Europe (Utilities)	17	28

Tracking Risk	Correlation	ETF Liquidity (10 Mn)	ETF % Bid-Ask Spread	ETF Hist. Volatility	Index Hist. Volatility	Index Basket Return (21d)
1,90%	99,49%	1,31%	0,09%	18,80%	18,40%	1,50%
6,20%	92,34%	0,47%	1,41%	16,00%	13,90%	5,20%
7,90%	87,05%	3,27%	2,97%	16,00%	14,30%	4,40%
5,60%	93,34%	0,63%	0,07%	15,60%	15,30%	1,60%
12,80%	75,17%	2,97%	0,25%	19,40%	14,00%	3,80%
4,80%	96,76%	0,84%	0,12%	19,10%	18,20%	3,30%
7,20%	91,99%	2,24%	0,16%	18,20%	17,60%	5,70%
6,00%	97,50%	0,68%	0,11%	27,00%	27,00%	6,80%
6,80%	92,09%	0,55%	0,15%	17,10%	16,80%	6,70%
4,30%	96,50%	0,95%	0,11%	15,30%	13,30%	9,00%

Table 7: European: IndEXchange DJ EURO STOXX ETFs vs. Dow Jones Euro STOXX

ETF	Index	No. of Names in ETF	No. of Names in Index
IndEXchange DJ Euro-STOXX Banks Ex (ESBANK)	Dow Jones Euro STOXX (banks)	48	48
IndEXchange DJ Euro-STOXX Healthcare Ex (ESHEL)	Dow Jones Euro STOXX (Healthcare)	12	12
IndEXchange DJ Euro-STOXX Technologz Ex (ESTECH)	Dow Jones Euro TOXX (Technology)	17	16
IndEXchange DJ Euro-STOXX Telecommunications EX (ESTEL)	Dow Jones Euro STOXX (Telecommunications)	16	16

Table 8: European: Country Exposure ETFs vs. Various Indices

ETF	Index	No. of Names in ETF	No. of Names in Index
streetTRACKS AEX [AEXT]	AEX	24	24
Bel 20 Master Unit [BEL]	BEL 20	20	20
CAC 40 Master Unit [CACETF]	CAC 40	40	40
S&P/MIB Master Unit [ETFMIB]	MIB 30	40	30
IndEXchange DAX EX [GDAXEX]	DAX	30	30

Tracking Risk	Correlation	ETF Liquidity (10 Mn)	ETF % Bid-Ask Spread	ETF Hist. Volatility	Index Hist. Volatility	Index Basket Return (21d)
0.50%	99.94%	0.52%	1.41%	16.00%	16.10%	6.90%
1.50%	99.72%	2.97%	0.25%	19.40%	19.40%	3.10%
1.30%	99.89%	0.70%	0.11%	27.10%	27.40%	9.60%
0.10%	100.00%	0.55%	0.15%	17.10%	17.10%	7.10%

Tracking Risk	Correlation	ETF Liquidity (10 Mn)	ETF % Bid-Ask Spread	ETF Hist. Volatility	Index Hist. Volatility	Index Basket Return (21d)
0.50%	99.96%	0.75%	0.11%	16.40%	16.40%	3.90%
0.00%	100.00%	4.72%	0.22%	14.00%	14.00%	6.80%
0.10%	100.00%	0.28%	0.10%	16.10%	16.10%	4.50%
0.80%	99.86%	0.43%	0.08%	14.40%	14.30%	6.60%
0.00%	100.00%	0.28%	0.09%	17.90%	17.90%	4.10%

Table 8 (continued)

ETF	Index	No. of Names in ETF	No. of Names in Index
IndEXchange MDAX EX [MDAXEX]	MDAX	50	50
FRESCO DJ Germany Titans 30 [FDGETI]	DAX	30	30
HEX25 Index Share [IHEX25]	HEX25	25	25
XMTCH on SMI [XMTCH]	SMI	27	27
IndEXchange SMI Ex [EXSMI]	SMI	27	27
Fresco SMI [FRESMI]	SMI	27	27
XACT OMX [XOMX]	OMX	30	30
XACT SBX [XACTSBX]	OMX	75	30
streetTRACKS MSCI UK [STUK]	MSCI United Kingdom	138	151
IndEXchange FTSE 100 EX [FTSE_EX]	FTSE 100	102	102
iShares FTSE 100 [IFTSE]	FTSE 100	102	102
Fresco DJ UK Titans 50 [FDUKFI]	FTSE 100	102	50

Tracking Risk	Correlation	ETF Liquidity (10 Mn)	ETF % Bid-Ask Spread	ETF Hist. Volatility	Index Hist. Volatility	Index Basket Return (21d)
1.10%	99.77%	4.58%	0.30%	15.60%	15.60%	3.80%
0.40%	99.97%	0.28%	0.09%	17.80%	17.90%	4.10%
0.00%	100.00%	3.93%	0.25%	15.60%	15.60%	7.90%
0.00%	100.00%	0.49%	0.11%	15.30%	15.30%	4.90%
0.00%	100.00%	0.49%	0.11%	15.30%	15.30%	4.90%
0.00%	100.00%	0.49%	0.11%	15.30%	15.30%	4.90%
0.80%	99.90%	0.70%	0.32%	18.80%	18.80%	4.40%
2.00%	99.46%	0.74%	0.35%	18.20%	18.80%	4.40%
0.20%	99.99%	0.11%	0.14%	12.20%	12.20%	4.10%
0.00%	100.00%	0.11%	0.14%	12.40%	12.40%	4.10%
0.00%	100.00%	0.11%	0.14%	12.40%	12.40%	4.10%
0.80%	99.80%	0.13%	0.13%	12.50%	12.40%	4.10%

Table 9: European: Regional Exposure Europe ETFs vs. Various Indices

ETF	Index	No. of Names in ETF	No. of Names in Index
streetTRACKS Pan-Euro [ERO]	MSCI Pan Euro	267	267
streetTRACKS Pan-Euro[ERO]	MSCI Europe	267	563
streetTRACKS Pan-Euro[ERO]	FTSE Europe	267	514
EasyETF STOXX 50 Europe[SYSTX]	Dow Jones STOXX 50	50	50
iShares FTSE EuroTop 100[IETA]	FTSE EuroTop 100	101	103
iShares DJ STOXX 50[LDRSSTX]	Dow Jones STOXX 50	50	50
IndEXchange DJ STOXX 50[EXSTX]	MSCI Pan Euro	50	267
IndEXchange DJ STOXX 50[EXSTX]	MSCI Europe	50	563
IndEXchange DJ STOXX 50[EXSTX]	FTSE Europe	50	514
SPDR Europe 350 [SPE]	MSCI Europe	350	563
SPDR Europe 350 [SPE]	MSCI Pan Euro	350	267
SPDR Europe 350 [SPE]	FTSE Europe	350	514
UNICO i-tracker MSCIEurope [IMSEFI]	MSCI Europe	563	563
UNICO i-tracker MSCIEurope [IMSEFI]	FTSE Europe	563	514
Fresco STOXX 50 [FEU]	Dow Jones STOXX 50	50	50
Fresco STOXX 50 [FEU]	Dow Jones STOXX 50	50	50

Tracking Risk	Correlation	ETF Liquidity (10 Mn)	ETF % Bid-Ask Spread	ETF Hist. Volatility	Index Hist. Volatility	Index Basket Return (21d)
0.10%	100.00%	0.04%	0.24%	13.40%	13.40%	4.70%
0.50%	99.94%	0.04%	0.24%	13.40%	13.30%	4.70%
0.50%	99.92%	0.04%	0.24%	13.40%	13.30%	4.70%
0.00%	100.00%	0.08%	0.10%	13.70%	13.70%	4.30%
1.30%	99.53%	0.06%	0.10%	13.50%	13.70%	4.60%
0.00%	100.00%	0.08%	0.10%	13.70%	13.70%	4.30%
1.70%	99.24%	0.08%	0.11%	13.70%	13.40%	4.70%
2.00%	98.92%	0.08%	0.11%	13.70%	13.30%	4.70%
2.10%	98.85%	0.08%	0.11%	13.70%	13.30%	4.70%
0.40%	99.96%	0.04%	0.14%	13.50%	13.30%	4.70%
0.40%	99.96%	0.04%	0.14%	13.50%	13.40%	4.70%
0.40%	99.96%	0.04%	0.14%	13.50%	13.30%	4.70%
0.10%	100.00%	0.04%	0.37%	13.30%	13.30%	4.70%
0.30%	99.98%	0.04%	0.37%	13.30%	13.30%	4.70%
0.00%	100.00%	0.08%	0.10%	13.70%	13.70%	4.30%
0.00%	100.00%	0.08%	0.10%	13.70%	13.70%	4.30%

Table 10: European: Regional Exposure Eurozone ETFs vs. Various Indices

ETF	Index	No. of Names in ETF	No. of Names in Index
DJ Euro STOXX 50 MasterUnit [MSE]	Dow Jones Euro STOXX 50	50	50
Beta1 MSCI Euro [B1EU]	MSCI Euro	69	140
Beta1 MSCI Euro [B1EU]	MSCI EMU	69	299
EasyETF Euro STOXX 50[SYSTE]	Dow Jones Euro STOXX 50	50	50
Fresco EuroSTOXX 50[FSEUFI]	Dow Jones Euro STOXX 50	50	50
Fresco EuroSTOXX 50[FSEUFI]	MSCI Euro	50	140
IndEXchange DJ EuroSTOXX 50 [EXSTE]	MSCI Euro	50	140
IndEXchange DJ Eu-roSTOXX 50 [EXSTE]	MSCI EMU	50	299
iShares FTSE Euro 100[IEUR]	FTSE Euro 100	81	103
iShares DJ EuroSTOXX 50[LDRSSTE]	Dow Jones Euro STOXX 50	50	50
SPDR Euro [SPO]	MSCI Euro	174	140
SPDR Euro [SPO]	MSCI EMU	174	299
XMTCH on MSCI Euro [XMEZ]	MSCI Euro	140	140
XMTCH on MSCI Euro [XMEZ]	MSCI EMU	140	299
iShares MSCI EMU [EZU]	MSCI Euro	276	140
iShares MSCI EMU [EZU]	MSCI EMU	276	299
iShares S&P Europe 350 [IEV]	MSCI Europe	345	563
iShares S&P Europe 350 [IEV]	FTSE Europe	345	514

Tracking Risk	Correlation	ETF Liquidity (10 Mn)	ETF % Bid-Ask Spread	ETF Hist. Volatility	Index Hist. Volatility	Index Basket Return (21d)
0.10%	100.00%	0.10%	0.09%	16.30%	16.30%	5.40%
1.00%	99.83%	0.09%	0.09%	16.00%	15.50%	5.30%
1.50%	99.63%	0.09%	0.09%	16.00%	15.30%	5.40%
0.00%	100.00%	0.10%	0.09%	16.30%	16.30%	5.40%
0.10%	100.00%	0.10%	0.09%	16.30%	16.30%	5.40%
1.40%	99.70%	0.10%	0.09%	16.30%	15.50%	5.30%
1.40%	99.70%	0.10%	0.09%	16.30%	15.50%	5.30%
1.90%	99.46%	0.10%	0.09%	16.30%	15.30%	5.40%
0.50%	99.97%	0.08%	0.09%	15.90%	15.70%	5.20%
0.00%	100.00%	0.10%	0.09%	16.30%	16.30%	5.40%
0.40%	99.97%	0.08%	0.12%	15.60%	15.50%	5.30%
0.60%	99.95%	0.08%	0.12%	15.60%	15.30%	5.40%
0.10%	100.00%	0.08%	0.35%	15.50%	15.50%	5.30%
0.60%	99.93%	0.08%	0.35%	15.50%	15.30%	5.40%
0.70%	99.93%	0.35%	0.64%	15.20%	15.50%	5.30%
0.30%	99.98%	0.35%	0.64%	15.20%	15.30%	5.40%
0.40%	99.96%	0.05%	0.14%	13.40%	13.30%	4.70%
0.40%	99.96%	0.05%	0.14%	13.40%	13.30%	4.70%

Table 11: Japan: Japanese ETFs vs. Various Indices

ETF	Index	No. of Names in ETF	No. of Names in Index
iShares S&P/TOPIX 150[ITF]	MSCI Japan	149	344
iShares S&P/TOPIX 150[ITF]	TOPIX 150	149	150
iShares MSCI Japan [EWJ]	MSCI Japan	281	344
Fresco DJ Japan Titans 100[FDJPHU]	MSCI Japan	100	344
iShares Nikkei 225 [1329]	MSCI Japan	225	344
iShares Nikkei 225 [1329]	Nikkei 225	225	225

Table 12: US: Broad Based ETFs vs. Various Indices

ETF	Index	No. of Names in ETF	No. of Names in Index
iShares DJ US Total Market[IYY]	Dow Jones US TotalMarket	1617	1617
iShares Russell 3000 [IWV]	Russell 3000	2984	2992
iShares S&P 1500 [ISI]	S&P 1500	1500	1500

Tracking Risk	Correlation	ETF Liquidity (10 Mn)	ETF % Bid-Ask Spread	ETF Hist. Volatility	Index Hist. Volatility	Index Basket Return (21d)
1.40%	99.78%	0.24%	0.33%	21.00%	21.00%	0.40%
0.40%	99.99%	0.24%	0.33%	21.00%	21.10%	0.20%
0.30%	99.99%	0.19%	0.34%	21.00%	21.00%	0.40%
2.10%	99.54%	0.26%	0.33%	21.60%	21.00%	0.40%
4.80%	98.00%	0.37%	0.32%	23.00%	21.00%	0.40%
0.00%	100.00%	0.37%	0.32%	23.00%	23.00%	0.20%

Tracking Risk	Correlation	ETF Liquidity (10 Mn)	ETF % Bid-Ask Spread	ETF Hist. Volatility	Index Hist. Volatility	Index Basket Return (21d)
0.00%	100.00%	0.02%	0.08%	11.30%	11.30%	-0.10%
0.00%	100.00%	0.02%	0.08%	11.50%	11.50%	0.20%
0.00%	100.00%	0.02%	0.07%	11.30%	11.20%	0.10%

Table 13: US: Large-Cap ETFs vs. Various Indices

ETF	Index	No. of Names in ETF	No. of Names in Index
Diamond Trust Series 1 [DIA]	Dow Jones Industrial Average	30	30
iShares Russell 1000 [IWB]	Russell 1000	990	991
iShares S&P 500 [IVV]	S&P 500	500	500
iShares S&P 500 [IVV]	MSCI US	500	518
iShares S&P 100 [OEF]	S&P 100	100	100
Nasdaq-100 Index Tracking-Stock [QQQ]	Nasdaq 100	100	100
S&P Depository Receipts (SPDR) [SPY]	MSCI US	500	518
S&P Depository Receipts (SPDR) [SPY]	S&P 500	500	500
streetTRACKS Fortune 500[FFF]	Fortune 500	436	436
streetTRACKS Fortune 500[FFF]	MSCI US	436	518
streetTRACKS Fortune 500[FFF]	S&P 500	436	500
Vanguard Large-Cap [VV]	MSCI US	751	518
Fresco DJ US Large Cap[FDUSLC]	Dow Jones Industrial Average	261	30

Tracking Risk	Correlation	ETF Liquidity (10 Mn)	ETF % Bid-Ask Spread	ETF Hist. Volatility	Index Hist. Volatility	Index Basket Return (21d)
0.00%	100.00%	0.15%	0.07%	10.70%	10.70%	-1.00%
0.00%	100.00%	0.03%	0.07	11.00%	11.00%	0.20%
0.00%	100.00%	0.03%	0.06%	11.00%	11.00%	0.10%
0.50%	99.91%	0.03%	0.06%	11.00%	10.90%	-0.20%
0.00%	100.00%	0.06%	0.06%	10.80%	10.80%	-0.20%
0.00%	100.00%	0.06%	0.01%	18.60%	18.60%	2.00%
0.50%	99.91%	0.03%	0.06%	11.00%	10.90%	-0.20%
0.00%	100.00%	0.03%	0.06%	11.00%	11.00%	0.10%
0.00%	100.00%	0.03%	0.07%	10.60%	10.60%	0.00%
1.00%	99.62%	0.03%	0.07%	10.60%	10.90%	-0.20%
0.80%	99.80%	0.03%	0.07%	10.60%	11.00%	0.10%
0.40%	99.92%	0.03%	0.07%	10.90%	10.90%	-0.20%
2.80%	96.67%	0.04%	0.06%	10.70%	10.70%	-1.00%

Table 14: US: Mid-Cap ETFs vs. Various Indices

ETF	Index	No. of Names in ETF	No. of Names in Index
iShares Russell Mid-Cap[IWR]	Russell MidCap	792	792
iShares S&P MidCap 400 [IJH]	S&P MidCap 400	400	400
Standard & Poors MidCap 400 Depositary Receipts [MDY]	S&P MidCap 400	400	400
Vanguard Mid-Cap [VO]	S&P MidCap 400	452	400

Table 15: US: Small-Cap ETFs vs. Various Indices

ETF	Index	No. of Names in ETF	No. of Names in Index
iShares Russell 2000 [IWM]	Russell 2000	2001	2001
iShares S&P SmallCap 600[IJR]	S&P SmallCap 600	600	600
Vanguard Small-Cap [VB]	S&P SmallCap 600	1713	600

Tracking Risk	Correlation	ETF Liquidity (10 Mn)	ETF % Bid-Ask Spread	ETF Hist. Volatility	Index Hist. Volatility	Index Basket Return (21d)
0.00%	100.00%	0.06%	0.10%	12.40%	12.40%	1.50%
0.00%	100.00%	0.19%	0.12%	13.60%	13.60%	0.70%
0.00%	100.00%	0.19%	0.12%	13.60%	13.60%	0.70%
2.50%	98.47%	0.10%	0.10%	12.70%	13.60%	0.70%

Tracking Risk	Correlation	ETF Liquidity (10 Mn)	ETF % Bid-Ask Spread	ETF Hist. Volatility	Index Hist. Volatility	Index Basket Return (21d)
0.00%	100.00%	0.20%	0.22%	17.60%	17.60%	0.40%
0.00%	100.00%	0.39%	0.17%	16.90%	16.90%	0.50%
2.80%	98.61%	0.14%	0.18%	16.30%	16.90%	0.50%

Table 16: US: iShares Style ETFs vs. S&P Indices

ETF	Index	No. of Names in ETF	No. of Names in Index
iShares S&P 500/Barra Value [IVE]	S&P 500/Barra Value	333	333
iShares S&P 500/Barra Growth [IVW]	S&P 500/Barra Growth	167	167

Table 17: US: iShares Style ETFs vs. Russell Indices

ETF	Index	No. of Names in ETF	No. of Names in Index
iShares Russell 1000 Value[IWD]	Russell 1000 Value	697	697
iShares Russell 1000 Growth[IWF]	Russell 1000 Growth	620	621
iShares Russell 2000 Value[IWN]	Russell 2000 Value	1296	1296
iShares Russell 2000 Growth [IWO]	Russell 2000 Growth	1352	1352
iShares Russell MidCap Growth [IWP]	Russell MidCap Growth	483	483
iShares Russell MidCap Value [IWS]	Russell MidCap Value	562	562
iShares Russell 3000 Value [IWW]	Russell 3000 Value	1958	1993
iShares Russell 3000 Growth [IWZ]	Russell 3000 Growth	1921	1973

Tracking Risk	Correlation	ETF Liquidity (10 Mn)	ETF % Bid-Ask Spread	ETF Hist. Volatility	Index Hist. Volatility	Index Basket Return (21d)
0.00%	100.00%	0.06%	0.09%	11.20%	11.30%	-0.10%
0.00%	100.00%	0.06%	0.04%	11.20%	11.20%	0.30%

Tracking Risk	Correlation	ETF Liquidity (10 Mn)	ETF % Bid-Ask Spread	ETF Hist. Volatility	Index Hist. Volatility	Index Basket Return (21d)
0.00%	100.00%	0.05%	0.09%	10.40%	10.40%	0.20%
0.00%	100.00%	0.04%	0.05%	12.20%	12.20%	0.20%
0.00%	100.00%	0.45%	0.24%	15.80%	15.80%	0.00%
0.00%	100.00%	0.25%	0.20%	20.00%	20.00%	0.90%
0.00%	100.00%	0.09%	0.08%	14.90%	14.90%	1.90%
0.00%	100.00%	0.12%	0.11%	11.20%	11.10%	1.20%
0.00%	100.00%	0.05%	0.10%	10.70%	10.80%	0.20%
0.00%	100.00%	0.03%	0.07%	12.70%	12.70%	0.30%

Table 18: US: Select Sector SPDRs vs. S&P 500

ETF	Index	No. of Names in ETF	No. of Names in Index
Consumer DiscretionarySe-lect Sector SPDR [XLY]	S&P 500 (Consumer Dis-cretionary)	86	86
Consumer Staples Select Sec-tor SPDR [XLP]	S&P 500 (Consumer Sta-ples)	37	37
Energy Select Sector SPDR[XLE]	S&P 500 (Energy)	27	27
Financial Select SectorSPDR [XLF]	S&P 500 (Financials)	80	80
Health Care Select Sector SPDR [XLV]	S&P 500 (Health Care)	56	56
Industrials Select Sector SPDR [XLI]	S&P 500 (Industrials)	58	58
Materials Select Sector SPDR [XLB]	S&P 500 (Materials)	33	33
Technology Select Sector SPDR [XLK]	S&P 500 (Information Technology/Tele-communication Services)	90	90
Utilities Select Sector SPDR [XLU]	S&P 500 (Utilities)	33	33

Tracking Risk	Correlation	ETF Liquidity (10 Mn)	ETF % Bid-Ask Spread	ETF Hist. Volatility	Index Hist. Volatility	Index Basket Return (21d)
0.00%	100.00%	0.20%	0.07%	12.80%	12.80%	2.50%
0.90%	99.55%	0.36%	0.07%	9.10%	9.20%	0.80%
2.90%	98.69%	0.37%	0.08%	16.70%	15.60%	-3.10%
0.00%	100.00%	0.15%	0.08%	11.90%	11.90%	-0.30%
0.10%	99.99%	0.21%	0.07%	12.70%	12.70%	-1.90%
1.10%	99.60%	0.28%	0.07%	12.40%	12.40%	0.40%
0.30%	99.99%	0.71%	0.09%	16.90%	16.80%	-2.10%
0.30%	99.99%	0.09%	0.02%	17.60%	17.40%	0.80%
0.00%	100.00%	0.86%	0.11%	10.70%	10.70%	3.40%

Table 19: US: Select Sector SPDRs vs. MSCI US

ETF	Index	No. of Names in ETF	No. of Names in Index
Consumer Discretionary Select Sector SPDR [XLY]	MSCI US (Consumer Discretionary)	86	99
Consumer Staples Select Sector SPDR [XLP]	MSCI US (Consumer Staples)	37	33
Energy Select Sector SPDR[XLE]	MSCI US (Energy)	27	30
Financial Select Sector SPDR [XLF]	MSCI US (Financials)	80	101
Health Care Select Sector SPDR [XLV]	MSCI US (Health Care)	56	53
Industrials Select Sector SPDR [XLI]	MSCI US (Industrials)	58	55
Materials Select Sector SPDR [XLB]	MSCI US (Materials)	33	26
Technology Select Sector SPDR [XLK]	MSCI US (Information-Technology/Tele-communication Services)	90	91
Utilities Select Sector SPDR[XLU]	MSCI US (Utilities)	33	30

Tracking Risk	Correlation	ETF Liquidity (10 Mn)	ETF % Bid-Ask Spread	ETF Hist. Volatility	Index Hist. Volatility	Index Basket Return (21d)
2.90%	97.49%	0.20%	0.07%	12.80%	12.90%	0.10%
1.50%	98.66%	0.36%	0.07%	9.10%	9.20%	0.70%
2.80%	98.77%	0.37%	0.08%	16.70%	15.60%	-3.10%
0.70%	99.85%	0.15%	0.08%	11.90%	11.60%	-0.20%
1.00%	99.72%	0.21%	0.07%	12.70%	12.80%	-1.60%
1.50%	99.26%	0.28%	0.07%	12.40%	12.50%	0.30%
0.70%	99.91%	0.71%	0.09%	16.90%	16.80%	-2.10%
0.70%	99.93%	0.09%	0.02%	17.60%	17.70%	0.60%
0.70%	99.81%	0.86%	0.11%	10.70%	10.50%	3.50%

Table 20: US: Select Sector SPDRs vs. FTSE USA

ETF	Index	No. of Names in ETF	No. of Names in Index
Consumer Discretionary Select Sector SPDR [XLY]	FTSE USA (Cyclical Consumer Goods/Cyclical Services)	86	143
Consumer Staples Select Sector SPDR [XLP]	FTSE USA (Non-Cyclical Consumer Goods/Non-Cyclical Services)	37	127
Energy Select Sector SPDR [XLE]	FTSE USA (Resources)	27	35
Financial Select Sector SPDR [XLF]	FTSE USA (Financials)	80	127
Health Care Select Sector SPDR [XLV]	FTSE USA (Pharmaceuticals)	56	26
Industrials Select Sector SPDR [XLI]	FTSE USA (General Industrials)	58	47
Materials Select Sector SPDR [XLB]	FTSE USA (Chemcals/ Construction & Materials)	33	28
Technology Select Sector SPDR [XLK]	FTSE USA (Information Technology)	90	76
Utilities Select Sector SPDR [XLU]	FTSE USA (Utilities)	33	40

Tracking Risk	Correlation	ETF Liquidity (10 Mn)	ETF % Bid-Ask Spread	ETF Hist. Volatility	Index Hist. Volatility	Index Basket Return (21d)
3.10%	97.18%	0.20%	0.07%	12.80%	11.90%	0.10%
6.50%	77.62%	0.36%	0.07%	9.10%	10.20%	-1.00%
2.50%	99.04%	0.37%	0.08%	16.70%	15.80%	-3.30%
0.90%	99.79%	0.15%	0.08%	11.90%	11.40%	-0.20%
4.10%	95.58%	0.21%	0.07%	12.70%	13.90%	-2.50%
2.70%	98.08%	0.28%	0.07%	12.40%	13.30%	0.00%
6.50%	92.52%	0.71%	0.09%	16.90%	14.30%	0.10%
2.80%	99.28%	0.09%	0.02%	17.60%	19.30%	1.80%
1.10%	99.44%	0.86%	0.11%	10.70%	10.40%	3.20%

Table 21: US: iShares Dow Jones US Sector ETFs vs. Dow Jones US Sector

ETF	Index	No. of Names in ETF	No. of Names in Index
iShares DJ US Consumer Cyclical Sector [IYC]	DJ US Consumer Cyclical Sector	294	294
iShares DJ US Consumer Non-cyclical Sector [IYK]	DJ US Consumer Noncyclical Sector	99	99
iShares DJ US Energy Sector [IYE]	DJ US Energy Sector	57	81
iShares DJ US Financial Sector [IYF]	DJ US Financial Sector	295	295
iShares DJ US Healthcare Sector [IYH]	DJ US Healthcare Sector	172	172
iShares DJ US Industrial Sector [IYJ]	DJ US Industrial Sector	248	258
iShares DJ US Technology Sector [IYW]	DJ US Technology Sector	251	251
iShares DJ US Basic Materials Sector [IYM]	DJ US Basic Materials Sector	69	69
iShares DJ US TelecomSector [IYZ]	DJ US Telecom Sector	23	21
iShares DJ US Utilities Sector [IDU]	DJ US Utilities Sector	77	77

Tracking Risk	Correlation	ETF Liquidity (10 Mn)	ETF % Bid-Ask Spread	ETF Hist. Volatility	Index Hist. Volatility	Index Basket Return (21d)
0.00%	100.00%	0.13%	0.09%	12.40%	12.40%	0.30%
0.00%	100.00%	0.32%	0.07%	9.70%	9.70%	0.70%
1.30%	99.69%	0.44%	0.08%	16.50%	16.20%	-3.40%
0.00%	100.00%	0.12%	0.09%	11.60%	11.60%	0.20%
0.00%	100.00%	0.18%	0.08%	12.90%	12.90%	-1.80%
0.10%	99.99%	0.23%	0.08%	12.90%	12.90%	0.50%
0.00%	100.00%	0.08%	0.02%	20.30%	20.30%	1.60%
0.00%	100.00%	0.62%	0.11%	17.30%	17.30%	-2.90%
3.20%	97.89%	1.59%	0.10%	13.20%	14.70%	-2.10%
0.00%	100.00%	0.72%	0.13%	10.40%	10.40%	3.10%

Table 22: US: iShares Dow Jones US Sector ETFs vs. MSCI US

ETF	Index	No. of Names in ETF	No. of Names in Index
iShares DJ US Consumer Cyclical Sector [IYC]	MSCI US (Consumer Discretionary)	294	99
iShares DJ US Consumer-Non-cyclical Sector [IYK]	MSCI US (Consumer Staples)	99	33
iShares DJ US Energy Sector [IYE]	MSCI US (Energy)	57	30
iShares DJ US Financial Sector [IYF]	DJ US Financial Sector	295	295
iShares DJ US Healthcare Sector [IYH]	DJ US Healthcare Sector	172	172
iShares DJ US Industrial Sector [IYJ]	DJ US Industrial Sector	248	258
iShares DJ US Technology Sector [IYW]	DJ US Technology Sector	251	251
iShares DJ US Basic Materials Sector [IYM]	DJ US Basic MaterialsSector	69	69
iShares DJ US Telecom Sector [IYZ]	DJ US Telecom Sector	23	21
iShares DJ US Utilities Sector [IDU]	DJ US Utilities Sector	77	77

Tracking Risk	Correlation	ETF Liquidity (10 Mn)	ETF % Bid-Ask Spread	ETF Hist. Volatility	Index Hist. Volatility	Index Basket Return (21d)
2.00%	98.76%	0.13%	0.09%	12.40%	12.90%	0.10%
3.50%	93.23%	0.32%	0.07%	9.70%	9.20%	0.70%
2.20%	99.18%	0.44%	0.08%	16.50%	15.60%	-3.10%
0.90%	99.70%	0.12%	0.09%	11.60%	11.60%	0.20%
1.80%	99.07%	0.18%	0.08%	12.90%	12.80%	1.60%
2.30%	98.39%	0.23%	0.08%	12.90%	12.50%	0.30%
1.70%	99.76%	0.08%	0.02%	20.30%	19.30%	1.30%
1.60%	99.59%	0.62%	0.11%	17.30%	16.80%	2.10%
5.10%	94.97%	1.59%	0.10%	13.20%	15.60%	2.90%
1.30%	99.22%	0.72%	0.13%	10.40%	10.50%	3.50%

Table 23: US: iShares Dow Jones US Sector ETFs vs. S&P 500

ETF	Index	No. of Names in ETF	No. of Names in Index
iShares DJ US Consumer Cyclical Sector [IYC]	S&P 500 (Consumer Discretionary)	294	86
iShares DJ US Consumer-Non-cyclical Sector [IYK]	S&P 500 (Consumer Staples)	99	37
iShares DJ US Energy Sector [IYE]	S&P 500 (Energy)	57	27
iShares DJ US Financial Sector [IYF]	S&P 500 (Financials)	295	80
iShares DJ US Healthcare Sector [IYH]	S&P 500 (Health Care)	172	56
iShares DJ US Industrial Sector [IYJ]	S&P 500 (Industrials)	248	58
iShares DJ US Technology Sector [IYW]	S&P 500 (Information-Technology)	251	80
iShares DJ US Basic Materials Sector [IYM]	S&P 500 (Materials)	69	33
iShares DJ US Telecom Sector [IYZ]	S&P 500 (Telecommunication Services)	23	10
iShares DJ US Utilities Sector [IDU]	S&P 500 (Utilities)	77	33

Tracking Risk	Correlation	ETF Liquidity (10 Mn)	ETF % Bid-Ask Spread	ETF Hist. Volatility	Index Hist. Volatility	Index Basket Return (21d)
3.20%	96.92%	0.13%	0.09%	12.40%	12.80%	2.50%
4.00%	91.03%	0.32%	0.07%	9.70%	9.20%	0.80%
2.40%	99.02%	0.44%	0.08%	16.50%	15.60%	3.10%
1.40%	99.36%	0.12%	0.09%	11.60%	11.90%	0.30%
1.80%	99.62%	0.18%	0.08%	12.90%	12.70%	1.90%
2.20%	98.51%	0.23%	0.08%	12.90%	12.40%	0.40%
2.00%	99.67%	0.08%	0.02%	20.30%	19.10%	1.40%
1.40%	99.70%	0.62%	0.11%	17.30%	16.80%	2.10%
3.80%	97.00%	1.59%	0.10%	13.20%	14.90%	2.00%
1.20%	99.41%	0.72%	0.13%	10.40%	10.70%	3.40%

Table 24: iShares Goldman Sachs Sectors vs. Goldman Sachs Indices

ETF	Index	No. of Names in ETF	No. of Names in Index
iShares Goldman Sachs Natural Resources [IGE]	Goldman Sachs Natural Resources	120	120
iShares Goldman Sachs Networking [IGN]	Goldman Sachs Networking	33	33
iShares Goldman Sachs Semiconductor [IGW]	Goldman Sachs Semiconductor	52	52
iShares Goldman Sachs Software [IGV]	Goldman Sachs Software	46	46
iShares Goldman Sachs Tech [IGM]	Goldman Sachs Tech	226	226

Tracking Risk	Correlation	ETF Liquidity (10 Mn)	ETF % Bid-Ask Spread	ETF Hist. Volatility	Index Hist. Volatility	Index Basket Return (21d)
0.00%	100.00%	0.42%	0.10%	16.10%	16.10%	-2.90%
2.10%	99.79%	0.62%	0.10%	31.30%	31.70%	-0.30%
0.00%	100.00%	0.33%	0.06%	30.80%	30.80%	-0.80%
0.00%	100.00%	0.39%	0.00%	21.70%	21.70%	4.70%
0.00%	100.00%	0.07%	0.02%	20.40%	20.40%	1.50%

Table 25: US: Vanguard Sector VIPERS vs. MSCI Investable Market Sector Indices

ETF	Index	No. of Names in ETF	No. of Names in Index
Vanguard Consumer Discretionary [VCR]	MSCI US IMI Consumer Discretionary (Consumer Discretionary)	432	430
Vanguard Consumer Staples [VDC]	MSCI US IMI Consumer-Staples (Consumer Staples)	100	100
Vanguard Energy [VDE]	MSCI US IMI Energy (Energy)	113	113
Vanguard Financials [VFH]	MSCI US IMI Financials (Financials)	513	511
Vanguard Health Care [VHT]	MSCI US IMI Health Care (Health Care)	295	295
Vanguard Industrials [VIS]	MSCI US IMI Industrials (Industrials)	309	309
Vanguard Information Technology [VGT]	MSCI US IMI Information Technology (Information-Technology)	451	450
Vanguard Materials [VAW]	MSCI US IMI Materials (Materials)	117	115
Vanguard Telecommunication Services [VOX]	MSCI US IMI Telecommunication Services (Tele-communicationServices)	43	43
Vanguard Utilities [VPU]	MSCI US IMI Utilities (Utilities)	91	91

Tracking Risk	Correlation	ETF Liquidity (10 Mn)	ETF % Bid-Ask Spread	ETF Hist. Volatility	Index Hist. Volatility	Index Basket Return (21d)
0.00%	100.00%	0.13%	0.09%	13.10%	13.10%	2.60%
0.60%	99.79%	0..33%	0.08%	9.10%	9.10%	0.90%
1.75%	99.46%	0.33%	0.10%	17.20%	16.30%	-3.50%
0.00%	100.00%	0.12%	0.10%	11.50%	11.50%	0.20%
0.00%	100.00%	0.16%	0.08%	13.00%	13.00%	-1.60%
1.00%	99.72%	0.23%	0.10%	12.80%	12.70%	0.50%
0.00%	100.00%	0.07%	0.03%	20.10%	20.10%	1.20%
0.10%	100.00%	0.52%	0.11%	17.00%	17.00%	-2.10%
7.00%	90.12%	3.22%	0.18%	16.00%	14.60%	-1.80%
0.00%	100.00%	0.72%	0.13%	10.40%	10.40%	3.00%

Table 26: US: Vanguard Sector VIPERS vs. MSCI US Sector Indices

ETF	Index	No. of Names in ETF	No. of Names in Index
Vanguard Consumer Discretionary [VCR]	MSCI US Consumer Discretionary (Consumer Discretionary)	432	99
Vanguard Consumer Staples [VDC]	MSCI US Consumer Staples (Consumer Staples)	100	33
Vanguard Energy [VDE]	MSCI US Energy (Energy)	113	30
Vanguard Financials [VFH]	MSCI US Financials (Financials)	513	101
Vanguard Health Care [VHT]	MSCI US Health Care (Health Care)	295	53
Vanguard Industrials [VIS]	MSCI US Industrials (Industrials)	309	55
Vanguard Information Technology [VGT]	MSCI US Information Technology (Information Technology)	451	83
Vanguard Materials [VAW]	MSCI US Materials (Materials)	117	26
Vanguard Telecommunication Services [VOX]	MSCI US Telecommunication Services (Telecommunication Services)	43	8
Vanguard Utilities [VPU]	MSCI US Utilities (Utilities)	91	30

Tracking Risk	Correlation	ETF Liquidity (10 Mn)	ETF % Bid-Ask Spread	ETF Hist. Volatility	Index Hist. Volatility	Index Basket Return (21d)
2.90%	97.58%	0.13%	0.09%	13.10%	12.90%	0.10%
1.10%	99.22%	0.33%	0.08%	9.10%	9.20%	0.70%
3.40%	98.31%	0.33%	0.10%	17.20%	15.60%	-3.10%
1.10%	99.53%	0.12%	0.10%	11.50%	11.60%	-0.20%
1.90%	98.88%	0.16%	0.08%	13.00%	12.80%	-1.60%
2.50%	98.05%	0.23%	0.10%	12.80%	12.50%	0.30%
1.80%	99.65%	0.07%	0.03%	20.10%	19.30%	1.30%
2.00%	99.32%	0.52%	0.11%	17.00%	16.80%	-2.10%
8.90%	84.31%	3.22%	0.18%	16.00%	15.60%	-2.90%
1.50%	98.99%	0.72%	0.13%	10.40%	10.50%	3.50%

Table 27: Sector ETFs vs. Various Indices

ETF	Index	No. of Names in ETF	No. of Names in Index
iShares Nasdaq Biotechnology [IBB]	Nasdaq Biotechnology	139	151
Fresco DJ Industrial Average FDUSIA]	Dow Jones Industrial Average	30	30
Fresco DJ US Technology [FDUSTC]	Dow Jones US Technology	32	151
IndEXchange Dow Jones Industrial Average [EX INDUST]	Dow Jones Industrial Average	30	30
DJIA Master Unit [DJE]	Dow Jones Industrial Average	30	30
iShares Nasdaq Biotechnology [IBB]	Nasdaq Biotechnology	139	151

Table 28: International / Country Specific: iShares ETFs vs. MSCI Indices

ETF	Index	No. of Names in ETF	No. of Names in Index
iShares MSCI Australia [EWA]	MSCI Australia	70	72
iShares MSCI Austria [EWO]	MSCI Austria	18	13
iShares MSCI Belgium [EWK]	MSCI Belgium	21	20
iShares MSCI Brazil [EWZ]	MSCI Brazil	37	38
iShares MSCI Canada [EWC]	MSCI Canada	85	90

Tracking Risk	Correlation	ETF Liquidity (10 Mn)	ETF % Bid-Ask Spread	ETF Hist. Volatility	Index Hist. Volatility	Index Basket Return (21d)
0.90%	99.94%	0.70%	0.06%	22.90%	22.50%	-2.60%
0.00%	100.00%	0.15%	0.07%	10.70%	10.70%	-1.00%
2.80%	99.92%	0.11	0.00	18.90%	20.30%	1.60%
0.00%	100.00%	0.11	0.00	10.70%	10.70%	-1.00%
0.00%	100.00%	0.15	0.07	10.70%	10.70%	-1.00%
0.90%	99.94%	0.70	0.06	22.90%	22.50%	-2.60%

Tracking Risk	Correlation	ETF Liquidity (10 Mn)	ETF % Bid-Ask Spread	ETF Hist. Volatility	Index Hist. Volatility	Index Basket Return (21d)
2.30%	98.75%	0.68%	0.35%	14.50%	14.60%	8.00%
1.90%	99.37%	22.78%	0.38%	16.00%	16.50%	5.90%
0.70%	99.88%	4.97%	0.22%	13.90%	14.10%	6.70%
1.20%	99.94%	0.02%	1.35%	34.30%	34.20%	1.90%
0.50%	99.94%	0.79%	0.25%	15.20%	15.20%	3.70%

Table 28 (continued)

ETF	Index	No. of Names in ETF	No. of Names in Index
iShares MSCI France [EWQ]	MSCI France	57	57
iShares MSCI Germany [EWG	MSCI Germany	45	47
iShares MSCI Hong Kong [EWH]	MSCI Hong Kong	37	37
iShares MSCI Italy [EWI]	MSCI Italy	41	41
iShares MSCI Japan [EWJ]	MSCI Japan	281	344
iShares MSCI Mexico [EWW]	MSCI Malaysia (Free)	70	70
iShares MSCI Malaysia (Free) [EWM]	MSCI Mexico	27	23
iShares MSCI Netherlands [EWN]	MSCI Netherlands	25	26
iShares MSCI Singapore [EWS]	MSCI Singapore	35	35
iShares MSCI South Africa [EZA]	MSCI South Africa	43	44
iShares MSCI South Korea [EWY]	MSCI South Korea	61	67
iShares MSCI Spain [EWP]	MSCI Spain	37	31
iShares MSCI Sweden EWD]	MSCI Sweden	44	44
iShares MSCI Switzerland [EWL]	MSCI Switzerland	36	35
iShares MSCI Taiwan [EWT]	MSCI Taiwan	97	100
iShares MSCI United Kingdom [EWU]	MSCI United Kingdom	150	151

Tracking Risk	Correlation	ETF Liquidity (10 Mn)	ETF % Bid-Ask Spread	ETF Hist. Volatility	Index Hist. Volatility	Index Basket Return (21d)
0.00%	100.00%	0.28%	0.11%	15.90%	15.90%	4.50%
0.70%	99.93%	0.31%	0.11%	17.50%	17.70%	4.00%
0.20%	99.99%	2.46%	0.45%	18.30%	18.30%	1.20%
0.40%	99.96%	0.49%	0.10%	14.20%	14.20%	6.70%
0.30%	99.99%	0.19%	0.34%	21.00%	21.00%	0.40%
0.00%	100.00%	20.92%	0.83%	12.00%	12.00%	1.90%
1.80%	99.52%	8.53%	0.52%	17.60%	18.10%	5.40%
1.30%	99.67%	0.61%	0.10%	15.30%	15.50%	3.70%
0.90%	99.84%	7.53%	0.68%	15.00%	15.20%	1.50%
1.40%	99.92%	3.06%	0.52%	33.80%	33.60%	7.10%
2.90%	99.49%	1.28%	0.26%	28.90%	28.40%	-0.50%
1.00%	99.87%	0.86%	0.14%	15.80%	16.30%	7.50%
0.00%	100.00%	0.75%	0.36%	19.90%	19.90%	3.60%
1.70%	99.39%	0.82%	0.38%	14.90%	15.20%	4.90%
0.60%	99.98%	1.39%	0.45%	26.70%	26.60%	-1.00%
0.10%	100.00%	0.11%	0.14%	12.20%	12.20%	4.10%

Table 29: International / Country Specific: iShares ETFs vs. Local Indices

ETF	Index	No. of Names in ETF	No. of Names in Index
iShares MSCI Australia [EWA]	All Ordinaries	70	481
iShares MSCI Austria [EWO]	ATX	18	20
iShares MSCI Belgium [EWK]	BEL 20	21	20
iShares MSCI Brazil [EWZ]	Bovespa	37	54
iShares MSCI Canada [EWC]	S&P/TSX 60	85	60
Shares MSCI France [EWQ]	CAC 40	57	40
Shares MSCI Germany [EWG]	DAX	45	30
iShares MSCI Hong Kong [EWH]	Hang Seng	37	33
iShares MSCI Italy [EWI]	MIB 30	41	30
iShares MSCI Japan [EWJ]	Nikkei 225	281	225
iShares MSCI Malaysia (Free) [EWM]	KLSE Composite	70	100
iShares MSCI Mexico [EWW]	Mexico IPC	27	33
iShares MSCI Netherlands [EWN]	AEX	25	24

Tracking Risk	Correlation	ETF Liquidity (10 Mn)	ETF % Bid-Ask Spread	ETF Hist. Volatility	Index Hist. Volatility	Index Basket Return (21d)
1.40%	99.54%	0.68%	0.35%	14.50%	14.10%	8.50%
1.90%	99.44%	22.78%	0.38%	16.00%	16.80%	6.30%
1.00%	99.76%	4.97%	0.22%	13.90%	14.00%	6.80%
9.90%	95.92%	0.02%	1.35%	34.30%	35.00%	-1.30%
1.70%	99.41%	0.79%	0.25%	15.20%	15.40%	4.00%
0.90%	99.86%	0.28%	0.11%	15.90%	16.10%	4.50%
1.20%	99.80%	0.31%	0.11%	17.50%	17.90%	4.10%
6.00%	94.52%	2.46%	0.45%	18.30%	16.60%	1.20%
1.30%	99.61%	0.49%	0.10%	14.20%	14.30%	6.60%
4.70%	98.07%	0.19%	0.34%	21.00%	23.00%	0.20%
2.80%	97.34%	20.92%	0.83%	12.00%	11.50%	2.10%
2.80%	98.81%	8.53%	0.52%	17.60%	18.10%	4.80%
2.80%	98.67%	0.61%	0.10%	15.30%	16.40%	3.90%

Table 29 (continued)

ETF	Index	No. of Names in ETF	No. of Names in Index
iShares MSCI Singapore [EWS]	Straits Times	35	45
iShares MSCI South Africa [EZA]	MSCI South Africa	43	44
iShares MSCI South Korea [EWY]	KOSPI 200	61	200
iShares MSCI Spain [EWP]	IBEX	37	35
iShares MSCI Sweden [EWD]	OMX	44	30
iShares MSCI Switzerland [EWL]	SMI	36	27
iShares MSCI Taiwan [EWT]	Taiwan Weighted	97	652
iShares MSCI United Kingdom [EWU]	FTSE 100	150	102

Table 30: Australia: Australian ETFs vs. Various Indices

ETF	Index	No. of Names in ETF	No. of Names in Index
streetTRACKS S&P / ASX 200 [AUSTW]	S&P / ASX 200	200	198
streetTRACKS S&P/ASX 50 [AUSFY]	S&P / ASX 50	50	48

Tracking Risk	Correlation	ETF Liquidity (10 Mn)	ETF % Bid-Ask Spread	ETF Hist. Volatility	Index Hist. Volatility	Index Basket Return (21d)
2.20%	98.97%	7.53%	0.68%	15.00%	14.60%	1.70%
1.40%	99.92%	3.06%	0.52%	33.80%	33.60%	7.10%
4.30%	99.11%	1.28%	0.26%	28.90%	26.70%	0.90%
0.80%	99.89%	0.86%	0.14%	15.80%	16.00%	6.90%
2.80%	99.14%	0.75%	0.36%	19.90%	18.80%	4.40%
1.90%	99.26%	0.82%	0.38%	14.90%	15.30%	4.90%
3.70%	99.22%	1.39%	0.45%	26.70%	24.90%	-1.60%
0.70%	99.84%	0.11%	0.14%	12.20%	12.40%	4.10%

Tracking Risk	Correlation	ETF Liquidity (10 Mn)	ETF % Bid-Ask Spread	ETF Hist. Volatility	Index Hist. Volatility	Index Basket Return (21d)
1.00%	99.77%	0.51%	0.39%	14.30%	14.30%	8.50%
1.20%	99.66%	0.63%	0.32%	14.50%	14.50%	8.00%

Table 31: Hong Kong: Hong Kong ETFs vs. Various Indices

ETF	Index	No. of Names in ETF	No. of Names in Index
Tracker Fund of Hong Kong (TraHK) [2800]	MSCI Hong Kong	32	37
iShares MSCI China Tracker [2801]	Hang Seng Mainland	45	94
iShares MSCI China Tracker [2801]	MSCI China	45	60

Table 32: Asia: Coutry Specific vs. Various Indices

ETF	Index	No. of Names in ETF	No. of Names in Index
streetTRACKS STRAITS TIMES [EWS]	STRAITS TIMES	35	45
streetTRACKS STRAITS TIMES [EWS]	MSCI Singapore	35	35
Polaris Taiwan 50 [0050]	MSCI Taiwan	50	100

Table 33: Global: iShares S&P Global Sector ETFs vs. S&P 1200

ETF	Index	No. of Names in ETF	No. of Names in Index
iShares S&P Global Energy [IXC]	S&P Global 1200 (Energy)	53	58
iShares S&P Global Financial [IXG]	S&P Global 1200 (Financials)	214	226
iShares S&P Global Healthcare [IXJ]	S&P Global 1200 (Health Care)	82	84
iShares S&P Global Technology [IXN]	S&P Global 1200 (Information Technology)	122	128
iShares S&P Global Tele-communications [IXP]	S&P Global 1200 (Tele-communication Services)	41	42

Tracking Risk	Correlation	ETF Liquidity (10 Mn)	ETF % Bid-Ask Spread	ETF Hist. Volatility	Index Hist. Volatility	Index Basket Return (21d)
5.70%	95.15%	1.64%	0.41%	16.30%	18.30%	1.20%
5.60%	98.02%	2.49%	0.65%	27.30%	25.10%	-0.80%
0.80%	99.97%	2.49%	0.65%	27.30%	26.80%	-1.60%

Tracking Risk	Correlation	ETF Liquidity (10 Mn)	ETF % Bid-Ask Spread	ETF Hist. Volatility	Index Hist. Volatility	Index Basket Return (21d)
2.20%	98.97%	7.53%	0.68%	15.00%	14.60%	1.70%
0.90%	99.84%	7.53%	0.68%	15.00%	15.20%	1.50%
1.80%	99.78%	1.64%	0.45%	26.30%	26.60%	-1.00%

Tracking Risk	Correlation	ETF Liquidity (10 Mn)	ETF % Bid-Ask Spread	ETF Hist. Volatility	Index Hist. Volatility	Index Basket Return (21d)
0.70%	99.89%	0.40%	0.10%	13.40%	13.10%	-0.80%
0.30%	99.97%	0.09%	0.13%	10.50%	10.50%	2.40%
0.10%	99.99%	0.15%	0.10%	10.70%	10.70%	-0.10%
1.00%	99.86%	0.10%	0.07%	17.60%	17.30%	1.70%
0.40%	99.95%	0.68%	0.17%	12.80%	12.70%	3.30%

Table 34: Global: iShares S&P Global Sector ETFs vs. S&P 1200

ETF	Index	No. of Names in ETF	No. of Names in Index
iShares S&P Global Energy [IXC]	MSCI World (Energy)	53	66
iShares S&P Global Financial [IXG]	MSCI World (Financials)	214	320
iShares S&P Global Healthcare [IXJ]	MSCI World (Health Care)	82	117
iShares S&P Global Technology [IXN]	MSCI World (Information Technology)	122	182
iShares S&P Global Telecommunications [IXP]	MSCI World (Telecommunication Services)	41	42

Table 35: Global: iShares S&P Global Sector ETFs vs. FTSE World

ETF	Index	No. of Names in ETF	No. of Names in Index
iShares S&P Global Energy [IXC]	FTSE World (Oil & Gas)	41	51
iShares S&P Global Financial [IXG]	FTSE World (Financials)	214	288
iShares S&P Global Healthcare [IXJ]	FTSE World (Pharmaceuticals)	82	49
iShares S&P Global Technology [IXN]	FTSE World (Information Technology)	122	120
iShares S&P Global Telecommunications [IXP]	FTSE World (Telecommunication Services)	41	59

Tracking Risk	Correlation	ETF Liquidity (10 Mn)	ETF % Bid-Ask Spread	ETF Hist. Volatility	Index Hist. Volatility	Index Basket Return (21d)
1.00%	99.76%	0.40%	0.10%	13.40%	13.10%	-0.80%
0.80%	99.74%	0.09%	0.13%	10.50%	10.30%	2.50%
0.70%	99.76%	0.15%	0.10%	10.70%	10.60%	0.20%
1.20%	99.78%	0.10%	0.07%	17.60%	17.20%	1.70%
1.60%	99.21%	0.68%	0.17%	12.80%	12.80%	2.90%

Tracking Risk	Correlation	ETF Liquidity (10 Mn)	ETF % Bid-Ask Spread	ETF Hist. Volatility	Index Hist. Volatility	Index Basket Return (21d)
11.80%	57.88%	0.50%	0.13%	12.40%	13.30%	0.10%
1.20%	99.40%	0.09%	0.13%	10.50%	10.30%	2.80%
3.60%	95.06%	0.15%	0.10%	10.70%	11.60%	-0.30%
1.90%	99.45%	0.10%	0.07%	17.60%	18.10%	2.40%
2.20%	98.53%	0.68%	0.17%	12.80%	12.30%	3.50%

Table 36: Global: Regional ETFs vs. Various Indices

ETF	Index	No. of Names in ETF	No. of Names in Index
streetTRACKS DJ Global Titans [DGT]	DJ Global Titans	45	50
iShares S&P Global 100 [IOO]	S&P Global 100	97	100
BLDRS Asia 50 ADR Index [ADRA]	MSCI Pacific	50	504
BLDRS Developed Markets 100 ADR Index [ADRD]	MSCI World	100	1673
BLDRS Emerging Markets 50 ADR Index [ADRE]	MSCI EMF	50	726
BLDRS Europe 100 ADR Index [ADRU]	MSCI Europe	100	563
iShares MSCI EAFE [EFA]	MSCI EAFE	781	1065
iShares MSCI EMF [EEM]	MSCI EMF	249	728
iShares MSCI EAFE [EFA]	FTSE All World ex US	781	2243
iShares MSCI Pacific ex – Japan [EPP]	MSCI Pacific ex – Japan	157	160
iShares MSCI Pacific ex – Japan [EPP]	FTSE Asia Pacific ex – Japan	157	866
iShares S&P Latin America 40 [ILF]	S&P Latin America	37	40
UNICO i-tracker MSCI World [IMSWLD]	MSCI World	292	1673
UNICO i-tracker MSCI World [IMSWLD]	FTSE World	292	1784
Dow Jones Global Titans 50 Master Unit [MGT]	Dow Jones Global Titans 50	50	50
EasyETF Global Titans 50 [SYG]	Dow Jones Global Titans 50	50	50
IndEXchange DJ Global Titans Ex [TITAN]	Dow Jones Global Titans 50	50	50

Tracking Risk	Correlation	ETF Liquidity (10 Mn)	ETF % Bid-Ask Spread	ETF Hist. Volatility	Index Hist. Volatility	Index Basket Return (21d)
3.20%	95.78%	0.27%	0.06%	10.60%	9.30%	0.60%
0.60%	99.79%	0.06%	0.09%	10.00%	9.90%	1.40%
14.60%	67.80%	20.15%	0.24%	18.50%	17.90%	1.80%
6.20%	92.07%	2.85%	0.16%	13.80%	9.70%	1.60%
8.83%	64.56%	3.43%	0.22%	20.60%	32.90%	1.90%
9.10%	77.37%	2.91%	0.16%	13.80%	13.30%	4.70%
0.20%	99.99%	0.07%	0.21%	12.90%	12.80%	3.80%
4.29%	56.08%	4.10%	0.94%	17.60%	32.90%	1.90%
1.70%	99.09%	0.07%	0.21%	12.90%	12.50%	3.60%
1.50%	99.32%	0.50%	0.41%	13.00%	13.10%	5.70%
9.90%	77.57%	0.50%	0.41%	13.00%	15.70%	2.60%
45.10%	65.45%	5.15%	0.34%	20.80%	55.90%	-9.00%
0.70%	99.73%	0.06%	0.22%	9.40%	9.70%	1.60%
1.10%	99.36%	0.06%	0.22%	9.40%	9.70%	2.00%
0.00%	100.00%	0.06%	0.07%	9.30%	9.30%	0.60%
0.00%	100.00%	0.06%	0.07%	9.30%	9.30%	0.60%
0.20%	99.98%	0.07%	0.08%	9.30%	9.30%	0.60%

Sources: Morgan Stanley Quantitative Derivative Strategies, MSCI, FTSE, Dow Jones, S&P, various local index providers, and corresponding ETF managers

Notes: All ETF and index compositions are based on actual holdings as of the date of this report. Base currency is USD. All calculations are based on daily returns of the current constituent stocks over previous year, except for the returns of indices which are measured over the last 21 days. ETF liquidity is based on bottom-up aggregations of the average traded volumes of an ETF's underlying stocks over the last 14 days. ETF % Bid-Ask Spread is based on bottom-up aggregations of the average percentage bid-ask spreads of an ETF's underlying stocks over the last 14 days. Cash components in ETFs are not included in our analysis. In some cases, when an index basket is combined by several sectors / industries (e.g. Technology Select Sector SPDR vs. MSCI IT & MSCI Telecom Services), the index is re-constituted on a (free-float adjusted) market cap weighted basis.

Appendix B: Dow Jones EURO STOXX 50SMEX Prospectus

Dow Jones EURO STOXX 50SMEX

DETAILED
SALES PROSPECTUS
including Contract Terms.

INDEXCHANGE Investment AG
January 2005

INDEXCHANGE

Names and addresses.

Investment Management Company.

INDEXCHANGE Investment AG
Apianstraße 5
85774 Unterföhring (Munich), Germany

Phone: +49 (0) 89 92694 - 8888
Fax: +49 (0) 89 92694 - 8302

E-mail: info@indexchange.com
www.indexchange.com

Munich Commercial Register B 134 527

Legal Representatives.

Götz Kirchhoff
Thomas Meyer zu Drewer

Depository bank (Paying agent and custodian).

Bayerische Hypo- und Vereinsbank AG
Am Tucherpark 16
80538 Munich, Germany
Phone: +49 (0) 89 378 - 0

Auditors.

KPMG Deutsche Treuhand-Gesellschaft
Aktiengesellschaft
Wirtschaftsprüfungsgesellschaft
Munich office
Ganghoferstr. 29
80339 Munich, Germany
Phone: +49 (0) 89 9282 – 00

Designated Sponsors.

Bayerische Hypo- und Vereinsbank AG
Equity Linked Index Group
Arabellastraße 12
81925 Munich, Germany
Phone: +49 (0) 89 378 - 14117

Lehman Brothers International (Europe)
Rathenauplatz 1
60313 Frankfurt/Main, Germany
Phone: +49 (0) 69 1530 - 7141

Archelon Deutschland GmbH
Reuterweg 16
60313 Frankfurt/Main, Germany
Phone: +49 (0) 69 7408 - 7301

Optiver V.O.F.
De Ruyterkade 112
1011 AB Amsterdam, The Netherlands
Phone: +31 (0) 20 557 – 1122

BNP Paribas Equities
20 Bd des Italiens
75009 Paris, France
Tel: +33 (0) 1 4014 – 1746

Flow Traders B.V.
Postbus 10646
1011 EP Amsterdam, The Netherlands
Tel: +31 (0) 20 799 – 6799

Timber Hill (Europe) AG
Gotthardstr. 3
6300 Zug, Switzerland
Tel: +41 (0) 41 726 - 5097

Full Prospectus including Terms and Conditions.

Wertpapierkennnummer:
(Securities Identification Number)

Dow Jones EURO STOXX 50^{SMEX} 593 395

The most recent Prospectus, the General Terms and Conditions, and Special Conditions form the basis for the purchase or sale of fund units. It is not permitted to issue information or statements differing from this Prospectus. Any purchase or sale of units based on information or statements not contained in the Prospectus is at the sole risk of the seller. This Prospectus is supplemented by the latest annual report. If the reporting date of the latest annual report is more than eight months ago, then the most recent semi-annual report must also be made available.

The contractual relationship between Investment Management Company and investor as well as the pre-contractual relationship are subject to German law.

In accordance with Section 23 Paragraph 2 of the General Terms and Conditions, if the investor has no general place of jurisdiction in Germany, the place of jurisdiction for disputes arising from the contractual relationship shall be the registered office of the Investment Management Company. According to Section 123 of the German Investment Act (InvG – *Investmentgesetz*), sales documents must be drawn up in the German language or must include a German translation.

Contents.

Prospectus.

1. General provisions.

The **Dow Jones EURO STOXX 50^{SMEX}** investment fund (hereinafter referred to as "the investment fund") is a "Directive-compliant Investment Fund" as defined by the German Investment Act (InvG). It is managed by INDEXCHANGE Investment AG (hereinafter referred to as the "Company").

The management of the investment fund consists primarily of investing funds that investors have deposited with the Company in accordance with the principle of risk diversification in various assets separated from the assets of the Company. The investment fund does not form part of the bankruptcy estate of the Investment Management Company.

The German Investment Act and the Terms and Conditions, which govern the legal relationship between the investors and the Company, stipulate in what kind of assets the Company may invest the funds and which provision it must follow in making such investments. The Terms and Conditions comprise a General and a Special part ("General Terms and Conditions" and "Special Conditions"). The use of the Terms and Conditions by an investment fund normally requires the approval of the Federal Banking Supervisory Authority (BaFin). An exception to this is the provision in the "Special Conditions" that treats the fees and reimbursement of expenses that may be charged to the investment fund. For the investment fund, this is Section 8 of the Special Conditions (for details on fees and reimbursement of expenses see "Issue and redemption prices and expenses" and "Management and miscellaneous expenses").

1.1 Sales documents.

The full Prospectus and the simplified Prospectus, the Terms and Conditions, the Articles of Association and the current annual and semi-annual reports can be obtained free of charge from INDEXCHANGE Investment AG, Apianstr. 5, 85774 Unterföhring, Germany.

Additional information on the investment limits of this investment fund, risk management methods and the latest developments concerning risks and returns of the most important categories of assets may be obtained in electronic form from the Company.

1.2 Terms and Conditions.

The Terms and Conditions are printed in this Prospectus.

The Company is entitled to change the Terms and Conditions. Amendments to these Terms and Conditions require the approval of BaFin, with the exception of rules regarding fees and reimbursement of expenses. Amendments to the investment policies of the investment fund also require the approval of the Supervisory Board of the Company.

All planned amendments shall be published in the online Federal Gazette (*Bundesanzeiger)* and on www.indexchange.com.

The amendments shall take effect no earlier than three months after their publication, provided no earlier date is determined by BaFin. Amendments to rules for fees and reimbursement of expenses shall take effect no earlier than 13 months after their publication. Amendments to the current investment policies of the investment fund also take effect no earlier than 13 months after their publication and are only permitted under the condition that the Investment Management Company offers investors the opportunity to exchange at no cost their units for units in investment funds with comparable investment policies.

2. Management Company.

2.1 Company, legal form and registered office.

The investment fund is managed by INDEXCHANGE Investment AG, whose registered office is in Unterföhring near Munich. The Company was incorporated on 23 October 2000.

INDEXCHANGE Investment AG is an Investment Management Company pursuant to the German Investment Act (InvG). Its legal form is that of a German public limited company (AG).

INDEXCHANGE Investment AG was authorised to manage securities index investment funds on 22 December 2000. After coming into conformity with the Investment Act, the Company has been authorised since 30 July 2004 to manage Directive-Compliant Security Index Investment Funds and Mixed Investment Funds (Non-Directive-Compliant Security Index Investment Funds).

2.2 Shareholders' equity, Supervisory Board and Management Board.

The share capital of the Company is 10 million Euros, fully paid up.

The shareholders' equity amounts to 11 million Euros. No payments with regard to the subscribed shares are outstanding.

The Supervisory Board comprises three members:

- Jens-Peter Neumann, Chairman,
  Member of the Corporate & Markets sector board of Bayerische Hypo- und Vereinsbank AG, Munich;
- Hans-Günther Bonk, Deputy Chairman
  Managing Director of the Corporate & Markets sector of Bayerische Hypo- und Vereinsbank AG, Munich;
- Vassilios Pappas
  Managing Director of the Corporate & Markets sector of Bayerische Hypo- und Vereinsbank AG, Munich.

The members of the Supervisory Board have unanimously appointed the following two persons as members of the Management Board:

- Götz Kirchhoff, Poing, born in 1953,
  formerly Managing Director of Allfonds Bayerische Kapitalanlagegesellschaft mbH, Munich
  (since November 1996; previously of the merged Allfonds Gesellschaft für Investmentanlagen mbH, Unterföhring)
- Thomas Meyer zu Drewer, Unterföhring,
  born in 1960,
  formerly Head of Fund Management, Equities and Bonds, at Activest Investmentgesellschaft mbH, Munich
  (since November 1999; previously under a different company name).

3. Licensor and licence agreement.

3.1 Licensor and licence agreement.

The Dow Jones EURO STOXX 50^{SM} (hereinafter referred to as the "underlying index") is a registered trademark of STOXX Ltd. and Dow Jones & Company, Inc. (hereinafter referred to as "licensor") and is thus protected against unauthorised use. The licensor grants licences for the use of its index as an underlying valuation tool for capital market products.

The Company has concluded a licence agreement with the licensor which grants the Company the right to use the index underlying the investment fund. This licence agreement has an unlimited term.

3.2 Disclaimer of liability by the licensor.

The investment fund is not sponsored, promoted, sold or distributed by the licensor.

Aside from the licensing of the underlying index and the permitted use of the trademark in connection with naming the investment fund, the licensor has no connection whatsoever with the Company.

The licensor does not guarantee the accuracy or completeness of the underlying index or other information contained therein and accepts no liability for mistakes, omissions or interruptions in the underlying index. The licensor gives no direct or indirect guarantee of the results the Company achieves through the use of the underlying index or of the other data contained therein. The licensor provides no direct or indirect guarantee and assumes no liability as regards the marketability, suitability or use for a specific purpose of the underlying index or the data contained therein.

Without any restriction to the above and in no circumstances can the licensor accept responsibility for any damages caused by or in connection with the underlying index or the investment fund it underlies. This disclaimer of liability also applies to indirect losses, special damages or consequential losses (including loss of profits) in relation to the underlying index or the investment fund it underlies, even if the licensor has been made aware of the assertion of such a claim.

No third party shall benefit from any contracts or agreements between the licensor and the Company.

4. Custodian Bank.

4.1 General.

The Investment Act requires segregation of duties between the management and the custody of the investment fund. The Investment Management Company has commissioned another credit institution as custodian of the assets of the investment fund.

The custodian bank holds the assets for unit holders in custody, separated for each fund in blocked investment accounts or in blocked accounts. Specifically, the custodian bank must ensure that the issue and redemption of units and the calculation of unit values comply with provisions of the Investment Act and the Terms and Conditions. The custodian bank must also ensure that the equivalent value for transactions undertaken for the investment fund is placed in their custody within the usual periods and that the income from the investment fund is used in accordance with the provisions of the Investment Act and the Terms and Conditions. The custodian bank must also examine whether investment in blocked accounts with another bank is consistent with the Investment Act and the Terms and Conditions. If this is the case, it is obliged to grant its approval for the investment.

The custodian bank assesses the value of the fund and the unit value in cooperation with the Company.

4.2 Company, legal form, registered office and main activities.

Bayerische Hypo- und Vereinsbank AG, with its registered office at Am Tucherpark 16, Munich, shall act as the custodian bank for the investment fund. The custodian bank is a credit institution under German law. Its main activities are deposits and securities transactions.

5. Launch date, term and investment objective of the investment fund.

5.1 Launch date and term.

The investment fund was launched on 27 December 2000 and is of unlimited duration. The investors own an equity interest in the assets of the investment fund as co-owners in proportion to the number of units held.

5.2 Investment objective.

The objective of the investment fund is to achieve the same investment performance as the underlying index. For this purpose, the Fund shall track the underlying index as closely and as completely as possible.

The Fund adopts a passive management strategy to achieve these objectives. In contrast to the active management approach, the underlying index is used as the basis for making decisions on the purchase and sale of assets and their respective weightings in the investment fund. The passive management strategy and trading units on an exchange limits management fees and transaction costs charged to the investment fund.

5.3 Achievability of investment objectives.

No assurance can be given that the investment objectives will be achieved.

One obstacle to replicating the performance of the underlying index is the fact that the underlying index is a statistical model based on certain calculation assumptions. These include that no transaction costs will be incurred when securities are purchased or sold. In addition, management fees and some tax payments are deducted from the fund unit prices, whereas they are ignored completely in the underlying index.

Detailed information about the underlying index may be obtained in printed or electronic form from the Company or from the licensor.

6. Investment principles.

6.1 General.

The Company may only purchase assets for the investment fund that are oriented towards replicating the underlying index, while maintaining an appropriate risk diversification. The underlying index has been recognised by the German Federal Banking Supervisory Authority and meets the following requirements of the Investment Act:

- The composition of the index is sufficiently diversified.
- The index represents an adequate benchmark for the market to which it relates.
- The index has been published in an appropriate manner.

Details of the composition of the underlying index at the end or middle of the respective financial year are also presented in the most recent annual report or semi-annual report for the investment fund.

Because of the relationship between this investment fund and its underlying index and because certain issuer and investment limits may be exceeded as a result, the principle of risk diversification finds only limited application.

6.2 Effects of index adjustments.

In order to replicate the underlying index as closely as possible, fund management must make all changes in the composition and weighting of the underlying index for the investment fund.

At its discretion, fund management may assess when the investment fund should be adjusted and whether an adjustment is appropriate in consideration of the investment objective.

6.3 Replication of the index and priority of direct duplication.

To replicate the underlying index, only the following assets may be acquired:

- Securities included in the security index or introduced to it following a change to the index (index securities),
- Securities issued on the underlying index (index certificates),
- Futures contacts on the underlying index (index futures), and
- Investment fund units pursuant to Section 8 of the "General Terms and Conditions".

In replicating the underlying index, within the meaning of a direct duplication of the index, priority is to be given to investments in index securities over investments in other assets listed above approved for use in replicating indices. The underlying index may only be replicated using assets that indirectly replicate the index for purposes of maintaining the investment restrictions listed in the second sentence under point 8.2.

6.4 Duplication percentage.

In order to replicate the underlying index, the duplication percentage must not be less than 95% of the total assets in the investment fund as defined in Point 6.3. Index futures shall be included in the calculation of the duplication percentage with their weighted market risk in accordance with the simple approach in accordance with the statutory instrument on risk management and risk measurement in the investment fund (hereinafter referred to as "DerivateV") issued pursuant to Section 51 Paragraph 1 InvG. The duplication percentage reflects the proportion of the above-named securities, certificates, futures contracts and investment units in the investment fund which matches the weighting of the underlying index.

7. Investment instruments in detail.

7.1 Securities.

The Company may acquire, on behalf of the investment fund, securities of domestic and foreign issuers,

1. if they are admitted for official trading on a stock exchange in a member state of the European Union or in another state abiding by the agreement concerning the European Economic Area, or which are included on another regulated market in a member state of the European Union or in another state abiding by the agreement concerning the European Economic Area;
2. if they are approved for trading on a stock exchange specified in the appendix to the Special Conditions of this Fund or on a regulated market in the same countries.

New issues of securities may be acquired if admission for official trading on one of the aforementioned stock exchanges or regulated markets must be applied for in accordance with their issue conditions, and the admission or inclusion will take place within a year after their issue.

7.2 Bank accounts.

The Company may also hold, on behalf of the investment fund, bank accounts with a maturity not exceeding twelve months. These accounts, which must be in the form of blocked accounts, must be maintained at a financial institution which has its registered office in a member state of the European Union or in a country abiding by the agreement concerning the European Economic Area.

7.3 Futures contracts on the underlying index.

7.3.1 General.

The Company may only acquire on behalf of the investment fund futures contracts as defined in Point 6.3. No transactions for the investment fund may be made for purposes of hedging. The Company shall use index futures for purposes of efficient replication of the underlying index, when and to the extent that it is contractually permissible and in the interests of the investors.

7.3.2 Limitation of market risk.

Index futures are subject to the market risk associated with the unfavourable development of market prices for the investment fund. In calculating the potential market risk arising from the acquisition of index futures, the Company uses the simple approach as defined in the Derivative Regulation (DerivateV – *Derivateverordnung*). Through the use of index futures, the potential market risk of the investment fund could double.

7.3.3 Over-the-counter (OTC) transactions.

The Company may purchase index futures on an exchange, on another organised market or over the counter as a so-called OTC transaction. OTC transactions may only be undertaken with suitable banks and financial institutions on the basis of standard general contracts. For index futures purchased other than on a stock exchange, the counterparty risk of a contract party is limited to 5% of the value of the investment fund. If the contract party is a financial institution which has its registered office in the European Union, the European Economic Area or a state that is not a member of either of those organisations with comparable levels of governmental supervision, the counterparty risk may total 10% of the value of the investment fund. Index futures purchased other than on a stock exchange where the contract partner is the central clearinghouse of a stock exchange or another organised market are not calculated in the counterparty limits if the index futures are valued daily at market prices with a daily margin settlement.

8. Issuer limits and investment restrictions.

8.1 Issuer limits.

The Company must comply with the limitations and restrictions specified in the Investment Act and in the Terms and Conditions while managing assets.

The Company may invest up to 20% of the assets of the investment fund in securities from a single issuer (debtor). This limit may be increased to up to 35% of the value of the investment fund for securities from a single issuer. An investment up to this limit is permissible only for one individual issuer (debtor).

For assets based on an underlying index, the market price of the index securities shall be attributed to the respective issuer limits on a pro rata basis. Index futures shall be attributed to the issuer limits in accordance with Sections 18 and 20 DerivateV.

8.2 Investment restrictions.

The Company may invest no more than 5% in bank accounts in accordance with the General Terms and Conditions. A minimum of 95% of the investment fund must be invested in assets as defined in Point 6.3 on the security index.

The Company may invest no more than 10% of the assets of the investment fund in:

- Securities which are not admitted to official trading on a stock exchange or are not listed on an organised market;

- New issues of securities whose planned admission has not yet taken place.

9. Securities loans.

Assets available in the investment fund may be loaned at market rates to third parties. If the securities are transferred to a third party for an unlimited period, the Company may give notice to terminate the loan at any time. It must be agreed contractually that assets of the same type, value, and volume should be returned to the investment fund at the end of the loan period. It is required for an asset transfer loan that sufficient collateral be granted to the investment fund. Cash balances can be assigned or pledged or securities can be assigned or pledged to satisfy this requirement. The investment fund is entitled to the income from the collateral.

The borrower is also obliged to pay the interest accrued on the borrowed securities upon maturity of the loan to the custodian bank for account of the investment fund. If securities are lent for a fixed period, such lending is limited to 15% of the value of the investment fund. The securities transferred to one borrower may not exceed 10% of the value of the investment fund.

The Investment Management Company may not grant cash loans to third parties for account of the investment fund.

10. Borrowing.

On behalf of all the investors, the Company may subscribe to short-term loans for amounts of up to 10% of the investment fund, if the terms of the loan are at market rates and subject to approval of the conditions of the loan by the custodian bank.

11. Valuation.

11.1 General regulations for asset valuation.

Assets listed on stock exchanges or included on another organised market and subscription rights are valued at their respective market values unless otherwise indicated under "Special valuation rules".

Assets not listed on stock exchanges or included on another organised market or for which no tradable value is available are valued at current market values, which shall be assessed with due care using appropriate valuation models and taking into consideration current market conditions, unless otherwise indicated under "Special valuation rules".

11.2 Special valuation rules for bank accounts, time deposits, investment units and loans.

As a rule, bank accounts are stated at face value.

Time deposits are valued at the yield price if the time deposit can be terminated at any time and repayment upon termination is at the yield price.

Investment units are valued at redemption price.

The market price of the loaned securities shall be applied to value repayment claims arising from securities loans.

Assets denominated in foreign currencies shall be converted to Euros based on the Reuters AG afternoon fix for the currency.

12. Performance.

The graphic shows the performance of the underlying index over the last 10 years. The performance of the investment fund is indicated from the launch date.

Past performance of the investment fund is not a predictor of future results.

Source: Bloomberg/INDEXCHANGE

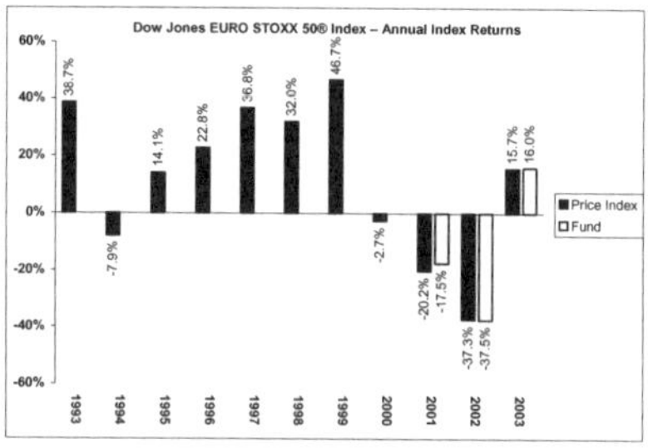

13. Risk disclaimer.

13.1 General.

The assets in which the Investment Management Company invests for account of the investment fund contain both opportunities for growth and risks. Losses may be incurred if the market value of the assets decreases in relation to the purchase price. If the investor sells units in the investment fund at a point in time at which the value of the assets owned by the investment fund has decreased in relation to the purchase price, he will not receive all of the money he invested in the investment fund. Although each investment fund seeks steady growth, this cannot be guaranteed. However, investor risk is limited to the amount invested. The investor will not be required to make any payments beyond the sum invested.

13.2 Risk of loss.

If the underlying index decreases in value, the unit holder is fully exposed to the risk of falling market prices of his fund units. The Company will not use hedging transactions to limit losses (no active management).

13.3 Risk of deviation.

Temporary unavailability of certain equities on the market or other exceptional circumstances may lead to a deviation from the exact index weighting. As a result, the investment fund would not be able to completely replicate the performance of the underlying index.

13.4 Concentration risk.

The underlying index of the investment fund concentrates investments on a particular regional market. This makes the investment fund exclusively dependent on the performance of this regional market and not on the overall market.

13.5 Market risk.

The price or market value performance of financial products is especially dependent on the performance of the capital markets, which in turn are influenced by the general state of the global economy and by the economic and political conditions in the respective countries. Irrational factors such as sentiment, opinions and rumours have an effect on general price performance, particularly on a stock exchange.

13.6 Issuer and counterparty risk.

The default of an issuer or of a counterparty may result in losses for the investment fund. Issuer risk describes the effect of the particular developments of the respective issuer which, in addition to the general trends on the capital markets, have an effect on the price of a security. Even if securities are carefully selected, losses may result if issuers become insolvent. Counterparty risk contains the risk that the counterparty to a contract partially or completely defaults on his liabilities. This applies to all contracts that are entered into for account of the investment fund.

13.7 Settlement risk.

Especially when unlisted securities are acquired or when settlement takes place through a transfer agent, there is the risk that settlement will not be executed as expected because a counterparty fails to pay or deliver on time or in accordance with the agreement.

13.8 Currency risk.

If assets of an investment fund are invested in currencies other than the fund currency, the investment fund receives yields, repayment and proceeds from such investments in the respective currency. If the value of this currency falls in relation to the fund currency, this reduces the value of the investment fund.

13.9 Custodial risk.

When assets are held in custody, especially in foreign countries, there is a risk of loss resulting from the insolvency, violation of due diligence or improper behaviour on the part of the Custodian or Sub-custodian.

13.10 Inflation risk.

All assets are subject to devaluation through inflation.

13.11 Legal and tax risk.

The legal and tax treatment of funds may change in ways that cannot be predicted or influenced.

13.12 Change to Terms and Conditions; liquidation or merger.

The Company reserves the right in the Terms and Conditions for the investment fund to change the Terms and Conditions. In addition, it is possible, in accordance with the Terms and Conditions, to completely liquidate the investment fund or to merge it with another investment fund which it also manages. For the investor this entails the risk that the planned holding period will not be realised.

13.13 Risk of suspension of redemption.

Investors may request the redemption of their units from the Company on any valuation day. The Company may temporarily suspend redemption of units for a limited time in exceptional circumstances and then redeem the units at a later date at the applicable price at that time. This price may be lower than the price before suspension of redemption.

14. Profile of a typical investor.

Investments in the investment fund are only suitable for experienced investors able to evaluate the risk and the value of the investment. The investor must be willing and able to accept substantial fluctuations in the value of the units and the possibility of a substantial loss of capital. The investment horizon should be at least seven years.

15. Units.

The rights of the investors are registered exclusively in global certificates when the investment fund is set up. These global certificates shall be held in custody by a central securities depository. No claim can be made by an investor for the delivery of individual unit certificates. The acquisition of units is only possible in conjunction with depository custody. The units are bearer fund units and certify the claims of the owner vis-à-vis the Company.

16. Issue and redemption of units by the Company.

16.1 Issue of units.

The number of units issued is, in principle, not restricted. Units may be acquired from the Designated Sponsors listed on the inside cover. The fund units shall be issued by the custodian bank at the issue price, which corresponds to the net asset value per fund unit plus an issue premium. The Company reserves the right to temporarily suspend or terminate the issue of units.

16.2 Redemption of units.

Investors may request the redemption of units from the Company on any valuation day, independent of the minimum investment amount. Redemption orders must be submitted to the custodian bank or the Company. The Company is obligated to redeem the units at the currently valid redemption price that corresponds to the unit value, less a redemption fee, if applicable.

16.3 Settlement of issue and redemption of units.

Settlement takes place no later than the valuation date following receipt of the redemption order.

16.4 Suspension of redemption of fund units.

The Company may temporarily suspend redemption of units in exceptional circumstances when suspension appears necessary to protect the interests of the investors. Exceptional circumstances include, for example, if there is an unscheduled closing of a stock exchange on which a significant portion of the securities of the investment fund is traded or when the assets of the investment fund cannot be valued.

The Company reserves the right to redeem or exchange the units at the current price only after it has promptly sold assets held by the investment fund with due consideration of the interests of all investors.

The Company shall inform investors of the suspension and resumption of redemption through publication in the online *Bundesanzeiger* and on the Internet at www.indexchange.com.

17. Stock exchanges and markets.

17.1 General.

The units of the investment fund are admitted for (official) trading on the following stock exchanges:

- Frankfurt Stock Exchange

  Deutsche Börse AG
  Neue Börsenstr. 1
  60487 Frankfurt am Main, Germany
  Phone: +49 (0) 69 2101 - 0
  Fax: +49 (0) 69 2101 - 2005

- SWX Swiss Exchange

  Selnaustr. 30
  8021 Zurich, Switzerland
  Phone: +41 (0) 58 854 - 5454
  Fax: +41 (0) 58 854 - 5455

- Euronext Paris

  39 rue Cambon
  75039 Paris Cedex 01, France
  Phone: +33 (0) 1 - 4927 – 1000
  Fax: +33 (0) 1 - 4927 - 1433

It is also possible that units may be traded on other markets.

Deutsche Börse AG calculates the net asset value of the investment fund continuously during trading hours. The Company provides Deutsche Börse AG with the information required to calculate the indicative net asset value once a day.

The market price underlying trade on a stock exchange or dealing in other markets is not determined exclusively by the value of the assets held in the investment fund. Supply and demand are also factors in the price. For this reason, the market price may deviate from the calculated unit price.

17.2 Function of the Designated Sponsors

The Designated Sponsors, or Market Makers, ensure sufficient liquidity for both buyers and sellers. A Designated Sponsor provides a purchase (bid) price and a sales (offer) price at which investors can purchase or sell fund units at any time.

17.3 Risk of stock exchange trading.

The obligation of the Designated Sponsors to maintain liquidity is limited to certain volumes (minimum quotation volumes) and maximum spreads. The minimum quotation periods of bid and offer prices do not usually extend to the entire effective trading period. Consequently, there may be short interruptions in the provision of prices, with the result that an order may be executed outside the quality criteria specified for that stock exchange.

17.4 Issue and redemption of units on the stock exchange.

Investors can place orders on the relevant stock exchange with their banks or brokers to purchase or sell units of the investment fund. Investors are generally charged for this service. The Company has no control over these charges.

No issue premiums or redemption fees apply to units purchased on the stock exchange. Normal costs and fees associated with stock exchange trading and custody are not affected by the above.

18. Issue and redemption prices and expenses.

18.1 Issue and redemption prices.

For the calculation of unit issue and redemption prices, on each valuation day the custodian bank determines the value of the assets of the investment fund less liabilities (net asset value).

Unit value is calculated by dividing the net asset value by the number of units in circulation.

All days on which the stock exchanges are open are valuation days for units of the investment fund.

18.2 Suspension of calculation of issue and redemption prices.

The Company may temporarily suspend calculation of the issue and redemption prices under the same conditions as for redemption of units. These conditions are explained in more detail under Point 16.4 (suspension of redemption of units).

18.3 Issue premium

When the issue price is determined, an issue premium of up to 5% of the net asset value shall be added to the unit value. This issue premium may reduce or completely offset performance gains, particularly on short-term investments. The issue premium is basically a fee for the distribution of the units of the investment fund. The Company may pay the issue premium forward as compensation for services provided by intermediaries.

18.4 Publication of issue and redemption prices.

The issue and redemption prices are published regularly at www.indexchange.com.

18.5 Costs incurred on the issue and redemption of units.

No additional charges shall be levied for the issue and redemption of units by the Company or the custodian bank. Issue and redemption are carried out at issue price (unit value plus issue premium) and redemption price.

If third parties redeem the fund units, there may be charges associated with the redemption of fund units. If units are purchased from third parties, there may also be additional costs beyond the issue price.

19. Management and miscellaneous fees.

19.1 Operating expenses.

The Company receives operating expenses from the investment fund. These expenses are charged at 0.15% of the average value of the investment fund. This charge covers the following fees and expenses:

- Fee for the management of the investment fund (fund management, administrative activities);
- Custodian fee;
- Licence fees for the use of the underlying index;
- Expenses for the publication and shipment of certain annual and semi-annual investor reports;
- Expenses for the publication of the annual and semi-annual reports, the issue and redemption prices and distributions, if applicable;
- Expenses for audit of the investment fund by the Company's auditors;
- Expenses for the publication of the basis for taxation and certification that the tax information was determined in accordance with German tax law;
- Distribution costs.

The operating expenses may be taken from the investment fund at any time.

19.2 Other expenses.

The following expenses may also be charged to the investment fund:

- Expenses resulting from the purchase and sale of assets;
- Normal bank custody fees, including the normal bank charges for the custody of foreign securities abroad and related taxes, if applicable;
- Ongoing expenses related to account management.

19.3 Composition of the total expense ratio.

The management costs incurred by the investment fund (excluding transaction costs) are disclosed in the annual report and are expressed as the total expense ratio (TER). The TER is composed of:

- General expenses that are charged for management of the investment fund in accordance with Point 19.1;
- Delivery fees for index adjustments;
- Customary bank custody fees, including the customary bank charges for the custody of foreign securities abroad and related taxes, if applicable;
- Ongoing expenses related to account management.

20. Details on the acquisition of other investment units.

In addition to the fee for managing the investment fund, a management fee is charged for the other investment units held by the investment fund.

This management fee can, but is not required to, include the costs listed under Point 19.1. In addition, other fees, expenses, taxes, commissions and other expenses not included in the management fee are to be paid separately by investors in the investment fund. In addition to the expenses listed under Points 19.1 and 19.2, fees may also be charged for the assertion and enforcement of legal claims and for taxes resulting in connection with the management and custody of the other investment units. It is possible that a significant portion of the fees paid will be paid out as a portfolio commission to brokers of other investment units.

Issue premiums and redemption fees that have been charged to the investment fund for the purchase and redemption of units are published in the annual and semi-annual reports. Also published are the fees charged to the investment fund as a management fee for units held in the investment fund, when such fees are charged by a domestic or foreign investment management company or a company to which the Company is linked by an equity interest.

The investment fund is not a sub-fund of an umbrella fund.

21. Unit classes.

All units issued have the same rights. There are no unit classes.

22. Regulations for the calculation and application of earnings.

The Company applies a so-called income netting procedure for the investment fund. This means that the proportional income accruing during the financial year which the acquirer of the fund units must pay as part of the issue price and which the seller of the units receives as payment as part of the redemption price is continuously netted. The expenses incurred are accounted for in the calculation of the income netting procedure.

The income netting procedure serves to adjust for fluctuations in the relationship between income and other assets, which are caused through net fund inflow or outflow due to the sale or redemption of units. Otherwise, every net fund inflow would reduce the return on net assets of the investment fund and every outflow would increase those returns.

The overall effect of the income netting procedure is that the amount of the distribution per unit is not influenced by the unpredictable performance of the investment fund or the number of units in circulation. In income netting, it is accepted that investors who buy units shortly before the distribution date receive back that portion of the issue price attributed to returns in the form of a distribution and that they have to pay taxed on that portion, despite the fact that the capital paid in by them did not contribute to the returns.

23. Financial year and distributions.

The financial year of the investment fund begins on 1 May and ends on 30 April of each year.

23.1 Distribution mechanism.

The Company shall distribute to the investors the interest, dividends and income from investment units, as well as fees from loans and securities repurchase agreements received on behalf of the investment fund each year in (month of distribution). Capital gains and other income may also be included in the distribution.

23.2 Distribution certificate.

If units are held in custody at the Custodian Bank, the Custodian Bank's branches credit the distributions to the account at no charge. If the investment account is maintained at another bank or savings bank, there may be additional expenses.

24. Liquidation and transfer of the investment fund.

24.1 General.

Investors are not entitled to request the liquidation of the investment fund. However, the Company may, upon thirteen months' notice, cease management of an investment fund through publication in the online *Bundesanzeiger* and in the annual report or semi-annual report.

Moreover, the right of the Company to administer the investment fund shall expire if insolvency proceedings concerning the assets of the Company are opened or with the entering into legal force of the decision by the court which rejects a petition to open insolvency proceedings for lack of assets in accordance with Section 26 of the Insolvency Act (*Insolvenzverordnung*). In these cases, powers over the investment fund assets will be transferred to the custodian bank that liquidates the investment fund, or, with the authorisation of BaFin, management of the investment fund can be transferred to another investment management company.

24.2 Procedure for the liquidation of an investment fund.

The issue and redemption of fund units will be discontinued.

Proceeds from the sale of investment fund assets less the investment fund's liabilities and liquidation costs will be distributed to the investors, whereupon investors shall be entitled to claim their share of the proceeds on sale of the investment fund assets in proportion to fund units owned.

After a period of 12 months, the custodian bank is entitled to deposit unclaimed liquidation proceeds at the competent district court for the Company.

On the day on which its right to manage lapses, the Company shall prepare a liquidation report that meets the requirements of an annual report. No later than three months after the date of liquidation of the investment fund, the liquidation report shall be published in the online *Bundesanzeiger* and on www.indexchange.com.

24.3 Transfer of all assets of the investment fund.

All assets of the investment fund may be transferred to another investment fund at the end of the financial year. As well, all assets of another investment fund may be transferred to the investment fund at the end of the financial year of the other investment fund.

The other investment fund must also be managed by the Company. Its investment policies and limits, the issue premium and redemption fees and the fees to be paid to the investment management company and the custodian bank must not deviate significantly from those of the investment fund.

24.4 Procedure for the transfer of an investment fund.

On the transfer date, the values of the acquiring and the transferring funds are calculated, the exchange ratio is established, and the entire procedure is reviewed by an auditor. The exchange ratio is determined based on the ratio between the net asset value of the transferred fund and that of the acquired fund as of the date of the transfer. The investor receives the number of units in the new investment fund in accordance with the value of his units in the transferring investment fund.

All the assets of one investment fund may only be transferred to another with the authorisation of BaFin.

25. Summary of tax regulations.

Detailed procedures for the taxation of income earned by investment funds are published in the annual reports.

The following general description is based on current tax regulations. However, we accept no responsibility for any changes in tax treatment as a result of legislative or judicial actions or decrees issued by the tax authorities.

As a special purpose fund (*Zweckvermögen*), the investment fund is exempt from German corporation tax and trade tax. Taxable income of the investment fund is nonetheless treated as investment income (*Einkünfte aus Kapitalvermögen*) in the tax returns of the investors. If the units are included in operating assets (*Betriebsvermögen*), the income will be taxable as operating income (*Betriebseinnahmen*). Under current tax regulations, taxable income and investment income are calculated differently. For example, a distinction must be made whether the applicable date for the receipt of income occurs at the time of distribution or reinvestment of earnings.

25.1 Private unit holders (resident taxpayers).

25.1.1 Realised gains on the sale of securities and from futures contracts.

The investor is not subject to tax on gains on the sale of securities and from futures contracts realised through an investment fund (Section 2 Paragraph 3 No. 1 InvStG).

25.1.2 Interest and related income.

The investor is subject to tax on interest and related income, whether such income is distributed or reinvested.

Distributed or reinvested income from the investment fund is partially subject to interest withholding tax (*Zinsabschlagsteuer*) and the solidarity surcharge (*Solidaritätszuschlag*), which consists simply of a tax prepayment that can be offset against the investor's final income tax liability. However, it is not charged against the total taxable distribution and reinvestment of earnings of the investment fund, but specifically on interest income.

Domestic and foreign dividends, capital gains from securities transactions, subscription rights for shares in corporations, profits on futures contracts and income which the Federal Republic of Germany does not have the right to tax in accordance with treaties on double taxation remain exempt from interest withholding tax.

Details on interest withholding tax payable for distributed or reinvested income from the investment fund can be found in the annual report and the publications of the basis of taxation.

Interest withholding tax will not apply if the investor is resident in Germany for tax purposes and presents an application for a tax allowance (*Freistellungsauftrag*) at the bank where his account is maintained, provided that the taxable income concerned does not exceed 1,421 Euros (for individuals) or 2,842 Euros (for married couples).

The same applies to those who submit a tax exemption certificate (*NV-Bescheinigung*) and foreign investors upon proving their status as a non-resident taxpayer.

If the units of a distributing or accumulating investment fund are held by a domestic investor in a domestic investment account with the Investment Management Company or at another bank, interest withholding tax will not be withheld by the custodian bank if an official application for a tax allowance made out in a sufficiently high amount or a tax exemption certificate issued by the tax authorities for a period of three years is presented before the specified distribution date. In this case the gross amount of the distribution will be credited to the investor.

If the investment fund reinvests income, the interest withholding tax will be based on 30% of the taxable reinvested investment fund income and will be withheld by the Investment Management Company itself. Issue and redemption prices will be correspondingly reduced by the interest withholding tax at the end of the financial year. If the units are held in a custody account with a German bank, investors who submit an application for a tax allowance made out in a sufficiently high amount or an exemption certificate to their custodian bank before the end of the financial year of the investment fund will have the interest withholding tax credited to their account.

If the application for a tax allowance or an exemption certificate is not presented or not presented in time, the investor will still receive a tax certificate from the custodian bank stating the amount of tax withheld and paid on interest income and the solidarity surcharge. The investor then has the opportunity to offset this amount of interest withholding tax against his income tax liability on submission of his income tax return. This also applies to the income in excess of the application for a tax allowance.

25.1.3 German and foreign dividends.

Only half of the amount of German and foreign dividends that are distributed or reinvested by the investment fund are subject to taxation (so-called half-income system – *Halbeinkünfteverfahren*). Upon distribution or reinvestment, a capital gains tax of 20% and the solidarity surcharge is deducted from all German dividends, that is, including the non-taxable half; the capital gains tax is immediately refunded to the investor if the fund units are held in custody at a German bank and they have been presented with an application for a tax allowance made out in a sufficiently high amount or a tax exemption certificate. Otherwise, the unit holder can have the withholding tax and the solidarity surcharge offset against his personal income tax liability, on submission of the tax certificate from his custodian bank.

25.1.4 Negative taxable income.

If the overall taxable income of the investment fund is negative, the investment fund carries this amount forward and may use it to offset future positive taxable income in future years. It is not possible to allocate negative taxable income directly to the investor. These negative amounts thus have no effect on the income tax of the investor until the assessment period (tax year) in which the financial year of the investment fund ends for which the investment fund offsets the negative taxable income is over, or in which the distribution for the financial year of the investment fund is made. It is not possible for the investor to apply these amounts to his income tax prior to this time.

25.1.5 Capital gains for investors.

Investors must pay tax on profits from the sale of units if they are held privately for less than twelve months. Losses incurred under equivalent conditions can be offset against capital gains within the income from private capital transactions of the previous year or of future years.

25.2 Units held in operating assets (resident taxpayers).

25.2.1 Realised gains on the sale of securities and from futures contracts.

Investors are not subject to tax on realised gains on the sale of securities and from futures contracts if these profits are reinvested. If these profits are distributed, investors must take them into account in their taxes. The capital gains on stocks are completely (for incorporated investors) or half (for other business investors, such as sole traders) exempt from taxes. The full amount of capital gains on bonds and profits from futures contracts are subject to tax.

25.2.2 Interest and related income.

The investor is subject to tax on interest and related income, whether such income is distributed or reinvested.

If units are held in operating assets, exemption or compensation of interest withholding tax and a refund of the capital gains tax is only possible with submission of an application for a tax allowance. Otherwise, the investor receives a tax certificate on the interest withholding tax and the allowable capital gains tax.

25.2.3 German and foreign dividends.

Dividends from German and foreign public limited companies, which are distributed in respect of units held in operating assets or which are reinvested are tax-free for corporations. Sole traders are taxed on only half the amount of the dividends, as are private investors (half-income system).

25.2.4 Negative taxable income.

If the overall taxable income of the investment fund is negative, the investment fund carries this amount forward and may use it to offset future positive taxable income in future years. It is not possible to allocate negative taxable income directly to the investor. These negative amounts thus have no effect on the income tax or corporation tax of the investor until the assessment period (tax year) in which the financial year of the investment fund ends for which the investment fund offsets the negative taxable income is over, or in which the distribution for the financial year of the investment fund is made. It is not possible for the investor to apply these amounts to his income tax or corporation tax prior to this time.

25.2.5 Capital gains for investors.

Gains from the sale of fund units held in operating assets are tax-free for corporations provided it involves dividends and investment fund gains realised from German and foreign shares (so-called equity income). Sole traders are subject to taxation for half of these capital gains.

The Investment Management Company publishes the equity income as a percentage of the investment unit price.

25.3 Non-resident taxpayers.

If an investor who is not resident in Germany holds investment fund units in a German custody account with a German bank, the units will be exempt from the deduction of interest withholding tax, provided that he can furnish proof of his status as a non-resident. Any possible capital gains tax credit or refund for foreign investors is dependent on existing double taxation treaties between the country in which the residence or corporate headquarters of the investor is located and the Federal Republic of Germany. If the custodian bank has no knowledge of the investor's status as a non-resident or proof of this is not provided on time, the foreign investor is forced, by way of a refund procedure in accordance with Section 37, Paragraph 2 of the Fiscal Code ("AO"), to apply for a refund of the interest withholding tax paid. The responsibility lies with the tax office of the custodian bank/Investment Management Company.

If reinvesting investment fund units are held by a foreign investor in a domestic bank, he will receive a 30% refund of interest withholding tax paid upon proving his status as a non-resident. If the refund application is delayed, a refund can be applied for in accordance with Section 37, Paragraph 2 of the Fiscal Code ("AO"), as is the case with a delay in proof of the status as a non-resident.

25.4 Solidarity surcharge.

A solidarity surcharge of 5.5% is levied on the capital gains tax payable and interest withholding tax payable on dividends or reinvestments. This solidarity surcharge can be offset against income tax.

If no capital gains tax is due or a refund is made of capital gains tax during reinvestment – such as with a sufficient application for a tax allowance, tax exemption certificate or proof of status as a non-resident taxpayer – no solidarity surcharge will be deducted or the solidarity surcharge withheld will be refunded.

25.5 Foreign withholding tax.

Withholding tax is sometimes withheld on foreign income of the investment fund in the country of origin.

The Investment Management Company may deduct the allowable withholding tax and advertising costs through the investment fund. In such cases, the foreign withholding tax may not be either allowed or deducted by the investor.

If the Investment Management Company elects not to deduct the foreign withholding tax at the fund level, on application by the investor, the allowable foreign withholding tax can be deducted from total income or will be credited against the portion of German income or corporation tax attributable to the corresponding foreign income.

25.6 Separate determination, external audit.

The basis of taxation calculated for the investment fund shall be separately determined. The investment company must submit an assessment return (*Feststellungserklärung*) to this end to the competent tax authorities. Amendments to the assessment return, e.g. amendments made in the course of an external audit (Section 11 Paragraph 3 InvStG) by the tax authorities shall be effective for the financial year in which the amended assessment can no longer be contested.

The tax allocation of this amended assessment to the investor is then carried out at the end of the financial year or on the distribution day for that financial year.

25.7 Tax on interim income.

The tax on interim income was reinstated on 1 January 2005. For investors, this means that when units are redeemed or sold, the interest income earned by the investment fund and included in the redemption price is subject to capital gains tax. Conversely, investors can reduce their tax liability by reporting as negative income from capital assets the portion of the purchase price paid upon acquisition of units that pertains to interest income earned by the investment fund.

This ensures that the respective shares of interest income attributable to investors acquiring and redeeming (or selling) units are only subject to tax if those investors actually held investment fund units during the period of time in which that investment fund earned that interest income. To prevent duplicate taxation of interim income, i.e. once as a capital gain on an asset held and then a second time as a capital gain upon the disposal of an asset, any interim income included in a purchase price at the time of an acquisition shall be deducted from the acquisition cost, and any interim income included in a redemption price at the time of a redemption or sale shall deducted from that price.

25.8 Results of the merger of investment funds.

Investment funds may be merged. Investors in the transferring investment fund receive units in the acquiring investment fund in exchange for their units in the transferring fund. This exchange does not result in the disclosure of undisclosed accruals. However, this marks the beginning of a new speculation period (period of capital tax gains liability) for investors whose units in the transferring investment fund were acquired within one year of the transfer date.

25.9 Transparent, semi-transparent and non-transparent taxation.

The above-mentioned tax principles (so-called transparent taxation) only apply if the basis for taxation as defined in Section 5 Paragraph 1 Sentence 1 InvStG is made known.

If the information in accordance with Section 5 Paragraph 1 No. 1 Letter c or f InvStG has not been made available, the income is 100% taxable (so-called semitransparent taxation).

If the disclosure requirement in accordance with Section 5 Paragraph 1 InvStG is breached other than in a case of semi-transparent taxation, then the distributions and 70% of the surplus amount shall be recognised for investors when this surplus amount is between the first redemption price of the investment units determined during the calendar year and the last redemption price determined during the calendar year; at least 6% of the last redemption price determined in the calendar year shall be recognised (so-called non-transparent taxation).

25.10 Holdings in other investment funds.

If the investment fund generates earnings from units of other investment funds (target funds), then for tax purposes these earnings shall be considered to have been generated by the investment fund itself.

Non-transparent taxation may also be applied if the disclosure requirement in accordance with Section 5 Paragraph 1 InvG was not fulfilled by the target fund.

Determination of equity income shall be based on the asset structure of the target fund.

25.11 Notice.

The information on taxes is based on current tax law and regulations. The information is directed towards individuals who are fully subject to income tax or corporation tax in Germany. However, we accept no responsibility for any changes in tax treatment as a result of legislative or judicial actions or decrees issued by the tax authorities.

26. Outsourcing.

The company has outsourced the following activities to other companies:

- Human resources
- Auditing
- Compliance
- IT support
- Financial accounting

27. Annual and semi-annual reports; auditors.

The annual and semi-annual reports can be obtained from the Company and the Custodian Bank.

KPMG Deutsche Treuhandgesellschaft AG Wirtschaftsprüfungsgesellschaft, Munich, has been appointed to audit the investment fund and annual reports.

28. Payments to unit holders; distribution of reports and other information

The contract with the custodian bank ensures that investors receive distributions, if dividends are provided for by the investment fund, and that units can be redeemed. The investor information mentioned in this prospectus may be obtained as described under Point 1.1.

29. Other funds managed by the Investment Management Company.

The Company also manages the following public investment funds that are not included in this Prospectus:

a) Directive-Compliant Investment Funds

eb.rexx® Jumbo Pfandbriefe^{EX}

eb.rexx® Government Germany^{EX}

eb.rexx® Government Germany 1.5-2.5^{EX}

eb.rexx® Government Germany 2.5-5.5^{EX}

eb.rexx® Government Germany 5.5-10.5^{EX}

DAX$^{®EX}$

MDAX$^{®EX}$

TecDAX$^{®EX}$

Dow Jones STOXX 50^{SMEX}

Dow Jones Global Titans 50^{SMEX}

Dow Jones STOXX^{SM} 600 Institutional^{EX}

b) Mixed Investment Funds

SMI$^{®EX}$

FTSE 100$^{TM\ EX}$

Dow Jones Industrial Average^{SMEX}

Dow Jones EURO STOXX^{SM} Banks^{EX}

Dow Jones EURO STOXX^{SM} Health Care^{EX}

Dow Jones EURO STOXX^{SM} Technology^{EX}

Dow Jones EURO STOXX^{SM} Telecommunications^{EX}

Dow Jones STOXX^{SM} 600 Automobiles & Parts^{EX}

Dow Jones STOXX^{SM} 600 Banks^{EX}

Dow Jones STOXX^{SM} 600 Basic Resources^{EX}

Dow Jones STOXX^{SM} 600 Chemicals^{EX}

Dow Jones STOXX^{SM} 600 Construction & Materials^{EX}

Dow Jones STOXX^{SM} 600 Financial Services^{EX}

Dow Jones STOXX^{SM} 600 Food & Beverage^{EX}

Dow Jones STOXX^{SM} 600 Health Care^{EX}

Dow Jones STOXX^{SM} 600 Industrial Goods & Services^{EX}

Dow Jones STOXX^{SM} 600 Insurance^{EX}

Dow Jones STOXX^{SM} 600 Media^{EX}

Dow Jones STOXX^{SM} 600 Oil & Gas^{EX}

Dow Jones STOXX^{SM} 600 Personal & Household Goods^{EX}

Dow Jones STOXX^{SM} 600 Retail^{EX}

Dow Jones STOXX^{SM} 600 Technology^{EX}

Dow Jones STOXX^{SM} 600 Telecommunications^{EX}

Dow Jones STOXX^{SM} 600 Travel & Leisure^{EX}

Dow Jones STOXX^{SM} 600 Utilities^{EX}

Instruction on the right of cancellation under Section 126 InvG. (doorstep selling)

1. If the purchaser of units is required to make a declaration of intent concerning the purchase as a result of oral negotiations outside of the permanent business premises of those selling or brokering the sale, this declaration is binding only if he does not cancel it in writing to the Investment Management Company within a period of two weeks; this is also true when the person who sells the units or brokered the sale does not have any permanent business premises.
2. Sending the revocation prior to the deadline is sufficient for observing the time limit. The two-week period does not commence until the full Prospectus is offered to the investor and a copy of the application form has been delivered. If there is a dispute as to whether or at what time the full Prospectus was offered to the investor or the copy of the application form was delivered, the burden of proof rests with the seller.
3. The right of cancellation does not apply if the seller can prove that
   a) the purchaser acquired the units as part of his commercial operations or
   b) he called on the purchaser to conduct negotiations leading to the sale of the units as a result of a previous request (Section 55 Paragraph 1 of the Industrial Code (*Gewerbeordnung*).
4. If the right of cancellation is exercised after the investor has made payment, the Investment Management Company is obliged to repay the investor's costs – incrementally as the purchased units are transferred back, if necessary – in addition to an amount corresponding to the value of the purchased units the day after the cancellation was received.
5. The right of cancellation cannot be waived.
6. The provisions of paragraphs 1 to 5 also apply for the sale of units by the investor.

General Terms and Conditions.

General Terms and Conditions governing the legal relationship between the investors and INDEXCHANGE Investment AG, Apianstr. 5, D-85774 Unterföhring bei München (hereinafter referred to as the "Company"), for Directive-compliant security index investment funds (hereinafter referred to as "Investment Funds") set up by the Company. These General Terms and Conditions are valid only in connection with the "Special Conditions" established for the corresponding investment fund.

Section 1 – Principles.

1. The Company is an Investment Management Company subject to the German Investment Act (InvG – Investmentgesetz).
2. It will invest the funds placed by the investors in its own name for the joint account of the investors in accordance with the principle of risk diversification in assets permitted by the InvG and separated from its own assets in the form of an investment fund. Global certificates (fund units) will be issued by the Company regarding the rights of the investors resulting therefrom.

Section 2 – Depository bank.

1. The Company will appoint a financial institution as depository bank; the depository bank acts independently of the Company and solely in the interest of the investors.
2. The depository bank is obliged to carry out the duties required by the InvG and these Terms and Conditions.

Section 3 – Fund management.

1. The Company acquires and manages the assets in its own name for the joint account of the investors. The Company applies due care and diligence of a prudent businessman. While performing its duties, it acts independently of the depository bank and exclusively in the interests of the investors and the integrity of the markets.
2. The Company is entitled to acquire assets with the funds invested by the investors and to resell these assets and reinvest the proceeds; it is further entitled to undertake all other legal actions resulting from the management of said assets.
3. The Company may not grant loans for the joint account of the investors nor guarantees or sureties; it may not sell assets as defined in Sections 47, 48 and 50 InvG that are not part of the investment fund when the transaction is concluded. Section 51 InvG continues to apply.

Section 4 – Investment policies.

1. The Company may only acquire such assets on behalf of the investment fund that are designed to track a security index (security index) approved by the Federal Banking Supervisory Authority (Supervisory Authority) while maintaining an appropriate level of risk. The security index will be recognised, specifically if
   a) the composition of the security index is adequately diversified;
   b) the index represents an adequate benchmark for the market to which it relates; and
   c) the index has been published in an appropriate manner.

   The Company sets forth in the provisions of the contract which assets may be acquired for the investment fund.
2. The investment fund may only acquire securities included in a security index or introduced to it following a change thereto (index securities); securities, issued on these index securities or on the underlying index; and derivatives on securities, money-market instruments, investment units pursuant to Section 8, recognised financial indices, interest rates, foreign exchange rates or currencies, in which the investment fund may invest as stated in the Terms and Conditions. In replicating the underlying index, within the meaning of a direct duplication of the index, priority is to be given to investments in index securities over investments in other assets listed in Sentence 1 approved for use in replicating indices. The underlying index may only be replicated using securities or derivatives which indirectly replicate the index for purposes of maintaining the restrictions listed in Section 11 Paragraph 6.
3. In order to replicate the security index, the duplication percentage must not be less than 95% of the total assets in the investment fund as defined in Paragraph 2 Sentence 1. Derivatives will be included in the calculation of the duplication percentage with their weighted market risk in accordance with the simple approach in accordance with the statutory instrument on risk management and risk measurement in investment funds (DerivateV) issued pursuant to Section 51 Paragraph 3 InvG.
4. The duplication percentage reflects the portion of securities and derivatives according to Section 51 Paragraph 1 InvG in the investment fund that corresponds with the security index in terms of weighting. The duplication percentage is defined as being equal to 100 less one half of the sum of the differences between the weighting of the securities in the index and the applicable weighting of the securities included in the total assets of the investment fund, added up for all securities and applicable values of derivatives according Section 51 Paragraph 1 InvG in the investment fund and for all securities in the index.

$$DP = 100\% - \frac{\sum_{i=1}^{n} \left| W_i^I - W_i^F \right|}{2}$$

DP = duplication percentage in %

n = number of equity classes in the Fund and in the index (upper summation limit)

I = index

F = Fund

W_i^I = weighting of equity i in index I in %

W_i^F = applicable weighting of equity i in the equity portion of the fund in %

$\sum$ = sum symbol

i = summation index; stands for the individual classes of equities from i = 1 (lower summation limit) to i = n (upper summation limit)

Section 5 – Securities.

Provided that the "Special Conditions" do not include any additional restrictions, the Company may, subject to Section 52 InvG, only acquire securities if

a) they are admitted for official trading on a stock exchange in a member state of the European Union or in another state abiding by the agreement concerning the European Economic Area, or which are included on another regulated market in a member state of the European Union or in another state abiding by the agreement concerning the European Economic Area;

b) they are approved for trading on a stock exchange specified in the appendix to the "Special Conditions" or on a regulated market in the same countries;

c) application for admission for official trading on one of the aforementioned stock exchanges or one of the aforementioned regulated markets is planned in accordance with the issue conditions, and the admission or inclusion will take place within a year after their issue;

d) they are equities to which the investment fund is entitled in a capital increase from Company assets;

e) they were acquired as a result of the exercise of subscription rights.

Section 6 – Money market instruments.

1. Provided that the "Special Conditions" do not include any additional restrictions, the Company may acquire, subject to Section 52 InvG, on behalf of the investment fund, instruments normally dealt in on the money market and interest-bearing securities with a residual term of no more than twelve months at the time of their acquisition or whose interest rate, in accordance with the issue conditions, is regularly – and at least once each twelve-month period – adjusted to reflect current market conditions (money market instruments). Money market instruments may only be acquired for the investment fund if they are issued

   a) by the German Federal Government, investment funds of the German Federal Government or the German Federal States, another member state of the European Union or another state abiding by the agreement concerning the European Economic Area;

   b) by another domestic local or regional authority or a regional government or local or regional authority of another member state of the European Union or another state abiding by the agreement concerning the European Economic Area;

   c) by the European Union or a country belonging to the Organization for Economic Co-operation and Development;

   d) by a central bank of a member state of the European Union or a country abiding by the agreement concerning the European Economic Area, the European Central Bank or the European Investment Bank;

   e) by an international organisation of which the Federal Republic of Germany is also a full member;

   f) by a company whose securities are admitted to official trading on a domestic or foreign stock exchange or listed on an organised market;

   g) by a credit institution which has its registered office in a member state of the European Union or another state abiding by the agreement concerning the European Economic Area or by a credit institution which has its registered office in a non-member state, provided that it is subject to the prudential rules considered by the Supervisory Authority as equivalent to those laid down in Community law;

   h) by a Company, whose capital and reserves amount to at least EUR 10 million and which presents its annual accounts in accordance with the Fourth Directive 78/660/EEC of 25 July 1978 on the annual accounts of certain types of companies, last amended by Directive of the European Parliament and of the Council 2003/51/EC of 18 June 2003;

   i) by a group company within the meaning of Section 18 of the German Stock Corporation Act (Aktiengesetz) if another company from the same group that satisfies the requirements of letters f), g) or h) has guaranteed the interest rate and repayment of these money market instruments;

   j) by an entity whose operations are dedicated to the placement of securitisation vehicles on the market provided that the entity has credit lines from a credit institution for purposes of ensuring liquidity

   and the issue or issuer of such instruments is itself regulated for the purpose of protecting investors and savings.

2. The Company may also acquire, on behalf of the investment fund, money market instruments for which an issuer as designated in Paragraph 1 Letter a) to e) or g) has guaranteed the interest rate and repayment.

Section 7 – Bank accounts.

The Company may hold, on behalf of the investment fund, bank accounts with a maturity not exceeding twelve months. The accounts, which must be in the form of blocked accounts, may be maintained at a credit institution which has its registered office in a member state of the European Union or another state abiding by the agreement concerning the European Economic Area; the accounts may also be held at a credit institution which has its registered office in a non-member state, provided that it is subject to the prudential rules considered by the Supervisory Authority as equivalent to those laid down in Community law. If not otherwise specified in the "Special Conditions", these bank accounts may be denominated in foreign currencies.

Section 8 – Investment fund units.

1. If not otherwise specified in the "Special Conditions", the Company, on behalf of an investment fund, may acquire units in other Directive-compliant domestic investment funds and foreign EC investment fund units as defined in the InvG. Units in other domestic investment funds and foreign investment fund units that are not EC investment fund units as well as units in joint-stock investment companies with variable capital may be acquired provided that

   a) such units are authorised under laws which provide that they are subject to supervision for the protection of the investors and that cooperation between authorities is sufficiently ensured;

   b) the level of protection for the investor is equivalent to that provided for an investor in a Directive-compliant domestic investment fund as defined in the InvG and in particular that the rules on asset segregation, borrowing, lending, and uncovered sales of transferable securities and money market instruments are equivalent to the requirements of Directive 85/611/EEC.

   c) the business of the companies and funds in question is reported in annual and semi-annual reports to enable an assessment to be made of the assets and liabilities, income and operations over the reporting period;

d) an unlimited number of units are offered to the public and the investors are entitled to redeem the fund units.

2. The Company may only acquire for the investment fund units in domestic investment funds and joint-stock investment companies with variable capital, EC investment fund units and foreign investment fund units if, in accordance with the fund rules or articles of association of the company, the joint-stock investment company or the foreign investment company, no more than a total of 10% of the value of their assets are invested in units of other domestic investment funds, joint-stock investment companies with variable capital or foreign investment funds as defined in Section 50 InvG.
3. The Company may only acquire for the investment fund such units in domestic investment funds and joint-stock investment companies with variable capital, EC investment fund units and foreign investment fund units if the fund rules or articles of association of the company, the joint stock-investment company or the foreign investment company are equivalent to the investment conditions of the investment fund.

Section 9 – Derivatives.

1. The Company has established in the "Special Conditions" whether and in what volume transactions of derivatives may be undertaken on behalf of the investment fund. The Company will observe the guidelines of the DerivateV when derivatives are used.
2. No derivatives transactions for the investment fund may be made for purposes of hedging.

Section 10 – Other investment instruments.

The Company may invest no more than 10% of the assets of the investment fund in

a) securities which are not admitted to official trading on a stock exchange or are not listed on an organised market;

b) money market instruments from issuers who do not fulfil the requirements of Section 48 InvG;

c) equities that meet the requirements of Section 47 Paragraph 1 Nos. 3 and 4 InvG;

d) receivables from loans that are not money market instruments as defined in Section 48 InvG, that are parts of a whole loan and for which a promissory note has been issued (borrowers' note loans), provided that these receivables may be assigned at least twice after acquisition for the investment fund and that the loan was granted

- to the German Federal Government, to an investment fund of the German Federal Government, to a German Federal State, to the European Communities or to a country belonging to the Organisation for Economic Co-operation and Development;
- to another domestic local or regional authority or a regional government or local or regional authority of another member state of the European Union or another state abiding by the agreement concerning the European Economic Area, for which a zero weighting has been announced in accordance with Article 44 of Directive 2000/12/EC of the European Parliament and of the Council of 20 March 2000 relating to the taking up and pursuit of the business of credit institutions;
- to another authority or public body with its registered office in Germany or in another member state of the European Union or in another state abiding by the agreement concerning the European Economic Area;
- to companies, whose securities are admitted to official trading on a domestic or foreign stock exchange; or
- to other debtors, provided that one of the locations listed in Letter d), first through third bullet points, has guaranteed the interest rate and repayment.

Section 11 – Issuer and investment restrictions.

1. The Company must comply with the limitations and restrictions specified in the InvG and in the Contract Terms while managing assets.
2. The Company may invest up to 20% of the assets of the investment fund in securities from a single issuer (debtor).
3. The limit stipulated in Paragraph 2 may be increased to up to 35% of the value of the investment fund for securities from a single issuer (debtor). An investment up to the limit under Sentence 1 is permissible only for one individual issuer (debtor).
4. For assets based on an underlying index, the market price of the index securities will be attributed to the respective issuer limits on a pro rata basis. The same method will be used for assets based on a single index security or a basket of index securities. Derivatives pursuant to Section 51 Paragraph 1 InvG will be attributed to the issuer limits in accordance with Sections 18 and 19 DerivateV.
5. The Company may invest up to 5% of the value of the investment fund in bank accounts or money market instruments as defined in Sections 6 and 7, if not otherwise specified in the "Special Conditions".
6. If not otherwise specified in the "Special Conditions", the investment fund must invest at least 95% in assets in accordance with Section 4 Paragraph 2 Sentence 1 on a security index.

Section 12 – Borrowing.

On behalf of all the investors, the Company may subscribe to short-term loans for amounts of up to 10% of the investment fund, if the terms of the loan are at market rates and subject to approval of the conditions of the loan by the depository bank. For this purpose short-term loans will include amounts that the Company has received as borrower in conjunction with a repurchase transaction.

Section 13 – Loans.

1. The Company may grant a securities loan on behalf of the investment fund to a securities borrower at an arm's length fee for an unlimited or limited period, subject to the transfer of sufficient collateral. The market price of the securities to be transferred plus the market value of the securities already transferred to the same securities borrower as a securities loan on behalf of the investment fund must not exceed 10% of the value of the investment fund. The market value of securities subject to short-term transfers plus the market value of the securities previously transferred as short-term

securities loans on behalf of the investment fund may not exceed 15% of the value of the investment fund.

2. If the collateral for the securities transferred is maintained in accounts, the Company may make use of the opportunity to invest these accounts in money market instruments as defined in Section 48 InvG in the currency of the account. The investment fund is entitled to the income from the collateral.
3. The Company may also utilise an organised system for brokerage and settlement of securities loans supplied by a company identified by a securities custody bank or specified in the "Special Conditions" whose corporate objective is the settlement of international securities transactions for third parties, and which deviates from the requirements of Sections 54 and 55 InvG, if this system's regulations guarantee that investors' interests are upheld.
4. Any right of the Company to grant loans in relation to assets that the investment fund may acquire will be governed in the "Special Conditions".

Section 14 – Securities repurchase agreements.

1. The Company may conclude securities repurchase agreements with banks or financial institutions for valuable consideration as specified under Section 340 b, Paragraph 2 of the German Commercial Code ("HGB") on behalf of the investment fund.
2. The object of the securities repurchase agreements must include securities that may be acquired by the investment fund.
3. The repurchase agreements must have a maximum term of 12 months.
4. Any right of the Company to conclude securities repurchase agreements in relation to other assets that the investment fund may acquire in accordance with the Contract Terms will be governed in the "Special Conditions".

Section 15 – Transfer of all assets of the investment fund to another investment fund.

1. The Company may transfer all the assets of this investment fund to another investment fund or this investment fund may acquire all the assets of another investment fund if
   a) both investment funds are managed by the Company;
   b) the investment principles and limits under the Contract Terms for these investment funds do not deviate significantly from one another;
   c) the compensation owed to the Company and to the depository bank as well as the issue surcharge and redemption fees do not deviate significantly from one another;
   d) the transfer of all assets of the investment fund is carried out at the end of the financial year of the transferring fund (transfer date), the values of the acquiring and the transferring funds are calculated on the transfer date, the exchange ratio is established, the assets and liabilities are acquired and the entire transfer procedure is reviewed by an auditor, and the Supervisory Authority has approved the transfer of the assets and confirmed that the interests of the investors have been adequately protected.
2. The exchange ratio is determined based on the ratio between the net asset value of the transferred fund and that of the acquired fund as of the date of the transfer. The new units of the acquiring fund will be deemed to have been issued to investors of the transferring fund as of the beginning of the day following the transfer date.
3. Paragraph 1 Letter c does not apply to the consolidation of separate investment funds into a single investment fund with various unit classes. In this case, instead of the exchange ratio described in Paragraph 2 Sentence 1, the percentage breakdown of the unit class in the investment fund will be calculated.

Section 16 – Unit certificates.

1. The unit certificates will be bearer certificates, each of them representing one or more investment units.
2. The units vary in their regulations with respect to appropriation of earnings, issue premiums, redemption charges, unit currency, management fees, or a combination of these characteristics (unit classes). The Company details are laid out in the "Special Conditions".
3. At a minimum, the unit certificates will bear the handwritten or facsimile signatures of the Company and the depository bank. In addition, they will bear the original signature of a supervisory person from the depository bank.
4. The units are transferable. When a unit certificate is transferred, the rights attached thereto are also transferred. The Company will always assume that the owner of the unit certificate is the beneficiary.
5. Rights of investors established on creation of the investment fund or rights of investors of a unit class established on creation of the unit class that are not securitised in global certificates, but rather in individual unit certificates or in multiple certificates, will be governed by provisions of the "Special Conditions".

Section 17 – Issue and redemption of units, suspension of redemption.

1. In principle, the number of units issued and the corresponding unit certificates are not restricted. The Company retains the right to temporarily suspend or terminate the issue of units.
2. Units may be acquired from the Company, the depository bank, or from third parties.
3. Investors may demand the redemption of their units from the Company. The Company is obligated to redeem units at the currently valid redemption price on behalf of the investment fund. The redemption agency is the depository bank.
4. The Company nevertheless retains the right to suspend redemption of units in exceptional circumstances when suspension appears necessary to protect the interests of the investors.

Section 18 – Issue and redemption prices.

1. For the calculation of unit issue and redemption prices, the value of assets (net asset value) included in the investment fund will be determined at times specified in the "Special Conditions" and divided by the number of units in circulation (unit value). If special unit classes for the investment fund are introduced in accordance with Section 16, Paragraph 2, then the unit value and the issue and redemption prices will be determined separately. Asset valuation will be performed in

accordance with the principles mentioned in the InvG for valuation calculations.

2. The issue price corresponds to the unit value plus sales charge, if any, as set forth in the "Special Conditions". The redemption price corresponds to the unit value less redemption fee, if any, as set forth in the "Special Conditions". If the investor is to pay any other costs besides the issue premium and the redemption fee, the amount and calculation of such fees are set forth in the "Special Conditions".
3. The settlement date for purchase and redemption orders is no later than the next value date following the receipt of the purchase or redemption order, if not otherwise specified in the "Special Conditions".

Section 19 – Expenses.

Fees and other expenses payable to the Company, the depository bank and third parties, which can be charged to the investment fund, are specified in the "Special Conditions". The "Special Conditions" detail the manner, the amount, and the calculation basis for any fees in excess of those specified in the preceding sentence.

Section 20 – Accounting.

1. The Company will publish an annual report with a profit and loss statement no later than three months after the end of the financial year of the investment fund in accordance with Section 44, Paragraph 1 InvG.
2. The Company will publish a semi-annual report no more than two months after the end of the first half of the financial year in accordance with Section 44, Paragraph 2 InvG.
3. If the right to manage the investment fund is transferred to another company during the financial year, the Company must prepare an interim report for the period to the transfer date that meets the requirements of an annual report in accordance with Section 44 Paragraph 1 InvG.
4. The reports can be obtained from the Company and the depository bank and other locations to be listed in the sales prospectus; they will also be published in the online *Bundesanzeiger* (Federal Gazette) as well as in a financial or daily newspaper with sufficient circulation or in the electronic information media designated in the sales prospectus.

Section 21 – Termination and winding up of the investment fund.

1. The Company may give notice of at least thirteen months to cease management of the investment fund through publication in the online *Bundesanzeiger* and in the annual report or semi-annual report.
2. The right of the Company to manage the investment fund lapses when the termination becomes effective. In this case, the investment fund and/or the right to sell the investment fund assets are transferred to the depository bank, which will wind up the assets and distribute them to the investors. The depository bank can claim fees due to the Company during the winding-up period. With the approval of the Supervisory Authority, the depository bank can refrain from this assignment, in which case management of the investment fund will be transferred to another company in accordance with the existing contract terms.
3. The Company must prepare a liquidation report for the period to the date on which its right to manage lapses in accordance with Section 38 InvG, which fulfils the requirements of an annual report under Section 44 Paragraph 1 InvG.

Section 22 – Changes to Contract Terms.

1. The Company is entitled to change the Contract Terms.
2. Changes in these Contract Terms require the prior approval of the Supervisory Authority, with the exception of rules regarding fees owed to the Company, the depository bank and third parties, and other expenses charged to the investment fund (Section 41, Paragraph 1 Sentence 1 InvG). Changes under Sentence 1 Investment Principles that affect the investment fund require the prior approval of the Supervisory Board of the Company.
3. All planned changes will be published in the online *Bundesanzeiger* as well as in a financial or daily newspaper with sufficient circulation or in the electronic information media designated in the sales prospectus and will take effect no earlier than three months after their publication – with the exception of changes according to Paragraphs 4 and 5 – provided no earlier date is given with the approval of the Supervisory Authority. The planned changes and their effective dates must be published in accordance with Sentence 1.
4. Changes to rules for expenses and fees payable to the Company, the depository bank, and third parties (Section 41, Paragraph 1 InvG) will take effect 13 months after publication. The publication will be governed by Paragraph 3, Sentence 2 hereto.
5. Changes to the current investment principles will take effect 13 months after publication. The publication will be governed by Paragraph 3, Sentence 2 hereto.

Section 23 – Place of performance, jurisdiction.

1. The place of performance is the registered office of the Company.
2. If the investor has no general place of jurisdiction in Germany, the place of jurisdiction will be the registered office.

Special Conditions.

Special Conditions governing the legal relationship between the investors and INDEXCHANGE Investment AG, Apianstr. 5, D-85774 Unterföhring bei München (hereinafter referred to as the "Company"), for the Directive-compliant security index investment fund **Dow Jones EURO STOXX 50^{SMEX}** (hereinafter referred to as the "Investment Fund") set up by the Company. These Special Conditions are valid only in connection with the "General Terms and Conditions" established for the corresponding investment fund.

Investment policies and restrictions.

Section 1 – Assets.

1. The Company may acquire the following assets for the investment fund:
   a) securities pursuant to Section 47 InvG,
   b) bank accounts pursuant to Section 49 InvG,
   c) derivatives pursuant to Section 51 InvG,
   d) investment fund units pursuant to Section 8 of the "General Terms and Conditions".

   1. The purpose of the equity and equity index certificate selection for the investment fund is to replicate the Dow Jones EURO STOXX 50^{SM} (price index) (hereinafter referred to as the underlying index) while maintaining an appropriate level of risk.
2. Certificates for individual securities pursuant to Section 47 InvG, money-market instruments pursuant to Section 49 InvG and other investment instruments pursuant to Section 52 InvG may not be acquired for the investment fund.

Section 2 – Loans and securities repurchase agreements.

1. With regard to the investment principles and restrictions, Sections 13 and 14 of the "General Terms and Conditions" must be taken into consideration.
2. Securities repurchase agreements pursuant to Section 14 of the "General Terms and Conditions" are not entered into.

Section 3 – Investment restrictions.

With regard to the investment restrictions, Section 11 of the "General Terms and Conditions" must be taken into consideration. Investments in investment units as defined in Section 4 Paragraph 2 and Section 8 of the "General Terms and Conditions" may be made for the investment fund.

Section 4 – Use of financial instruments.

1. The Company may only invest in futures contracts on the underlying index for the investment fund. In these transactions, the Company may under no circumstances deviate from the investment objectives listed in the "General Terms and Conditions" or in the Sales Prospectus.
2. In calculating the upper limit of market risk for the use of derivatives pursuant to Paragraph 1, the Company uses the simple approach as defined in the Derivative Regulation (DerivateV - Derivateverordnung). The investment fund's weighted interest-rate and equity risk or currency risk, as calculated pursuant to Section 16 of the DerivateV, may at no time exceed twice the value of the investment fund.
3. The Company will use the derivatives listed in Paragraph 1 for purposes of efficient portfolio management and to produce additional returns, when and to the extent that it considers this to be in the interests of the investors.
4. No derivatives transactions may be made for purposes of hedging.

Unit classes.

Section 5 – Unit classes.

All units have the same rights; there will not be different unit classes as specified under Section 16, Paragraph 2 of the "General Terms and Conditions".

Unit certificates, issue price, redemption price, redemption of units and costs.

Section 6 – Unit certificates.

The investors own an equity interest in the assets of the investment fund as co-owners in proportion to the number of units held.

Section 7 – Issue and redemption price.

1. Issue and redemption prices will be determined on each trading session. On public holidays that fall on trading sessions, as well as on 24 and 31 December each year, the Investment Management Company and the depository bank may refrain from determining the value; details are dealt with in the Sales Prospectus.
2. The issue premium is 5% of the unit value. The Company is free to charge a lower issue premium.
3. Any price determined by the stock exchange may deviate from the calculated price of the fund units. When acquiring shares through the stock exchange, no issue surcharge within the meaning of Paragraph 2 is calculated. However, transaction costs, over which the company has no control, will be charged. Amounts paid in bank commissions, brokerage fees or market fees depend on the individual agreements between the investor and his own bank or broker.
4. Purchase and redemption orders received by the Company or depository bank by 3:00 p.m. (C.E.T.) will be settled at the issue or redemption price determined on the following trading session. For the determination of the issue or redemption price, the prices on the day the purchase or redemption order is accepted will be applied to the assets held in the investment fund.

Section 8 – Expenses[1].

1. For managing the investment fund, the Company will receive a fee of 0.15% per annum of the net asset value determined each trading session from the investment fund in accordance with Section 19, Paragraph 1 of the "General Terms and Conditions". The Company is free to charge a lower management fee. The management fee will be paid in advance in monthly instalments by the investment fund.
2. The management fee specified in Paragraph 1 will cover services rendered by the Company for the investment fund, including fees payable for the licence agreement with STOXX Limited, as well as expenses of the depository bank, legally required printing, mailings, and publications associated with the investment fund, and for annual report audits conducted by auditors of the Company.

[1] This provision is not subject to the approval of BaFin.

3. The following expenses are not covered by Paragraph 1 hereto:
   a) expenses resulting from the purchase and sale of assets (transaction costs);
   b) normal bank custody fees, including the normal bank charges for the custody of foreign securities abroad and related taxes, if applicable;
   c) ongoing expenses related to account management.

   Such expenses will be charged to the investment fund in addition to the management fee in accordance with Paragraph 1 hereto.
4. The Company will publish in the annual report and in the semi-annual report the amount of the issue surcharges and redemption fees that have been charged to the investment fund during the reporting period for the purchase and redemption of units as defined in Section 8 of the "General Terms and Conditions". When units are purchased that are managed, directly or indirectly, by the Company itself or by any other company with which the Company is linked by a significant direct or indirect equity interest, the Company or the other company may not levy issue surcharges or redemption fees for the purchase or redemption. The Company will publish in the annual report and in the semi-annual report the fees charged as management fees for the units held in the investment fund, when such fees are charged by the Company itself, by another investment management company, a variable capital joint-stock investment company or another company, to which the Company is linked by means of a significant direct or indirect equity interest, or by a foreign investment company, including its management company.

Earnings appropriation and financial year.

Section 9 – Distribution of income.

1. The Company will distribute interest, dividends and income from investment units, as well as fees from loans and securities repurchase agreements received on behalf of the investment fund, taking into account the relevant income netting. Capital gains and other income, taking into account the relevant income netting, may also be used for distributions.
2. Distributable income pursuant to Paragraph 1 may be carried forward for distribution in subsequent financial years if the amount of the income carried forward does not exceed 15% of the value of the corresponding investment fund at the end of the financial year. Income from truncated financial years may be carried forward in its entirety.
3. In the interest of maintaining equity or replicating the index, some income, or in exceptional cases, all income, may be set aside for reinvestment in the investment fund.
4. Distributions will be made annually within three months after the close of the financial year.

Section 10 – Financial year.

The financial year of the investment fund begins on 1 May and ends on 30 April.

List of stock exchanges with official trading and other regulated markets.

Country	Stock exchanges in European countries which are not member states of the European Union and which are not parties to the agreement on the European Economic Area
Switzerland	Switzerland Electronic Stock Exchange

Country	Stock exchanges in non-European countries
Argentina	Buenos Aires
Australia	ASX (Sydney, Hobart, Melbourne, Perth)
Brazil	São Paulo, Rio de Janeiro
Chile	Santiago
China	Hong Kong Stock Exchange
India	Bombay, Calcutta, Delhi, Madras
Indonesia	Jakarta Stock Exchange
Japan	Tokyo, Osaka, Nagoya, Kyoto, Fukuoka, Niigata, Sapporo, Hiroshima
Canada	Toronto, Vancouver, Montreal
Korea	Seoul
Malaysia	Kuala Lumpur
Mexico	Mexico City
New Zealand	Wellington, Christchurch/Invercargill, Auckland
Peru	Lima
Philippines	Manila
Singapore	Singapore Stock Exchange
South Africa	Johannesburg
Taiwan	Taipei
Thailand	Bangkok
USA	American Stock Exchange (AMEX), New York Stock Exchange (NYSE), Pacific Stock Exchange, Philadelphia, Chicago, Boston, Cincinnati

Country	Regulated markets in countries which are not member states of the European Union and which are not parties to the agreement on the European Economic Area
Japan	Over the Counter Market
Canada	Over the Counter Market
Korea	Over the Counter Market
Switzerland	Bern Stock Market
USA	NASDAQ system, Over the Counter Markets (markets organised by the NASD, such as the over-the-counter equity market, municipal bond market, government securities market, corporate bonds, and public direct participation programs)
	Over the Counter Market of the members of the International Securities Market Association (ISMA), Zurich

Appendix C: ETF Websites

Links for Information on ETFs in Australia	
Streettracks	www.streettracks.com.au
Australian Stock Exchange	www.asx.com.au
S&P/ASX	www.standardandpoors.com
Links for Information on ETFs in Canada	
iUnits	www.ishares.net
TD — Exchange Traded Funds	www.tdassetmanagement.com
Toronto Stock Exchange	www.tse.ca
S&P / TSX / TSE	www.spglobal.com
Links for Information on ETFs in Europe	
Fund Sites	
Beta1	www.beta1.com
EasyETF	www.easyETF.com
TrackinDex	www.trackindex.com/
Fresco	www.frescoshares.com
iShares	www.ishares.net
LDRS	www.ldrs-funds.com
Global Sector LDRs	www.globalsectors.com
HEX 25 ETF	www.hex25.com
IndEXchange	www.indexchange.com
MasterUnit	www.masterunit.com
SPDR Europe	www.spdreurope.com
StreetTRACKS	www.statestreetfrance.com
XACT OMX	www.xactfonder.com

Xmtch SMI	www.xmtch.ch
Unico i-tracker	www.unico-fonds.com
Exchange Sites	
Borsa Italiana	www.borsaitalia.it
Deutsche Boerse	www.deutsche-boerse.com
Euronext Amsterdam	www.euronext.com
Euronext Brussels	www.euronext.com
Euronext Paris	www.euronext.com
Helsinki Stock Exchange	www.hexgroup.com
London Stock Exchange	www.londonstockexchange.com
NASDAQ Europe	www.nasdaqeurope.com
Stockholm Stock Exchange	www.omgroup.com
Swiss Stock Exchange	www.swx.com
Virt-x	www.virt-x.com
Index Sites	
Dow Jones	www.djindices.com
Dow Jones Stoxx	www.stoxx.com
E. Capital Partners	www.e-cpartners.com
MSCI	www.msci.com
Standard & Poor's	www.spglobal.com
iBOXX	www.iboxx.com
Links for Information on ETFs in South Africa	
Satrix	www.satric.co.za
South African Stock Exchange	www.jse.co.za
Links for Information on ETFs in Hong Kong	
SSGA TraHK	www.ssgaasia.com/eng/
iShares	www.ishares.com.hk
MSCI	www.msci.com
Hong Kong Stock Exchange	www.hkex.com.hk

Links for Information on ETFs in India	
Benchmark Asset Management	www.benchmarkfunds.com
Prudential ICICI	www.pruiciciamc.com/
Unit Trust of India	www.unittrustofindia.com
Mumbai Stock Exchange	www.bseindia.com
National Stock Exchange of India	www.nse-india.com
Links for Information on ETFs in Israel	
Tali 25	www.zakai.com/tali/
Tel-Aviv Stock Exchange	www.tase.co.il
Links for Information on ETFs in Japan	
Tokyo Stock Exchange	www.tse.or.jp
Osaka Stock Exchange	www.ose.or.jp
Barclays Global Investors	www.barclaysglobal.co.jp
Daiwa Asset Management	www.daiwa-am.co.jp
Nikko Asset Management	ww.nikko-am.co.jp
Nomura Asset Management	www.nomura-am.co.jp
FTSE	www.ftse.com
Links for Information on ETFs in the Korea	
CJ Investment Trust Mgmt Co Ltd	www.cjitm.co.kr
Korea Investment Trust Mgmt Co Ltd	www.kitmc.com
Samsung Investment Trust Mgmt Co Ltd	www.samsungfund.com
LG Investment Trust Mgmt Co Ltd	www.lgfund.co.kr
Korean Stock Exchange	www.kse.or.kr/en_index.html
Links for Information on ETFs in Taiwan	
Polaris	http://sitc.polaris.com.tw
Links for Information on ETFs in Singapore	
StreetTRACKS	www.streettracks.com.sg
Singapore Exchange	www.sgx.com

iShares	www.ishares.com
Standard & Poor's	www.spglobal.com
Dow Jones	www.djindexes.com
MSCI	www.msci.com
Links for Information on ETFs in the US	
Fund Sites	
BLDRS	www.bldrsfunds.com
Fresco	www.frescoshares.com
iShares	www.ishares.com
Powershares	www.powershares.com.
Rydex	www.rydexfunds.com.
streetTRACKS	www.streetTRACKS.com
Select Sector SPDRs	www.spdrindex.com
VIPERS	www.vipers.vanguard.com
HOLDRS	www.holdrs.com
Exchanges	
American Stock Exchange	www.AMEX.com
Chicago Board Options Exchange	www.cboe.com
International Securities Exchange	www.iseoptions.com
NASDAQ	www.nasdaq.com
NASDAQ Liffe	www.nqlx.com
NYSE	www.nyse.com
Chicago Stock Exchange	www.chicagostockex.com
Pacific Exchange	www.pacificex.com
Index Sites	
Bank of New York	www.bnyadr.com
Dow Jones	www.djindices.com
Dow Jones Stoxx	www.stoxx.com
FTSE	www.ftse.com

MSCI	www.msci.com
Ryan Labs	www.ryanindex.com
Russell	www.russell.com
Standard & Poor's	www.spglobal.com
Wilshire	www.wilshire.com

Biographies

Catherine Barker is a member of Investment Solutions, part of the Global Index and Markets Group in Europe, which designs optimal investment and transactional solutions for Barclays Global Investors' strategic clients. Before joining Investment Solutions, Catherine was product manager for the European Cash Management team in London and was responsible for the development of new products and product strategy. Prior to joining Barclays Global Investors in 1999, Catherine was part of the Fixed Income Sales team at Morgan Stanley Asia in Singapore. Catherine has a BSc in economics from Bristol University.

Catherine Barker, Investment Solutions, Barclay Global Investors Limited, Murray House, 1 Royal Mint Court, London EC3N 4HH.

Stephane Barthelemy, CFA, is a portfolio manager at the Active Equity Management Unit. He is in charge of the Enhanced and Emerging Markets strategies. He joined the firm in December 1999 as an index portfolio manager, and he has been in charge of the management of the ETFs. He is graduated from the business school Ecole Supérieure de Commerce de Montpellier, with a specialisation in Finance. Prior his joining State Street Banque, Stéphane Barthélemy worked for more than three years at La Compagnie Financière Edmond de Rothschild Banque as Head of the Middle Office Structured Products department. He holds the Chartered Financial Analyst designation and has 8 years of experience in finance.

Stéphane Barthélemy, CFA
State Street Global Advisors, 1789 Chaussée de Wavre, 1160 Brussels.

Andrew Broadley heads the Investment Services Division of National Commercial Bank (NCB). He has spent the last 23 years in a variety of organizations.

He joined NCB in 2003 from Nedbank, the largest bank in South Africa, where he had been the Chief Investment Officer of Nedbank Syfrets Private Bank and previously the Chief Executive of Syfrets Private Bank.

Prior to that, Andrew was with the Orbis / Allan Gray asset management group. Orbis is a Bermuda-based fund manager which received the Standard & Poors first place award for investment performance over five and ten years in the Offshore Global Equity sector; Allan Gray Ltd is the largest privately-owned fund manager in South Africa, focused on equity stock-picking.

Andrew spent twelve years working in the UK and USA, which included seven years employed by Household Inc., which was in 2003 purchased by HSBC. He ran their insurance business in the UK which sold insurance through a variety of channels including 150 branches, third party distributors and direct mail / call centers.

He holds a Bachelor of Commerce degree from the University of Cape Town and is a Chartered Accountant.

Andrew Broadley, Division Head of Investment Services Division,
The National Commercial Bank, P.O. Box 15844 Jeddah
21454 Saudi Arabia.
www.alahli.com

Eleanor de Freitas joined Barclay Global Investors Europe's Index Strategy team in March 2003. Before returning to the UK she was a portfolio manager in the Developed International Equity Management Group in BGI's San Francisco office. Prior to joining BGI in June 2001, she spent over five years as a quantitative analyst at ING Barings where she played an instrumental role in developing their global quantitative equity research product. Eleanor graduated from St. Anne's College, Oxford University with a BA Hons Degree in Mathematics and has subsequently been awarded an MA Oxon.

Eleonore de Freitas, Investment Solutions, Barclay Global Investors Limited, Murray House, 1 Royal Mint Court, London EC3N 4HH.

Alain Dubois is responsible for the marketing of State Street ETFs in Europe. Based at State Street Global Advisors Limited (Brussels), he relocated to Belgium in 1999 after 4 years with State Street Bank in Boston where he held several positions within the custody bank. Before joining State Street, Alain was a program manager for the United Nations.

Alain holds a bachelor in International Relations from the University of Brussels, a Master in Law (LLM) from the University of Brussels and a Master in International Law from the University of Edinburgh.

Alain Dubois, Principal, Head of European ETFs, State Street Global Advisors, 1789 Chaussée de Wavre, 1160 Brussels.

Edwin J. Elton, *NYU Stern, Henry Kaufman Management Center, 44 West Fourh Street, New York, NY 10012.*

Martin J. Gruber, *NYU Stern, Henry Kaufman Management Center, 44 West Fourh Street, New York, NY 10012.*

Elisabeth Hehn, CEO, Value Investment Professionals AG, Zug, founded her independent company in Germany and since 1999 built up the institutional consultancy business, where she advises one of the most prestigious insurance companies world-wide, substantial German institutions such as pension funds and collective schemes in the area of innovative investment concepts. Parallel to that she provides product solutions like investment funds and certificates from her office in Zug, Switzerland. Between 1989 and 1999 she was responsible at Dresdner Bank Group and UBS for asset management, derivatives and the marketing of structured products as Head of OTC-Equity Derivatives Sales. She earned a PhD in statistical economics from Hagen University, Germany focusing on analysing and forecasting global equity and derivative market-trends, and specialising in ARCH and GARCH models. She has published numerous books and articles in the field of Asset Management as well as Hedge Funds and she is currently doing market research for the fund industry. Dr. Hehn is member of DVFA (Deutsche Gesellschaft für Finanzanalyse, the German Certified Financial Analyst Assiciation), DGF (Deutsche Gesellschaft für Finanzwirtschaft (DGF) e.V., German Finance Association), the committee of FinanzBetrieb, Handelsblattgruppe and she is working on projects in Behavioral Finance with Prof. R. Selten, Bonn University, Germany, Nobel prize winner, Prof. A. Sadrieh, Magdeburg University, Germany.

Elisabeth Hehn, Value Investment Professionals AG, Eichhofweg 1, 6318 Walchwil/Zug.

Markus Hübscher graduated from the University of Berne with a Masters in Economics and Business Administration. He has CEFA qualifications for being Certified EFFAS Financial Analyst. He joined the Economic Research Department of Credit Suisse in Zurich in 1986 where he was responsible for the economic analysis and research of various developed countries. In 1989 he was assigned to work with CS First Boston and CS Buckmaster & Moore in London. In 1991 he joined the Asset Management Department von Credit Suisse as Portfolio Manager for European Equities. In 1994, he launched the first, Indexed Equities and Fixed Income products for CSAM in Zurich. Since 1996 he is Head of the Quantitative Portfolio Management Unit at CSAM in Zurich and responsible for all index accounts and Exchange Traded Funds worldwide.

*Markus Hübscher, Head of Quantitative Portfolio Management,
Credit Suisse Asset Management, Credit Suisse Group, Paradeplatz 8,
P.O. Box 1, 8070 Zurich.*

Rainer Riess is Managing Director of Stock Market Business Development at Deutsche Börse and the Frankfurt Stock Exchange (FWB®). He is responsible for customer relations for traders, investors and issuers as well as the product offering of all cash market activities of Deutsche Börse AG, comprising of the electronic trading system Xetra® and the Frankfurt Stock Exchange specialist trading. Currently, almost 300 member institutions from 18 countries use the Xetra system. Altogether, the cash market of Deutsche Börse comprises of more than 50,000 stocks, bonds, exchange-traded and actively managed funds, certificates and warrants.

His past experience within Deutsche Börse Group has included managing the Primary Markets department for all listing business, creating the Neuer Markt and shaping the development of the German and European equity market and its regulatory structure. He worked on several product innovations such as the exchange-traded funds business (XTF® segment) and new index concepts, as well as the internationalisation, product and service strategy of Deutsche Börse AG. As a member of the CBOT/EUREX a/c/e Alliance management committee, he worked on the implementation of the Eurex system in the US.

Rainer Riess holds a Masters of Arts in Economics from the Johann Wolfgang Goethe University in Frankfurt and a Master of Business Administration from the University of Miami. He is a former Fulbright scholar.

*Rainer Riess, Managing Director of Stock Market Business Development,
Deutsche Börse AG, Neue Börsenstraße 1, 60487 Frankfurt am Main.*

Ute Brunner-Reumann studied law at Julius-Maximilians-University Würzburg. Afterwards, during her legal internships she worked, inter alia, for a leading French bank. Ute Brunner-Reumann received a Dr. iur. degree on "The Independence of the European Central Bank" at Julius-Maximilians-University Würzburg.

Since 2000, Ute Brunner-Reumann is associate in the Frankfurt office of Clifford Chance and admitted to the Frankfurt Bar.

Ute Brunner-Reumann has specialised on banking law. She mainly advises investment, commercial and universal banks as well as investment companies on all aspects of German, European and international banking and capital markets law. In particular, she works in the field of investment and regulatory law but also advises on structured products and alternative investments.

Ute Brunner-Reumann, Clifford Chance, Mainzer Landstraße 46, 60325 Frankfurt am Main.

Helge Staack, *MBFA, Director Deutsche Bank – Private Wealth Management, Product Management / Investment Solutions. Deutsche Bank AG, Taunusanlage 12, 60262 Frankfurt am Main.*

Printing and Binding: Strauss GmbH, Mörlenbach